The Book of Mormon:
The Keystone Scripture

RELIGIOUS STUDIES CENTER PUBLICATIONS

BOOK OF MORMON SYMPOSIUM SERIES

- The Book of Mormon: The Keystone Scripture
- The Book of Mormon: First Nephi, the Doctrinal Foundation

MONOGRAPH SERIES

- Nibley on the Timely and the Timeless
- Deity and Death
- The Glory of God Is Intelligence
- Reflections on Mormonism
- Literature of Belief
- The Words of Joseph Smith
- Book of Mormon Authorship
- Mormons and Muslims
- The Temple in Antiquity
- Isaiah and the Prophets
- Scriptures for the Modern World
- The Joseph Smith Translation: The Restoration of Plain and Precious Things
- Apocryphal Writings and the Latter-Day Saints

SPECIALIZED MONOGRAPH SERIES

- Supporting Saints: Life Stories of Nineteenth-Century Mormons
- The Call of Zion: The Story of the First Welsh Mormon Emigration
- The Religion and Family Connection: Social Science Perspectives

The Book of Mormon:
The Keystone Scripture

Papers from the First Annual Book of Mormon Symposium

Edited with an Introduction by Paul R. Cheesman
Assisted by S. Kent Brown and
Charles D. Tate, Jr.

Religious Studies Center
Brigham Young University
Provo, Utah

Library of Congress Catalog Card Number: 87-62541
ISBN 0-88494-637-1

First Printing, 1988

Produced and Distributed by
BOOKCRAFT, INC.
Salt Lake City, Utah

Printed in the United States of America

Contents

Preface ix

1 The Challenge of the Book of Mormon 1
Daniel H. Ludlow

2 What the Book of Mormon Tells Us About Jesus Christ 21
Robert J. Matthews

3 The Ministry of the Father and the Son 44
Robert L. Millet

4 A Comparison of Book of Mormon, Bible, and Traditional Teachings on the Doctrines of Salvation 73
Joseph F. McConkie

5 The Beginnings of Christianity in the Book of Mormon 91
Kent P. Jackson

6 The Three Nephite Churches of Christ 100
Rodney Turner

7 Fasting in the Book of Mormon and the Bible 127
Stephen D. Ricks

8 Faith, Hope, Charity 137
Larry E. Dahl

9 Love in the Book of Mormon 151
Gayle O. Brown

10 Before Columbus 164
George F. Carter

11 Categories of Evidence for Old World Contacts with Ancient America 187
Norman Totten

12 Cultural Parallels Between the Old World and the New World 206
Paul R. Cheesman

13 The Bering Strait and American Indian Origins ... 218
James R. Christianson

14 Book of Mormon–Transmission from Translator to Printed Text 237
George A. Horton, Jr.

15 "Lest Ye Become As the Nephites of Old" 256
Susan Black

Subject Index 269

Scripture Index 283

Preface

In response to President Jeffrey R. Holland's proposal that the Religious Studies Center hold an annual Book of Mormon Symposium on the Brigham Young University campus, the First Annual Book of Mormon Symposium was held on 27-28 September 1985. Outstanding papers were presented on Book of Mormon teachings that make it the keystone scripture of The Church of Jesus Christ of Latter-day Saints: its message on Jesus Christ, on the ministry of the Father and the Son, on the doctrines of salvation, and on faith, hope, and charity, among others. There were also several papers on pre-Columbian Old World contacts with the New World. Those papers are published in this volume.

The Book of Mormon contains sacred writings of some of the inhabitants of ancient America. Its stated purpose is to witness to the world that Jesus is the Christ. This keystone scripture proves that the Bible is true and confounds false doctrines by restoring to their original clarity plain and precious doctrines lost from the Bible. Its history and doctrines were compiled to help us know how to combat the false religious, educational, political, and philosophical concepts of our time.

The Book of Mormon is a great standard and proves that Joseph Smith was a prophet of God. Since the Book of Mormon was published over 150 years ago, it has withstood the criticisms and the praises of the world. The purpose of the symposium represented by this volume was to show there is much more we can learn from and about that scripture in the pursuit of truth and understanding.

The views expressed in these papers are the authors' own and are not necessarily those endorsed by The Church of Jesus Christ of Latter-day Saints, Brigham Young University, or the Religious Studies Center, collectively or individually.

PAUL R. CHEESMAN

The Challenge of the Book of Mormon 1

Daniel H. Ludlow

My topic for discussion here is "The Challenge of the Book of Mormon." The decision to use the word *challenge* came from a remark by President Spencer W. Kimball in his first press conference after he became President of the Church. He was asked by a reporter, "What problems are being faced by the Church today?" President Kimball's reply was, "We don't have any problems–only challenges."

In checking *Webster's Third New International Dictionary, Unabridged,* I found many definitions and synonyms for the word *challenge,* both as a verb and as a noun. Among the most interesting definitions are "to assert a right, title, or claim to" and "something that is to be striven for." Some of the synonyms that might have particular significance to our discussion today are *claim, protest,* and *test.*

If you would feel more comfortable with the plural "challenges" in the title, just insert it in your mind. The words of King Benjamin come to mind: "I cannot tell you all the things whereby ye may commit sin; for there are divers ways and means, even so many that I cannot number them" (Mosiah 4:29). In a somewhat similar manner,

Daniel H. Ludlow is director of correlation review for The Church of Jesus Christ of Latter-day Saints.

we cannot mention all of the challenges associated with the Book of Mormon. However, at any one time a specific person will probably be concerned with a particular single challenge. Also, after all other challenges are resolved, one will always remain: to learn to live the principles of righteousness contained in the Book of Mormon, which Joseph Smith said was "the keystone of our religion."

Some of the special challenges associated with the Book of Mormon which I hope to discuss with you today are as follows:

1. To learn everything we can about the Book of Mormon.
2. To learn for ourselves, by the power of the Holy Ghost, that Jesus Christ is the divine Son of God.
3. To learn the great principles of righteousness contained in the Book of Mormon.
4. To live these principles of righteousness.
5. To place our emphasis on the "weightier matters" pertaining to the Book of Mormon.
6. To teach these things to others.

In order to understand the major claims of the Book of Mormon, we need to understand some of the background and experiences of the four major writers associated with this book. Except for the few pages in the books of Enos, Jarom, and Omni, all the remainder of the Book of Mormon comes to us from the literary efforts of four persons: Nephi, Jacob, Mormon, and Moroni. It is true that some of these writers quote from other persons and sources, but it is also true that they had to decide to include these references for us to have them in our present Book of Mormon. Some interesting experiences shared by these four writers of the Book of Mormon include the following five points:

1. They are all witnesses of Jesus Christ (see 2 Nephi 11:2, 3; Mormon 1:15; Ether 12:22-33, 38-39). Two of these prophets, Nephi and Jacob, were witnesses of the pre-earthly Jesus Christ; the other two, Mormon and Moroni, were witnesses of the

resurrected Jesus Christ. Thus, all four writers of the Book of Mormon text serve as special types of witnesses of Jesus Christ's divinity.

2. They were all tutored by supernatural beings, either by pre-earthly spirit beings sent as angels, or by translated beings (see 1 Nephi 11; 2 Nephi 10:2-3, 7; 3 Nephi 28:26; Mormon 8:11).

3. They all had a vision of our day and wrote especially for and to us (see 2 Nephi 6:4-9; 25:3-8, 22; 26:16-24; Jacob 4:4, 13; Mormon 8:25-35; 9:26, 30-31; Moroni 1:4).

4. They all received heavenly counsel regarding what they should include in their writings (see 2 Nephi 28:1-3; 32:7; Jacob 2:11; Words of Mormon 1:3-9; 3 Nephi 26:11-12; 30:1; Mormon 5:9, 13; Ether 8:24-26; 13:13).

5. They all warned us that we will be held accountable for what we do with their words (see 2 Nephi 33:10-15; Jacob 6:1, 12-13; Mormon 3:14, 20-22; Moroni 10:24-34).

When we see these attributes and characteristics, the Book of Mormon should take on additional meaning for each of us. Have you ever had the experience, for example, of reading a chapter from Moroni and then closing your eyes and asking yourselves the question, "What was there in the experiences of Moroni, or what did Moroni see in vision concerning our day, that would prompt him to write this particular account?" When we do this, we find additional significance in the Book of Mormon, and its major assertions begin to make more sense.

One of the definitions that seem to apply to part of our discussion today is that a challenge is a *claim.* Thus, perhaps it would be well for us to begin with a review of the major claims made by the Book of Mormon. Unfortunately, many people both in and out of the Church have expended great amounts of time, energy, thought, and even money to prove or disprove claims of the Book of Mormon which are not made by the book itself.

Major Claims or Assertions of the Book of Mormon

The title page of the Book of Mormon claims that the book was "written . . . [for] the convincing of the Jew and Gentile that Jesus is the Christ, the Eternal God, manifesting himself unto all nations." First and foremost, then, the Book of Mormon claims to be a witness for the divinity of Jesus Christ.

This and other claims of the Book of Mormon can be listed as follows:

1. To be a witness for the divinity of Jesus Christ and to bring to the Jews and Gentiles the testimony that Jesus is the Christ.

2. To fulfill biblical prophecy and to be a witness for the Bible.

3. To convince the Lamanites that they are of the house of Israel; to show the remnant of the house of Israel what great things the Lord has done for their fathers; to teach them the covenants of the Lord made with their fathers, that they may know they are not cast off forever; to bring them the knowledge of a Savior through the testimony of the Nephites as well as that of the Jews.

4. To restore to the knowledge of mankind many plain and precious truths concerning the gospel of Jesus Christ.

5. To convince mankind that every person must be judged by his works; to test the faith of this generation; to help the faithful.

6. To help the people of this generation solve their problems; to provide mankind with secrets of national survival; to prepare the faithful for the second coming of Jesus Christ and the millennial reign.

Claims or Assertions Made by Others Concerning the Book of Mormon

Please note some of the many claims for the Book of Mormon that are not included in this list. The Book of Mormon does not claim to be primarily a history book, neither primarily an archaeological textbook nor a treatise on geography, economics, or political science. Neither is it a scientific paper on engineering or metallurgy or agriculture or warfare. We should not claim more for the book than what it claims for itself. Also, we should remember that the Book of Mormon tells only part of the story of a relatively small group of people in a limited geographical area during a relatively brief period of time.

Certainly the Book of Mormon contains some historical elements and geographical references, but not in the number or in the detail that some have hoped or others have claimed. Indeed, any items that might be historical or archaeological or geographical or political are incidental and are included in the book only to the degree that they contribute to one of the stated major purposes of the book.

For example, note the following:

1. We learn of the monetary system of the Nephites simply because two missionaries holding a street meeting are bribed by a heckler to deny the existence of Jesus Christ. The recorder feels we should understand the approximate worth of the bribe, so he briefly reviews their monetary system. Also, as you will recall, the incident is included so the reader can learn that God knows the thoughts of men, and he can reveal these thoughts to his representatives.

2. We learn of the weapons and strategy of war of these people primarily so the reader will understand that even though armies are well prepared for war, they still fight only with the strength of men unless God is on their side.

3. We learn of the crops and animals of these people primarily when they are leaving to establish new colonies in order to be free to worship their God.

It is obviously unfair for anyone to judge the Book of Mormon by what it does or does not teach concerning economics or defense or agriculture when these are not the areas emphasized by its writers. As well might we judge the competency of a brain surgeon by ascertaining what he knows about clothing and textiles, or judge a musician by what she knows concerning the water-retention qualities of different types of soils.

Note the insistence of the major writers of the Book of Mormon that it is not a history book:

> I, Nephi, do not give the genealogy of my fathers. . . . I desire the room that I may write of the things of God. For the fulness of mine intent is that I may persuade men to come unto . . . God. . . . Wherefore, the things which are pleasing unto the world I do not write, but the things which are pleasing unto God (1 Nephi 6:1, 3-5).
>
> These plates . . . are not the plates upon which I make a full account of the history of my people. . . . Upon the other plates should be engraven an account of the reign of the kings, and the wars and contentions of my people; wherefore these plates are for the more part of the ministry; and the other plates are for the more part of the reign of the kings and the wars and the contentions of my people (1 Nephi 9:2, 4).
>
> Many . . . sayings are written upon mine other plates; for a more history part are written upon mine other plates (2 Nephi 4:14).
>
> And if my people desire to know the more particular part of the history of my people they must search mine other plates (2 Nephi 5:33).

Subtitle: "Another Testament of Jesus Christ"

In keeping with the major claim of the Book of Mormon that it is a witness of the divinity of Jesus Christ, it is entirely appropriate that a subtitle has now been added to the book: "Another Testament of Jesus Christ."

I was living in Australia when I heard of the decision by the Brethren to include the subtitle. I was thrilled by the announcement, but was a little surprised that the word *testament* was chosen rather than the word *witness*. Many of us had become accustomed to referring to the Book of Mormon as a "second witness" to the divinity of Christ and to the Bible.

At the first opportunity, I checked the most comprehensive and complete dictionary I could find in the major library in Perth, Australia, and found some very interesting things concerning the etymology of the word *testament.* Among other things I learned that the word is derived from a prehistoric Italic compound whose first and second constituents respectively are akin to the Latin *tres* (three) and the Latin *stare* (to stand). Thus, the idea of three serving as a witness comprises part of the basic meaning of the word *testament.*

The appropriateness of the new subtitle impressed me: "*Another* testament." Not a first testament, nor a second testament, nor a third—but *another* testament. For some the Book of Mormon might be a second testament of the divinity of Jesus Christ, but for a different person it might be a third testament, or even a first. How appropriate that the word *testament* itself has inherent within it the idea of "three witnesses."

God's System of Witnesses

This is entirely consistent with the system of witnesses employed by the Lord himself. In Deuteronomy 19:15 we read, "At the mouth of two witnesses, or at the mouth of three witnesses, shall the matter be established." And in 2 Corinthians 13:1 and Doctrine and Covenants 6:28, we note the confirming words, "In the mouth of two or three witnesses shall every word be established."

The three members of the Godhead exemplify this law in witnessing or testifying of each other. In the New Testament the Savior testifies so frequently of the oneness of his Father and himself, and of his Father's work with his work, that traditional Christianity has come to believe that God the Father and Jesus Christ the Son are one in virtually all ways, including being one in substance. That they are not one in actual substance was made clear by the Savior's other statements in the New Testament, including his prayer to his Father to make his disciples one "even as we are one" (see John 17:22). This matter is further clarified in the first vision of Joseph Smith.

The members of the Godhead are one in many respects, however (such as in their goals, purposes, and ideals), and they are also one in testimony. Note the significance of the following statement of the resurrected Jesus Christ concerning this matter:

> The Father, and the Son, and the Holy Ghost are one; and I am in the Father, and the Father in me, and the Father and I are one. . . . And I bear record of the Father, and the Father beareth record of me. . . . And thus will the Father bear record of me, and the Holy Ghost will bear record . . . of the Father and me; for the Father, and I, and the Holy Ghost are one (3 Nephi 11:27, 32, 36).

Here the Savior makes two very important points: (1) the three members of the Godhead are one in the sense that they testify or witness of each other, and (2) if we accept or believe in any one of the members of the Godhead, we must accept or believe in the others, for they all testify of each other.

The Scriptures Testify of Each Other
and of the Members of the Godhead

The same divine law of witnesses applies also to the holy scriptures. The Holy Bible is one witness to the divinity of Jesus Christ, but where are the second and third witnesses? Latter-day Saints believe the Book of Mormon to be a second witness (the "American" witness) to the divine mission of the Savior, and we believe the third great witness is yet to come forth. The Lord taught of the existence of three scriptural witnesses in these words:

> For behold, I shall speak unto the Jews and they shall write it; and I shall also speak unto the Nephites and they shall write it; and I shall also speak unto the other tribes of the house of Israel, which I have led away, and they shall write it. . . . And it shall come to pass that the Jews shall have the words of the Nephites, and the Nephites shall have the words of the Jews; and the Nephites and the Jews shall have the words of the lost tribes of Israel; and the lost tribes of Israel shall have the words of the Nephites and the Jews. . . . And my word . . . shall be gathered in one (2 Nephi 29:12-14).

Thus there shall be three great scriptural witnesses brought forth by the Lord.

The relationship of these records to each other is also made clear in the Book of Mormon. In his farewell address, Mormon made the following statement to the Lamanites of this dispensation: "Therefore repent, and be baptized in the name of Jesus, and lay hold upon the gospel of Christ, which shall be set before you, not only in this record [i.e., the Book of Mormon] but also in the record which shall come unto the Gentiles from the Jews, which record [i.e., the Bible] shall come from the Gentiles unto you. For behold, this [the Book of Mormon] is written for the intent that ye may believe that [the Bible]; and if ye believe that [the Bible] ye will believe this [the Book of Mormon] also" (Mormon 7:8-9).

Here Mormon is saying that one of the major purposes of the coming forth of the Book of Mormon is to testify of the Bible, and he states that if we honestly accept one of these scriptures we will also accept the other, for the two scriptures testify of each other. This is also the testimony of Brigham Young:

> No man can say that this book (laying his hand on the Bible) is true . . . and at the same time say, that the Book of Mormon is untrue. . . . There is not that person on the face of the earth who has had the privilege of learning the Gospel of Jesus Christ from these two books, that can say that one is true, and the other is false. No Latter-day Saint, no man or woman, can say the Book of Mormon is true, and at the same time say that the Bible is untrue. If one be true, both are (*Journal of Discourses,* 1:38).

Special Witnesses to the Book of Mormon

The Lord has provided us with a series of witnesses to the scriptures themselves. With regard to the Book of Mormon, at least three types of human witnesses were promised by the Lord and have been provided (see 2 Nephi 11:3; 2 Nephi 27:12-14; Ether 5:2-4; D&C 5:11-15).

First of all, we have the life and testimony of the Prophet Joseph Smith as a witness that the Book of Mormon is true. The Prophet declared that the record was given to him by an angel sent from God and that he translated part of it by the gift and power of God (see Joseph Smith–History 1:30-54, 59, 67). Joseph Smith sealed this testimony with his own life.

Second, we have the testimonies of the three special witnesses–Oliver Cowdery, David Whitmer, and Martin Harris. These men testified that the record of the Book of Mormon had "been translated by the gift and power of God, for his voice hath declared it unto us; wherefore we know of a surety that the work is true." They also claimed that they had "seen the engravings . . . upon the plates; . . . they have been shown unto us by the power of God, and not of man. . . . An angel of God came down from heaven, and he brought and laid before our eyes, that we beheld and saw the plates, and the engravings thereon" (See "The Testimony of the Three Witnesses" in the front of the Book of Mormon). None of these three special witnesses ever denied his testimony of the things he had both seen and heard.

Then we have the testimonies of the eight special witnesses. They said Joseph Smith had shown them the plates and they had handled them with their own hands and had seen the engravings thereon: "And this we bear record with words of soberness, . . . that the said Smith has got the plates of which we have spoken" (See "The Testimony of Eight Witnesses" in the front of the Book of Mormon). Again, not one of these men ever denied his testimony.

These groups of special witnesses not only testify of each other, but they also serve as witnesses to the claims of Joseph Smith, including the truthfulness of the Book of Mormon. If we accept the testimony of any of these human witnesses, we must accept the Book of Mormon and also the Bible and the divinity of Jesus Christ.

The Holy Ghost Testifies of the Truth of These Things

In addition to the testimony of other people and of the scriptures, however, the Lord has promised us a "more sure witness" of the truth of these things. This more sure witness is that of the Holy Ghost. Paul tells us that no man knoweth of the things of God except by the Spirit of God (1 Corinthians 2:11), and in 1 John 5:6 we read, "It is the Spirit that beareth witness, because the Spirit is truth."

Thus the best and most effective way to discover truth in the spiritual and religious realm is to ask God. "Ask, and it shall be given you," the Savior said (Matthew 7:7), but James adds, "Let him ask in faith, nothing wavering" (James 1:6).

The last writer in the Book of Mormon gives us a specific formula by which we can gain a knowledge of the truth of spiritual things, including the knowledge of whether or not the Book of Mormon is true:

> Behold, I would exhort you that when ye shall read these things, if it be wisdom in God that ye should read them, that ye would remember how merciful the Lord hath been unto the children of men, from the creation of Adam even down until the time that ye shall receive these things, and ponder it in your hearts.
>
> And when ye shall receive these things, I would exhort you that ye would ask God, the Eternal Father, in the name of Christ, if these things are not true; and if ye shall ask with a sincere heart, with a real intent, having faith in Christ, he will manifest the truth of it unto you, by the power of the Holy Ghost.
>
> And by the power of the Holy Ghost ye may know the truth of all things (Moroni 10:3-5).

Surely the Lord has provided us with ample witnesses in our day that the work of this dispensation is true. He has borne his own testimony to us through his prophets and his divine Son; he has sent angels again to the earth with the glad tidings of the gospel; he has provided scriptural and human witnesses to his great work; and he has promised us a personal witness by his emissary the Holy Ghost if we are sincere and faithful. As the prophet Moroni stated, "All this shall stand as a testimony against the world at the last day" (Ether 5:4).

It now behooves us to examine honestly and sincerely these witnesses and their testimonies, and, if we do, the Lord has promised us we shall not find them wanting.

We have all heard the truism "God will force no man to heaven." It is also true that "God will force no man to obtain a testimony of the Book of Mormon."

One of the major purposes of our existence on this earth is to learn to walk by faith. To help us realize this purpose, the Lord has removed the memory of our pre-earthly existence; thus we can truly learn to develop our powers of faith in him here in this life. God does not let our faith go unanswered, however. He has promised that certain *evidences* or *witnesses* will "follow them that believe" (Mark 16:17-18); therefore, we can know our faith in him is not in vain, and we are encouraged in the further development of faith.

A Challenge for the Non-Believer: Gaining a Testimony of the Book of Mormon by the Power of the Holy Spirit

At the beginning of our discussion I mentioned that the challenge of the Book of Mormon differs from person to person, and from time to time. May I now speak briefly to those who face the test of finding out for themselves whether or not the Book of Mormon is true. Undoubtedly there will be several who read this chapter who do not *know* whether the book is true; these persons may or may not be members of the Church.

You will note that so far in our discussion we have emphasized that a testimony of the Book of Mormon is based on spiritual power. After all, the foremost claim of the Book of Mormon—that Jesus is the Christ and is the divine Son of God—is of a spiritual nature, and the things of the Spirit are known only through the power of the Spirit. You cannot gain or measure a spiritual truth, such as a testimony, by physical things alone. The charts of physical weights and measurements do not help in spiritual matters.

However, our Heavenly Father is willing to provide us with additional types of "witnesses" or "proofs" or "signs" that the claims of the Book of Mormon are true. But, as indicated in both ancient and modern scripture, these "proofs" come *after* the exercise of faith, which again is the result of spiritual power. As Moroni stated, "I . . . would show unto the world that faith is things which are hoped for and not seen; wherefore, dispute not because ye see not, for ye receive no witness until after the trial of your faith" (Ether 12:6).

Perhaps the two best-known definitions of faith in the scriptures come from Paul in the New Testament and Alma in the Book of Mormon: "Faith is the substance of things hoped for, the evidence of things not seen" (Hebrews 11:1), and "Faith is not to have a perfect knowledge of things; therefore if ye have faith ye hope for things which are not seen, which are true" (Alma 32:21).

You will note that *hope* is closely allied with faith in both of these definitions. Alma continues with his explanation: "If ye will awake and arouse your faculties, even to an experiment upon my words, and exercise a particle of faith, yea, even if ye can no more than desire to believe, let this desire work in you, even until ye believe in a manner that ye can give place for a portion of my words" (Alma 32:27).

Note the key words: *hope, desire, believe.* If you want to recognize and receive "proofs" of the Book of Mormon, you begin with the *hope* that the Book of Mormon is true. Then you *desire* to find out whether or not it is true. Then you start acting upon that desire until you come to *believe.* Then, and not until then, can you come to *know.*

There is a great misconception among some that the Lord is averse to giving signs or proofs. Evidently this idea comes from the words of the Lord in the New Testament: "An evil and adulterous generation seeketh after a sign" (Matthew 12:39; cf. 16:4). A key word in this verse is *seeketh.*

However, the scriptures also teach:

> And these signs shall *follow* them that *believe* (Mark 16:17; emphasis added).
>
> And they [the disciples] went forth, and preached every where, the Lord working with them, and *confirming the word with signs following* (Mark 16:20; emphasis added. These are the last words in Mark).
>
> I thought it good to shew the signs and wonders that the high God hath wrought toward me. How great are his signs! and how mighty are his wonders! (Daniel 4:2-3).
>
> Ye men of Israel, hear these words; Jesus of Nazareth, a man approved of God among you by miracles and wonders and signs, which God did by him in the midst of you, as ye yourselves also know (Acts 2:22).
>
> And many other signs truly did Jesus in the presence of his disciples, which are not written in this book (John 20:30).

The Lord is not averse to giving signs. He loves to give signs; he greatly desires to provide evidence; he is willing to prove all his works. But these signs, evidences, and proofs have real meaning and significance only to those who have faith. Signs follow faith, they do not precede it. Signs are given to help develop faith already present; they are not given to produce or replace faith. Thus, if we are interested in finding proof of the Book of Mormon, we should begin by *seeking faith* rather than by seeking signs.

If the world understood this principle and the scriptures pertaining to it, they would also understand why the Lord does not have the Book of Mormon plates displayed in the new Church museum, or why he does not send an angel to demonstrate the Urim and Thummim on television. Now we can better understand the words of the Lord to his prophet in March 1829: "I have reserved those things which I have entrusted unto you, my servant Joseph, for a wise purpose in me, and it shall be made known unto future generations; but this generation shall have my word through you" (D&C 5:9-10). And, in section 105: "It is expedient in me that they should be brought thus far for a trial of their faith" (vs. 105:19). This scripture ties in beautifully with Ether 12:6: "Ye receive no witness until after the trial of your faith."

The steps on how you can find and accept physical evidences or proofs concerning the Book of Mormon thus seem to be quite clear:

1. You *desire* to know that the Book of Mormon is true.
2. You *hope* the Book of Mormon is true.
3. You *read the Book of Mormon* and *ponder* its teachings (Moroni 10:3-5).
4. You *ask God* whether or not the Book of Mormon is true. (Who would know better than our Heavenly Father whether or not the Book of Mormon is indeed "Another Testament of Jesus Christ"?)

The degree to which you can or will accept an evidence or proof of the Book of Mormon will be in exact proportion to your *desire* to know if the Book of Mormon is true and in exact proportion to your *hope* that the Book of Mormon is true. However, even a *knowledge* or a *testimony* of the Book of Mormon alone is not enough.

A Challenge for the Believer: Becoming Converted to the Book of Mormon

Now may I speak briefly to those who already know that the Book of Mormon is true, who have already received a witness of its authenticity. Far too many of us who have this knowledge are content to rest in it—although we may want to have it nourished occasionally by the additional evidences or testimonies we receive at gatherings such as this symposium. However, we must go beyond knowledge alone to become truly converted to this book. We must not only believe and know the Book of Mormon is true; we must live the principles of righteousness contained in this sacred scripture.

Note the words of the Lord concerning this matter:

> And your minds in times past have been darkened because of unbelief, and because you have treated lightly the things you have received—
>
> Which vanity and unbelief have brought the whole church under condemnation.
>
> And this condemnation resteth upon the children of Zion, even all.
>
> And they shall remain under this condemnation until they repent and remember the new covenant, even the Book of Mormon and the former commandments which I have given them, not only to say, but to do according to that which I have written (D&C 84: 54-57).

Some may ask, "What is the difference between knowing that the Book of Mormon is true and being converted to the truths of the Book of Mormon?" My understanding is that a person can *know* something and not do anything about it. There is no causal relationship between *knowing* and *doing*. However, when a person is converted there is a change; his actions become 100 percent consistent with his knowledge. Otherwise he is not truly converted.

Our challenge as believers is to become truly converted, so that we not only can *say* that the Book of Mormon is true but will also *do* what the Lord has commanded to be written in his holy record.

A Challenge to Non-Believers and Believers: Living the Teachings of the Book of Mormon

And now may I speak to all of us—to the non-believer, the believer, and the believer who is also a doer.

The Savior was speaking of priorities when he said, "Wherefore, seek not the things of this world but seek ye first to build up the kingdom of God, and to establish his righteousness, and all these things shall be added unto you" (JST Matthew 6:38). A similar teaching is found in the book of Jacob in the Book of Mormon: "Before ye seek for riches, seek ye for the kingdom of God. And after ye have obtained a hope in Christ ye shall obtain riches, if ye seek them; and ye will seek them for the intent to do good—to clothe the naked, and to feed the hungry, and to liberate the captive, and administer relief to the sick and the afflicted" (Jacob 2:18-19). Again, the Savior was speaking of the relative importance of things when he asked: "What shall it profit a man, if he shall gain the whole world, and lose his own soul? Or what shall a man give in exchange for his soul?" (Mark 8:36-37).

Now may I paraphrase these scriptures and apply them to our topic here:

> Wherefore, seek not for those physical proofs that only establish the authenticity of the Book of Mormon; rather seek first to obtain the knowledge that "Jesus is the Christ, the Eternal God, manifesting himself unto all nations," and then shall the other proofs be added unto you.
>
> Before ye seek for the physical evidences of the Book of Mormon, seek ye for a spiritual testimony of its truthfulness. And after ye have obtained a testimony of its truthfulness by the power of the Holy Ghost, the physical evidences shall be made manifest unto you if ye seek them, for ye will seek them for the intent to do good—to interest the non-believer, to strengthen the believer, to liberate those bound down with false traditions, to free the honest in heart from incorrect teachings and doctrines, and to strengthen the believer and those who are wavering from the pressures of ridicule and persecution.
>
> And, what shall you be profited, if you gain a testimony of these truths, but do not live them? Or what shall you give in exchange for the truths of exaltation and eternal life?

Thomas à Kempis, in his classic *The Imitation of*

Christ, emphasized the importance of living the truths we know. He stated:

> Whosoever . . . would fully and feelingly understand the words of Christ, must endeavor to conform his life wholly to the life of Christ.
>
> Surely great words do not make man holy and just; but a virtuous life maketh him dear to God.
>
> I had rather *feel* compunction [another translation reads contrition] than know the definition thereof.

I believe there is a message there for each of us. I would rather *feel* the truths of the Book of Mormon, through trying to live them, than simply *know* they are true.

Don't Get on a "Hobbyhorse"

Another word of caution for all of us.

It was in the summer of 1955 that I first joined the faculty at Brigham Young University. At that time and shortly before, the leaders of the Church were cautioning us as members: "Do not get on a hobbyhorse in the Church. If you do, it will ride you right out of the Church and kingdom." Some of us have lived long enough to see the wisdom of this counsel. We have seen friends and family, students and colleagues, who have become so enamored over this program or that teaching that they have neglected the weightier things of pure testimony and righteous living.

My plea here would be that we would not repeat those errors in relationship to the Book of Mormon. May I illustrate my concern by quoting from a recent talk by Elder Robert L. Backman:

> In Africa, the natives have a unique, effective way to capture monkeys. They lop the top off a coconut, remove the meat, and leave a hole in the top of the coconut large enough for the monkey to put his paw in. Then they anchor the coconut to the ground with some peanuts in it. When the natives leave, the monkeys, smelling those delicious peanuts, approach the coconuts, see the peanuts in them, put their paws in to grasp the nuts, and attempt to remove the nuts—but find that the hole is too small for their doubled-up fists. The natives return with gunny sacks and pick up the monkeys—clawing, biting, screaming—but they won't drop the peanuts to save their lives.
>
> Do you know anyone who is caught in a monkey trap, where the things that matter the most are at the mercy of those things

> that matter the least? ("To the Young Men of the Church," *Ensign*, November 1980, p. 42).

I would repeat Elder Backman's concern: "Do you know anyone who is caught in a monkey trap, where the things that matter the most are at the mercy of those things that matter the least?"

Do you know of some who have become too enamored of the lack of proof of the Book of Mormon, or some at the other extreme who are so concerned about the abundance of physical evidences of the Book of Mormon that they believe faith and testimony of the Spirit are no longer necessary? Might some of us even see within ourselves such a great love of or longing for the tasty peanuts that we might be sacrificing some of our spiritual life for things that in the long run might not really be very important? If we do see this tendency in ourselves or in others, I pray that something we have heard or seen or thought or felt in this symposium will help us to seek, first and above all, those things which are of eternal worth.

Closing Statement and Testimony

In closing, I would like to bear my testimony concerning the Book of Mormon. May I introduce it by quoting several excerpts from President Kimball's masterful general conference address of April 1963, entitled "A Book of Vital Messages."

> There is a book I have read many times, yet each time I read it I find it engages my interest the more. . . . It is a story of courage, faith, and fortitude, of perseverance, sacrifice, and super-human accomplishments, of intrigue, of revenge, of disaster, of war, murder, and rapine, of idolatry, and of cannibalism, of miracles, visions, and manifestations, of prophecies and their fulfillment.
>
> I found in it life at its best and at its worst, in ever-changing patterns. . . .
>
> It is a fast-moving story of total life, of opposing ideologies, of monarchies and judgeships and mobocracies. . . . Class distinction is there with its ugliness, race prejudice with its hatefulness, multiplicity of creeds with their bitter conflicts. . . .
>
> Its story has a vital message to all people. The gentiles will find the history of their past and the potential of their destiny; and the Jewish people, the blueprint of their future. . . .

Archaeologists may be excited as they read of ruins of ancient cities, highways, and buildings; and there may yet be hidden buried gold and priceless records. . . .

Engineers will learn from this great book that those centuries ago, men erected buildings, temples, and highways with cement, and paved roads connected city to city and land to land. . . .

The psychologists may find studies in human behavior and the workings of the human mind and the rationalizing processes where men convince themselves that "good is bad, and that bad is good." Here they will watch history unfold for thousands of years and see not only episodes in the lives of individuals but causes and effects in a total history of races. . . .

This comprehensive book should be studied by politicians, government leaders, kings, presidents, and premiers to see the rise and fall of empires, and the difference between statesmanship and demagoguery. They will see nations born in war, live in war, deteriorate in war, and die in war through the centuries. They may find answers to problems of capital and labor, of dishonesty, graft and fraud, of dissensions, internal rupture, and civil wars. . . .

This single volume records for historians about twenty-six centuries of stirring life, not generally known even to the most highly trained professors of history. It tells of the ancestries of those whose spectacular monuments are now observed in South and Central America and in the Mexican jungles.

In this wondrous book, ministers and priests can find texts for sermons, and men generally can find final and authoritative answers to difficult questions. . . .

It is the word of God. It is a powerful second witness of Christ. And, certainly, all true believers who love the Redeemer will welcome additional evidence of his divinity.

This inspiring book was never tampered with by unauthorized translators or biased theologians but comes to the world pure and directly from the historians and abridgers. The book is not on trial—its readers are.

Here is a scripture as old as creation and as new and vibrant as tomorrow, bridging time and eternity; it is a book of revelations and is a companion to the Bible . . . and agrees in surprising harmony with [the] Bible in tradition, history, doctrine, and prophecy; . . . the two were written simultaneously on two hemispheres under diverse conditions. . . .

In the final chapter of the book is the never-failing promise that every person who will read the book with a sincere, prayerful desire to know of its divinity shall have the assurance.

The book of which I speak is the keystone of true religion, the ladder by which one may get near to God by abiding its precepts. It has been named "the most correct of any book on earth."

My beloved friends, I give to you the Book of Mormon. May you read it prayerfully, study it carefully, and receive for yourselves the testimony of its divinity (Conference Report, April 1963, pp. 63-68; cf. *Faith Precedes the Miracle* [Salt Lake City: Deseret Book Company, 1972], pp. 329-37).

This would be my prayer, and is also my testimony. I honestly believe, my dear brothers and sisters, that at the final judgment we will give our accountability as to what we have done with the Book of Mormon and its teachings. I believe the questions will be asked of us in about the following order, and the first time we have to answer "no" will be the point of our judgment.

1. Did you have opportunity to read the Book of Mormon while you lived on the earth? (All of us reading this would have to answer this question "Yes").
2. Did you read the Book of Mormon?
3. Did you learn the great principles of righteousness contained in the Book of Mormon?
4. Did you apply these principles in your life?
5. Did you teach these principles to your children and to others?

It may be that if we can honestly answer "yes" to all of these questions, we might then hear those gladsome words, "Well done, thou good and faithful servant: . . . enter thou into the joy of thy Lord" (Matthew 25:21).

The Book of Mormon is the word of God, Another Testament of Jesus Christ. May we learn it, and love it —and live it.

What the Book of Mormon Tells Us About Jesus Christ

2

Robert J. Matthews

What the Book of Mormon Tells Us About Jesus Christ is a subject so large that it could take a lifetime to review. It is a spiritual topic, associated with faith, belief, testimony, emotion, revelation, and personal conviction. The Book of Mormon is a pillar of revealed truth supporting and upholding the chief cornerstone, who is Jesus Christ. Elder Bruce R. McConkie once described it as a book that would *shake* the earth. It truly is the keystone scripture.

In this chapter, I desire to discuss some of the fundamental things that the Book of Mormon relates about Jesus Christ. I do not pretend to any secret or new information or interpretation. I come equipped only with the holy scriptures, a personal conviction, and a desire to share my thoughts in meekness and sincerity, and in a manner I hope will be informative to you and acceptable to our Heavenly Father. I cannot speak for the Church—my views are my own, but I believe them to be correct.

Robert J. Matthews is dean of Religious Education and professor of Ancient Scripture at BYU.

Life in a Spiritual Desert

We live in a day of great distress in many places. Earthquake, famine, war, wickedness, and bloodshed are occurring in many parts of the globe, among our fellow human beings, even at the very time we rest securely. It is distressing to realize that at this very moment most of the people of the earth live in a physical desert, without enough food, without comfortable homes and conveniences or the sustenance of a good life. Furthermore, to a far greater extent, they exist in a poverty-stricken spiritual desert without the saving principles of the gospel of Jesus Christ and the knowledge of God. There is even greater tragedy and calamity in the spiritual deserts of life than in the physical. Far too many people do not have the knowledge of Jesus Christ and the blessings of the gospel, and to make matters worse, most of them do not even know it. I am certain that permanent peace, an adequate supply of food, spiritual contentment, and lasting security can come to individuals, families, nations, and the whole earth only when they have a true knowledge of Jesus Christ and obey the gospel. The world is not going to solve its problems of war, famine, poverty, and unrest until mankind believes and obeys the gospel of Jesus Christ. The Book of Mormon teaches that salvation is not only individual, it is also global. As Nephi wrote, "Behold, all nations, kindreds, tongues, and people shall dwell safely in the Holy One of Israel if it so be that they will repent" (1 Nephi 22:28).

The World Needs the Savior

The world needs Jesus, but can find him only as individuals begin to seek after him to learn of his ways, to repent and to keep his commandments. It is an individual thing. The change must first take place in the heart, the mind, and the attitude of the individual; thus there is a special need to teach faith in Jesus Christ. Notice the words of Alma 4:18-19, wherein he gave up the judgment seat to another in order to allow himself more time to teach the word of God:

> Now Alma did not grant unto him the office of being high priest over the church but he retained the office of high priest unto himself; but he delivered the judgment-seat unto Nephihah.
>
> And this he did that he himself might go forth among his people, or among the people of Nephi, that he might preach the word of God unto them, to stir them up in remembrance of their duty, and that he might pull down, by the word of God, all the pride and craftiness and all the contentions which were among his people, seeing no way that he might reclaim them save it were in bearing down in pure testimony against them.

The superior effectiveness of teaching the gospel to get people to change is shown in Alma 31:5:

> And now, as the preaching of the word had a great tendency to lead the people to do that which was just—yea, it had had more powerful effect upon the minds of the people than the sword, or anything else, which had happened unto them—therefore Alma thought it was expedient that they should try the virtue of the word of God.

I note here the words of President Harold B. Lee, spoken at a student fireside in Logan, Utah, in 1971, in which he discussed a general breakdown of faith in Jesus Christ.

> Fifty years ago or more, when I was a missionary, our greatest responsibility was to defend the great truth that the Prophet Joseph Smith was divinely called and inspired and that the Book of Mormon was indeed the word of God. But even at that time there were the unmistakable evidences that there was coming into the religious world actually a question about the Bible and about the divine calling of the Master himself. Now, fifty years later, our greatest responsibility and anxiety is to defend the divine mission of our Lord and Master, Jesus Christ, for all about us, even among those who claim to be professors of the Christian faith, are those not willing to stand squarely in defense of the great truth that our Lord and Master, Jesus Christ, was indeed the Son of God. So tonight it would seem to me that the most important thing I could say to you is to try to strengthen your faith and increase your courage and your understanding of the place of the Master in the great Plan of Salvation.
>
> The vital necessity of having that testimony was put in language by a beloved colleague of ours, the late President Charles A. Callis, who was a member of the Quorum of the Twelve, and before that served for many years as president of the Southern States Mission. He said: "Beautiful flowers do not grow on a rosebush unless the parent bush has its roots firmly planted in rich, fertile soil, unless it is watered, cultivated, unless it is pruned and carefully cared for by a gardener. Just so, beautiful flowers of sobriety, honesty, integrity, and virtue do not blossom in a human soul

> unless the feet of that human soul are firmly planted in a divine testimony of the mission of the Lord and Savior, Jesus Christ." (Unofficial transcript, LDS Student Association fireside, Utah State University, 10 October 1971.)

Since we know that what President Lee said is correct, we have to agree that it is an important matter for us to consider exactly what the Book of Mormon says about Christ. The doctrine of Christ is being challenged in the world today, in very subtle ways.

The scriptures tell us who Jesus is and, even more important, *how* we can come to him and *why* we ought to come to him. All of the standard works echo the beautiful promise of Jeremiah 29:13-14, expressed in Felix Mendelssohn's marvelous oratorio *Elijah*: "If with all your heart ye truly seek me, ye shall surely find me, thus saith our God."

The Lord has revealed his value system to mankind, telling what he sees as right, and what he sees as wrong, and what ought to be done about it. It is in this spirit that I will discuss what the Book of Mormon says about Jesus.

Jesus Is the Savior of All the World

The title page of the Book of Mormon declares that the book was written for "the convincing of the Jew and Gentile that *Jesus* is the *Christ*, the *Eternal God*, manifesting himself unto all nations." That statement tells us who Jesus is. He is God and has been active among the peoples of the world. He is not an absentee landlord.

For many centuries the world has had the Old Testament, that tells of the God of Adam, and of Enoch, Noah, Abraham, Jacob, Joseph, Moses, and Elijah. This same God, who is often declared to be Jehovah, ministered as a heavenly being to the ancient Israelite prophets. This same Jehovah, who was then a spirit being, was also born into mortality and became Jesus Christ.

For many centuries the world has had the New Testament, which tells of Jesus' birth in Bethlehem and his mortal ministry among the Jews in the Holy Land of the Middle East. It tells of his unique and divine birth, his violent death, and his bodily resurrection from the dead.

In addition to the Bible we now have the Book of

Mormon, which tells of Jesus' personal ministry as a resurrected, glorified being among the ancient Nephites in America a few months after his ascension from among the Jews. It also reveals that Jesus said he was personally going to visit the ten lost tribes of Israel after he left the Nephites. We do not have the actual record of that event yet, but we will have it when the Lord sees fit. The Book of Mormon does not compete with the Bible, but is a second witness, sent forth by the Lord to prove that the Bible record is true.

Thus the Book of Mormon enlarges the scope of our understanding of Jesus as the Savior. His ministry was not limited to the Jews of the Middle East, but extended also to America and then to the place of the lost tribes. But the Book of Mormon does not stop there. It tells us that the Lord Jesus has been active all along, in various ways, giving to every nation as much of the gospel as it could absorb and handle. This has *not* always been done by a *personal visit*, for we learn from 3 Nephi 15 that the Lord did not manifest himself personally to the gentile nations, but sent his servants to teach them. Yet the Lord has been active in one way or another among all peoples, doing for them all that he could according to their willingness, capacity, and desire to receive and to believe. Note these words from 2 Nephi 29:

> Know ye not that . . . I rule in the heavens above and in the earth beneath; and I bring forth my word unto the children of men, yea, even upon all the nations of the earth? . . .
>
> Know ye not that the testimony of two nations is a witness unto you that I am God, that I remember one nation like unto another? Wherefore, I speak the same words unto one nation like unto another. . . .
>
> For I command all men, both in the east and in the west, and in the north, and in the south, and in the islands of the seas, that they shall write the words which I speak unto them; for out of the books which shall be written I will judge the world, every man according to their works, according to that which is written.
>
> For behold, I shall speak unto the Jews and they shall write it; and I shall also speak unto the Nephites and they shall write it; and I shall also speak unto the other tribes of the house of Israel, which I have led away, and they shall write it; and I shall also speak unto all nations of the earth and they shall write it.
>
> And it shall come to pass that the Jews shall have the words of the Nephites, and the Nephites shall have the words of the Jews;

> and the Nephites and the Jews shall have the words of the lost tribes of Israel; and the lost tribes of Israel shall have the words of the Nephites and the Jews.
>
> And it shall come to pass that my people, which are of the house of Israel, shall be gathered home unto the lands of their possessions; and my word also shall be gathered in one (2 Nephi 29:7-8, 11-14).

The prophet Alma expressed a desire to tell every nation personally about the gospel, but then realized that the Lord had made provision for that within each nation.

> O that I were an angel, and could have the wish of mine heart, that I might go forth and speak with the trump of God, with a voice to shake the earth, and cry repentance unto every people!
>
> Yea, I would declare unto every soul, as with the voice of thunder, repentance and the plan of redemption, that they should repent and come unto our God, that there might not be more sorrow upon all the face of the earth.
>
> But behold, I am a man, and do sin in my wish; for I ought to be content with the things which the Lord hath allotted unto me. . . .
>
> Why should I desire more than to perform the work to which I have been called?
>
> Why should I desire that I were an angel, that I could speak unto all the ends of the earth?
>
> For behold, the Lord doth grant unto all nations, of their own nation and tongue, to teach his word, yea, in wisdom, all that he seeth fit that they should have (Alma 29:1-3, 6-8).

The Book of Mormon tells us that the person we call Jesus Christ is the God of the whole world, and of all people, and has been working among all nations to the extent of their willingness and ability to receive, and in accordance with his own timetable.

When the time came for Jesus to be born among the Jews, angels announced his birth to shepherds, and a new star guided the wise men of East. These were almost "private" signs, since Jesus would be there among the Jews in person. Not everyone heard the angels or saw the star. To the Nephites in America a greater sign was given, so that they could know without a doubt that the Son of God had been born in the Holy Land. There was a day and a night and a day without any darkness. This was a public sign and everyone saw it. The night was as bright as noonday, even though the sun descended below the horizon (see Helaman 14:4; 3 Nephi 1:15-19). Also at his death there were, in America, severe destructions, storms, and three days of darkness, and the voice of God was audibly heard among the people (see 3 Nephi 9-10). And kings upon the islands of the sea were wrought upon to exclaim, "The God of nature suffers" (1 Nephi 19:12). All of these were signs to the peoples of the world that the Son of God had been born and, some 33 years later, that he had died. None of these things are spoken of in the biblical record because it informs us only of what happened among the Jews. Thus it is the Book of Mormon that gives us the wider viewpoint. When we obtain the record of the lost ten tribes and read their account of the Savior's ministry among them, we no doubt will learn of various signs and miraculous happenings that they experienced of the birth and death of Jesus Christ whereby they could know, in similar fashion to the Nephites.

The concept of the worldwide mission and activity of Jesus, as God of all mankind, gives us some insight into the role of the wise men spoken of in Matthew chapter 2. Their mission was unique. They could not be ordinary men. They were no doubt special emissaries, prophets, if you will, coming from a land east of Palestine, to carry back to their own people a firsthand, personal knowledge of the birth of their Lord, Jesus Christ. They were spiritual men, with a mission, who knew what they were looking for. They were indeed wise men from the East—not astrologers or magicians, but prophets or seers, which is the wisest class of all men. And theirs was the greatest of all quests, as they sought the Son of God, the fount of all wisdom. Because the Book of Mormon widens our horizon as to the ministry of Jesus, we are able to gain a viewpoint about the wise men from the East that we might not have realized from the Bible alone.

I mentioned earlier that Jesus is Jehovah, born into the world with a body of flesh and bones, clothed with mortality. I will comment further on what the Book of Mormon says about that topic and will refer to four basic sources: First, in 1 Nephi 19:7-10, Nephi was at this point telling of the sacred nature of the things he had written and quoted what several earlier prophets had said about the God of Israel coming to earth.

> For the things which some men esteem to be of great worth, both to the body and soul, others set at naught and trample under their feet. Yea, even the very God of Israel do men trample under their feet; I say, trample under their feet but I would speak in other words—they set him at naught, and hearken not to the voice of his counsels.
>
> And behold he cometh, according to the words of the angel, in six hundred years from the time my father left Jerusalem.
>
> And the world, because of their iniquity, shall judge him to be a thing of naught; wherefore they scourge him, and he suffereth it; and they smite him, and he suffereth it. Yea, they spit upon him, and he suffereth it, because of his loving kindness and his long-suffering towards the children of men.
>
> And the God of our fathers, who were led out of Egypt, out of bondage, and also were preserved in the wilderness by him, yea, the God of Abraham, and of Isaac, and the God of Jacob, yieldeth himself, according to the words of the angel, as a man, into the hands of wicked men, to be lifted up, according to the words of Zenock, and to be crucified, according to the words of Neum, and to be buried in a sepulchre, according to the words of Zenos, which he spake concerning the three days of darkness, which should be a sign given of his death unto those who should inhabit the isles of the sea, more especially given unto those who are of the house of Israel.

There is no mistaking the fact that Nephi wanted his readers to understand that the God of their fathers (Jehovah) would come to earth as the Messiah.

Second, we quote from King Benjamin's discourse the words given to him by an angel. This is Mosiah 3:5-10, given about 124 B.C.:

> For behold, the time cometh, and is not far distant, that with power, the Lord Omnipotent who reigneth, who was, and is from all eternity to all eternity, shall come down from heaven among the children of men, and shall dwell in a tabernacle of clay, and shall go forth amongst men, working mighty miracles, such as healing the sick, raising the dead, causing the lame to walk, the blind to receive their sight, and the deaf to hear, and curing all manner of diseases.
>
> And he shall cast out devils, or the evil spirits which dwell in the hearts of the children of men.
>
> And lo, he shall suffer temptations, and pain of body, hunger, thirst, and fatigue, even more than man can suffer, except it be unto death; for behold, blood cometh from every pore, so great shall be his anguish for the wickedness and the abominations of his people.
>
> And he shall be called Jesus Christ, the Son of God, the

> Father of heaven and earth, the Creator of all things from the beginning; and his mother shall be called Mary.
>
> And lo, he cometh unto his own, that salvation might come unto the children of men even through faith on his name; and even after all this they shall consider him a man, and say that he hath a devil, and shall scourge him, and shall crucify him.
>
> And he shall rise the third day from the dead; and behold, he standeth to judge the world; and behold, all these things are done that a righteous judgment might come upon the children of men.

King Benjamin's words are quite clear that the Creator, the God of their fathers, the Lord Omnipotent, was the very person who would be born of Mary and would be the Son of God, the Messiah.

Third, the prophet Abinadi suffered death about 148 B.C. for teaching, among other things, that the coming Messiah, or Christ, would be the God of their fathers born into mortality. We read in Mosiah 7:27-28:

> And because he said unto them that Christ was the God, the Father of all things, and said that he should take upon him the image of man, and it should be the image after which man was created in the beginning; or in other words, he said that man was created after the image of God, and that God should come down among the children of men, and take upon him flesh and blood, and go forth upon the face of the earth—
>
> And now, because he said this, they did put him to death; and many more things did they do which brought down the wrath of God upon them.

Fourth, when Jesus visited the Nephites after his resurrection, he told them that he himself was the person who had led ancient Israel and had visited the prophet Moses. In 3 Nephi 15:4-5 Jesus is quoted as saying:

> Behold, I say unto you that the law is fulfilled that was given unto Moses.
>
> Behold, I am he that gave the law, and I am he who covenanted with my people Israel.

The foregoing are not by any means all of the references in the Book of Mormon identifying Jesus as the ancient God of Israel known as Jehovah, but they are sufficient to establish the idea.

Jesus Rose from the Grave with His Physical Body

A major message of the Book of Mormon is that Jesus, who was slain, and whose body was very dead for three days, rose from the grave with his physical, tangible body and was from that time on very much alive. Not only did he rise from the grave with a live, warm, physical body, but because of his atonement all mankind will also rise from the dead, each individually in his own time.

The physical nature of Jesus' resurrected body is described in detail in 3 Nephi, in which Jesus said he had come among the Nephites to *show* them his body. He also said that he would visit the lost tribes to *show* them his body. Note the repeated emphasis on the word *show.* In 3 Nephi 10:18-19 we read:

> And it came to pass that in the ending of the thirty and fourth year, behold, I will show unto you that the people of Nephi who were spared, and also those who had been called Lamanites, who had been spared, did have great favors shown unto them, and great blessings poured out upon their heads, insomuch that soon after the ascension of Christ into heaven he did truly manifest himself unto them—
>
> Showing his body unto them, and ministering unto them; and an account of his ministry shall be given hereafter.

Also in 3 Nephi we have an account of the personal visit of Jesus to the Nephites. I will quote a brief part from 3 Nephi 11:6-17:

> And behold, the third time they did understand the voice which they heard; and it said unto them:
>
> Behold my Beloved Son, in whom I am well pleased, in whom I have glorified my name—hear ye him.
>
> And it came to pass, as they understood they cast their eyes up again towards heaven; and he was clothed in a white robe; and he came down and stood in the midst of them; and the eyes of the whole multitude were turned upon him, and they durst not open their mouths, even one to another, and wist not what it meant, for they thought it was an angel that had appeared unto them.
>
> And it came to pass that he stretched forth his hand and spake unto the people, saying:
>
> Behold, I am Jesus Christ, whom the prophets testified shall come unto the world.
>
> And behold, I am the light and the life of the world; and I

> have drunk out of that bitter cup which the Father hath given me, and have glorified the Father in taking upon me the sins of the world, in the which I have suffered the will of the Father in all things from the beginning.
>
> And it came to pass that when Jesus had spoken these words the whole multitude fell to the earth; for they remembered that it had been prophesied among them that Christ should show himself unto them after his ascension into heaven.
>
> And it came to pass that the Lord spake unto them saying:
>
> Arise and come forth unto me, that ye may thrust your hands into my side, and also that ye may feel the prints of the nails in my hands and in my feet, that ye may know that I am the God of Israel, and the God of the whole earth, and have been slain for the sins of the world.
>
> And it came to pass that the multitude went forth, and thrust their hands into his side, and did feel the prints of the nails in his hands and in his feet; and this they did do, going forth one by one until they had all gone forth, and did see with their eyes and did feel with their hands, and did know of a surety and did bear record, that it was he, of whom it was written by the prophets, that should come.
>
> And when they had all gone forth and had witnessed for themselves, they did cry out with one accord, saying:
>
> Hosanna! Blessed be the name of the Most High God! And they did fall down at the feet of Jesus, and did worship him.

There were about 2500 persons who saw and felt his physical body on that occasion (see 3 Nephi 17:25). Even at three or four seconds each, "one by one," that would take several hours. The passage we have just read is one of the greatest scriptural records in our possession. It is clear that "showing" himself involved more than having them merely look. It was sight, sound, touch, and a witness of the Spirit.

In 3 Nephi 16:1-3 Jesus told why he was going to visit the lost tribes:

> And verily, verily, I say unto you that I have other sheep, which are not of this land, neither of the land of Jerusalem, neither in any parts of that land round about whither I have been to minister.
>
> For they of whom I speak are they who have not as yet heard my voice; neither have I at any time manifested myself unto them.
>
> But I have received a commandment of the Father that I shall go unto them, and that they shall hear my voice, and shall be numbered among my sheep, that there may be one fold and one shepherd; therefore I go to show myself unto them.

This theme is repeated in 3 Nephi 17:4:

> But now I go unto the Father, and also to show myself unto the lost tribes of Israel, for they are not lost unto the Father, for he knoweth whither he hath taken them.

The Book of Mormon Presents Nearly One Hundred Names for the Savior

The Book of Mormon contains approximately one hundred different names and titles that describe Jesus. Each of these has a different meaning or shade of meaning from the others. For example, he is called the Son of God, the Creator, the Lamb, the Messiah, the Advocate, the Shepherd, the Judge, the Holy One of Israel, the Great Spirit, the Redeemer, the Omnipotent, the Father, the Rock, the True Vine, the Law, and so on. I have mentioned only fifteen–about 15 percent of the total. Being the Creator is not the same as being the Shepherd or the Messiah, or the Law. These names identify different functions. Like the keys on a piano, each of these names bears a relationship and resemblance to the others, but each also manifests a meaning and tone of its own which is different from those of the ones next to it.

Because of its richness, the Book of Mormon plays a virtual symphony about Jesus. It tells a great variety of things. Its revelation of Christ is not a monotone. These one hundred names are used over and over again, until altogether there are almost 3500 instances wherein the Savior is mentioned. We could not strike two keys of a piano and feel that we had played a great musical composition. It takes all the keys played in numerous combinations to produce great music. In like manner, the wide range of names and the combinations in which they are presented make the Book of Mormon one of the greatest witnesses and records of Jesus Christ that can be found anywhere in the world. It truly is another witness, bearing record of who he is, what he said, what he did, why he did it, and *why* it is important. All of these things, including his second coming, are carefully documented, outlined, specified, and clarified in the pages of the Book of Mormon. It is a spiritual, Christ-centered symphony.

I am indebted to Susan Black for the statistics that the Book of Mormon contains 6580 verses and 3471 references to the Savior. I had myself previously analyzed 1 Nephi to find how many names were used to describe the Savior and how many times he was referred to. When I suggested to Susan several years ago that she might want to continue the study, she very willingly completed it through the remainder of the book. As a result of searching out the names for Jesus, she said she more perfectly sensed that the real message of the Book of Mormon is about Christ, and she expressed her feelings in these words:

> Reading the Book of Mormon this way has opened up many new ideas for me. How exciting it has been to read the Book of Mormon in this manner. It has proven to me that although it is interesting to note the travels of Lehi, and study the cultural remains of the ancient peoples, far and away the central figure of this revealed book is my Savior Jesus Christ.

Further, I am indebted to Monte S. Nyman for the information that of the 239 chapters in the Book of Mormon, only 6 do not contain some direct reference to the Savior.

There are at least three major reasons for reading the Book of Mormon: (1) to get the general story, (2) to absorb what it says about Jesus, and (3) to learn the other gospel principles contained in it.

It is worth noting that the actual term "Christ" does not occur in the Book of Mormon until 2 Nephi 10:3, and there it occurs as a direct revelation from an angel to the prophet Jacob. The combined term "Jesus Christ" appears first at 2 Nephi 25:19. The book of 1 Nephi alone has 23 terms for the Savior and uses these terms 150 times, but it does not use either "Jesus" or "Christ." That "Christ" should be his name was a revelation from the angel, and it seems to have been a new idea.

The Book of Mormon Tells How the Atonement Works

In addition to identifying Jesus as the Son of God

and the Redeemer, and many other titles and ramifications about him, one of the greatest things the Book of Mormon tells us is how the atonement of Jesus Christ works. And it explains that better than any other book. It tells how God can be both a merciful and a just God. The Atonement is explained in such a manner that we can begin to understand how mercy can be applied without robbing justice. The biblical prophets and Apostles understood these concepts, but unfortunately their writings have not come to us as clearly or as completely as they were had originally. We should be grateful, therefore, that these fundamental principles of God's plan of salvation for the human family are plainly taught in the Book of Mormon.

It would not help much to know the names for the Savior, and various other things about his character and greatness, unless we also knew how the atoning sacrifice works and how we can come to Jesus and be saved. It is in this category that the Book of Mormon makes a splendid contribution and offers perhaps its most magnificent message. We note a few examples. First is 2 Nephi 2:6-9:

> Wherefore, redemption cometh in and through the Holy Messiah; for he is full of grace and truth.
>
> Behold he offereth himself a sacrifice for sin, to answer the ends of the law, unto all those who have a broken heart and a contrite spirit; and unto none else can the ends of the law be answered.
>
> Wherefore, how great the importance to make these things known unto the inhabitants of the earth, that they may know that there is no flesh that can dwell in the presence of God, save it be through the merits, and mercy, and grace of the Holy Messiah, who layeth down his life according to the flesh, and taketh it again by the power of the Spirit, that he may bring to pass the resurrection of the dead, being the first that should rise.
>
> Wherefore, he is the firstfruits unto God, inasmuch as he shall make intercession for all the children of men; and they that believe in him shall be saved.

The Book of Mormon shows the relationship between the fall of Adam and the atonement of Jesus. They go hand in hand. Both were necessary, and both were foreknown in the premortal world. The following words are quoted from the sermon of King Benjamin:

> For behold, and also his blood atoneth for the sins of those who have fallen by the transgression of Adam, who have died not knowing the will of God concerning them, or who have ignorantly sinned. . . .

> And even if it were possible that little children could sin they could not be saved; but I say unto you they are blessed; for behold, as in Adam, or by nature, they fall, even so the blood of Christ atoneth for their sins.
>
> And moreover, I say unto you, that there shall be no other name given nor any other way nor means whereby salvation can come unto the children of men, only in and through the name of Christ, the Lord Omnipotent. . . .
>
> For the natural man is an enemy to God, and has been from the fall of Adam, and will be, forever and ever, unless he yields to the enticings of the Holy Spirit, and putteth off the natural man and becometh a saint through the atonement of Christ the Lord, and becometh as a child, submissive, meek, humble, patient, full of love, willing to submit to all things which the Lord seeth fit to inflict upon him, even as a child doth submit to his father (Mosiah 3: 11, 16-17, 19).

King Benjamin also explained that through the atonement of Jesus Christ we not only can *obtain* a remission of sins, but can *retain* a remission from day to day, as long as we live.

> As ye have come to the knowledge of the glory of God, or if ye have known of his goodness and have tasted of his love, and have received a remission of your sins, which causeth such exceedingly great joy in your souls, even so I would that ye should remember, and always retain in remembrance, the greatness of God, and your own nothingness, and his goodness and long-suffering towards you, unworthy creatures, and humble yourselves even in the depths of humility, calling on the name of the Lord daily, and standing steadfastly in the faith of that which is to come, which was spoken by the mouth of the angel.
>
> And behold, I say unto you that if ye do this ye shall always rejoice, and be filled with the love of God, and always retain a remission of your sins; and ye shall grow in the knowledge of the glory of him that created you, or in the knowledge of that which is just and true (Mosiah 4:11-12; see also Alma 4:14).

Alma further explained the effects of the fall of Adam:

> Now we see that Adam did fall by the partaking of the forbidden fruit, according to the word of God; and thus we see, that by his fall, all mankind became a lost and fallen people. . . .
>
> And we see that death comes upon mankind, yea, the death which has been spoken of by Amulek, which is the temporal death, nevertheless there was a space granted unto man in which he might repent; therefore this life became a probationary state; a time to prepare to meet God; a time to prepare for that endless state which

has been spoken of by us, which is after the resurrection of the dead (Alma 12:22, 24).

In explaining that the Atonement requires the life of a God, not of a man, Amulek said:

For it is expedient that an atonement should be made; for according to the great plan of the Eternal God there must be an atonement made, or else all mankind must unavoidably perish; yea, all are hardened; yea, all are fallen and are lost, and must perish except it be through the atonement which it is expedient should be made.

For it is expedient that there should be a great and last sacrifice; yea, not a sacrifice of man, neither of beast, neither of any manner of fowl; for it shall not be a human sacrifice; but it must be an infinite and eternal sacrifice. . . .

Therefore there can be nothing which is short of an infinite atonement which will suffice for the sins of the world. . . .

And behold, this is the whole meaning of the law, every whit pointing to that great and last sacrifice; and that great and last sacrifice will be the Son of God, yea, infinite and eternal.

And thus he shall bring salvation to all those who shall believe on his name; this being the intent of this last sacrifice, to bring about the bowels of mercy, which overpowereth justice, and bringeth about means unto men that they may have faith unto repentance.

And thus mercy can satisfy the demands of justice, and encircles them in the arms of safety, while he that exercises no faith unto repentance is exposed to the whole law of the demands of justice; therefore only unto him that has faith unto repentance is brought about the great and eternal plan of redemption (Alma 34:9-10, 12, 14-16).

Next we read in Alma 42:

And now, ye see by this that our first parents were cut off both temporally and spiritually from the presence of the Lord, and thus we see they became subjects to follow after their own will.

Now behold, it was not expedient that man should be reclaimed from this temporal death, for that would destroy the great plan of happiness.

Therefore, as the soul could never die, and the fall had brought upon all mankind a spiritual death as well as a temporal, that is, they were cut off from the presence of the Lord, it was expedient that mankind should be reclaimed from this spiritual death.

Therefore, as they had become carnal, sensual, and devilish, by nature, this probationary state became a state for them to prepare; it became a preparatory state.

And now remember, my son, if it were not for the plan of redemption, (laying it aside) as soon as they were dead their souls were miserable, being cut off from the presence of the Lord.

And now, there was no means to reclaim men from this fallen state, which man had brought upon himself because of his own disobedience. . . .

And thus we see that all mankind were fallen, and they were in the grasp of justice; yea, the justice of God, which consigned them forever to be cut off from his presence.

And now, the plan of mercy could not be brought about except an atonement should be made; therefore God himself atoneth for the sins of the world, to bring about the plan of mercy, to appease the demands of justice, that God might be a perfect, just God, and a merciful God also. . . .

And thus God bringeth about his great and eternal purposes, which were prepared from the foundation of the world. And thus cometh about the salvation and the redemption of men, and also their destruction and misery (Alma 42:7-12, 14-15, 26).

Helaman 14:16-19 says:

For all mankind, by the fall of Adam being cut off from the presence of the Lord, are considered as dead, both as to things temporal and to things spiritual.

But behold, the resurrection of Christ redeemeth mankind, yea, even all mankind, and bringeth them back into the presence of the Lord.

Yea, and it bringeth to pass the conditions of repentance. . . .

Therefore repent ye, repent ye, lest by knowing these things and not doing them ye shall suffer yourselves to come under condemnation, and ye are brought down unto this second death.

In 2 Nephi 2:24-27 we read:

But behold, all things have been done in the wisdom of him who knoweth all things.

Adam fell that men might be; and men are, that they might have joy.

And the Messiah cometh in the fulness of time, that he may redeem the children of men from the fall. . . .

Wherefore, men are free according to the flesh; and all things are given them which are expedient unto man, And they are free to choose liberty and eternal life, through the great Mediator of all men, or to choose captivity and death, according to the captivity and power of the devil; for he seeketh that all men might be miserable like unto himself.

What If There Were No Christ?

I once heard President David O. McKay say, "If Shakespeare were to come into the room we would all stand up, but if Jesus came in, we would kneel down and worship him." That categorizes the special and exalted role of our Savior.

Isaiah said, "The people that walked in darkness have seen a great light. They that dwell in the land of the shadow of death, upon them hath the light shined" (Isaiah 9:2; also quoted in the Book of Mormon, 2 Nephi 19:2).

What if there had been no Jesus, no Savior, no redemption? What would have been our fate? Could we have saved ourselves? We seem to be quite clear in our understanding that without Jesus there would have been no resurrection of the body from the dead, but what of our spirits? What would have become of our spirits if there had been no atonement by the Lord Jesus Christ? We find an answer to this in 2 Nephi 9:6-9:

> For as death hath passed upon all men, to fulfil the merciful plan of the great Creator, there must needs be a power of resurrection, and the resurrection must needs come unto man by reason of the fall; and the fall came by reason of transgression; and because man became fallen they were cut off from the presence of the Lord.
>
> Wherefore, it must needs be an infinite atonement—save it should be an infinite atonement this corruption could not put on incorruption. Wherefore, the first judgment which came upon man must needs have remained to an endless duration. And if so, this flesh must have laid down to rot and to crumble to its mother earth, to rise no more.
>
> O the wisdom of God, his mercy and grace! For behold, if the flesh should rise no more our spirits must become subject to that angel who fell from before the presence of the Eternal God, and became the devil, to rise no more.
>
> And our spirits must have become like unto him, and we become devils, angels to a devil, to be shut out from the presence of our God, and to remain with the father of lies, in misery, like unto himself; yea, to that being who beguiled our first parents, who transformeth himself nigh unto an angel of light, and stirreth up the children of men unto secret combinations of murder and all manner of secret works of darkness.

In no other place is it stated so clearly. Thus we realize that we would have been doomed to a life of misery, no matter what else we may have done. Because of the fall of Adam, a broken law would have prevented every son and daughter of Adam and Eve from escaping damnation.

We further read that there is no other name under heaven by which we could be saved except the name of

Jesus Christ. I take that to mean that we could not save ourselves, not in my name, not in yours. There is no other name. We find this taught not only in the New Testament in Acts 4:12, but also in at least seven places in the Book of Mormon, beginning hundreds of years before Christ came (see 2 Nephi 25:20; 31:21; Mosiah 3:17; 4:7-8; 5:8; Alma 38:9; Helaman 5:9). In other words, not only is there no other name now that the Atonement has been made, but there never has been any other name for salvation since the day that Adam fell.

I will note only two of these Book of Mormon references to give us the flavor of what is said. From Mosiah 3:17:

> And moreover, I say unto you, that there shall be no other name given nor any other way nor means whereby salvation can come unto the children of men, only in and through the name of Christ, the Lord Omnipotent.

And from chapter 4:6-8:

> I say unto you, if ye have come to a knowledge of the goodness of God, and his matchless power, and his wisdom, and his patience, and his long-suffering towards the children of men; and also, the atonement which has been prepared from the foundation of the world, that thereby salvation might come to him that should put his trust in the Lord, and should be diligent in keeping his commandments, and continue in the faith even unto the end of his life, I mean the life of the mortal body—
>
> I say, that this is the man who receiveth salvation, through the atonement which was prepared from the foundation of the world for all mankind, which ever were since the fall of Adam, or who are, or who ever shall be, even unto the end of the world.
>
> And this is the means whereby salvation cometh. And there is no other salvation save this which hath been spoken of; neither are there any conditions whereby man can be saved except the conditions which I have told you.

Our relationship to Jesus is not casual, it is crucial. It is not optional, it is absolute. If Jesus had not effected the Atonement, nothing we could do could make up for the loss.

The Book of Mormon Tells What an Anti-Christ Is

Not only does the Book of Mormon profusely tell about Jesus and his gospel; it also discusses the enemies of Christ and points out examples of anti-Christs. The message would not be complete if it did not do this. In Jacob 7 we read of Sherem (500 B.C.), who denied that there should be a Christ and that any person could know of things to come. He also denied that an atonement was necessary, or that God gives revelation to men.

In Alma 1 we read of Nehor (91 B.C.), who taught a generous doctrine that God had created everyone and had redeemed everyone, and thus we had no need to worry; that all people, regardless of their works, would be saved and have eternal life. The people paid him well for teaching this popular doctrine. Nehor was fashionable, rich, proud, and very popular, because he taught that which was pleasing to the carnal mind. He professed to have great humanitarian virtues; yet, when confronted about his doctrine by the aging Gideon, a member of the Church, Nehor, the great lover of mankind, became so angry that he slew Gideon with the sword.

And finally, in Alma 30 we read of Korihor (74 B.C.), another "learned" man who had much influence among the people. He ridiculed the ideas of a Christ, an atonement, a spirit of prophecy, and a need for repentance. He taught that there is no God, no need for Christ, no fall of Adam, and that only those things known and experienced by one's physical senses can be true. He further said that there was no sin, and no future judgment day or day of reckoning; that each person was saved only by his intellect, and when a man was dead that was the end. This man exhibited a materialistic viewpoint, trusting in the things of the world and of the mind of man in preference to the things of the Spirit and of God.

The false and subtle philosophies that influenced these three men are likewise present in our society today. We should be aware that the Book of Mormon tells us they are the enemies of Christ.

The Lord Supports His Servants in All Manner of Trials

Another thing the Book of Mormon tells us about Jesus is that he supports his people and lightens their burdens when they call on him for help. He hears and answers prayers of faith. We read in Mosiah 24:12-16, of Alma and his people, who were persecuted by Amulon and were forbidden to pray, and were also placed under heavy physical burdens. By their faith and prayers their burdens seemed to become light and eventually were lifted altogether.

The Compassion and Tenderness of Jesus

Jesus is concerned for the individual, and he knows that we need to prepare our minds in order to understand the gospel. Note these words in 3 Nephi 17:1-3:

> Behold, now it came to pass that when Jesus had spoken these words he looked round about again on the multitude, and he said unto them: Behold, my time is at hand.
>
> I perceive that ye are weak, that ye cannot understand all my words which I am commanded of the Father to speak unto you at this time.
>
> Therefore, go ye unto your homes, and ponder upon the things which I have said, and ask of the Father, in my name, that ye may understand, and prepare your minds for the morrow, and I come unto you again.

The people were not ready to receive all that Jesus had come to teach. Even with an excellent, perfect teacher, there is need for careful preparation on the part of the student. The passage continues in verses 5-9:

> And it came to pass that when Jesus had thus spoken, he cast his eyes round about again on the multitude, and beheld they were in tears, and did look steadfastly upon him as if they would ask him to tarry a little longer with them.
>
> And he said unto them: Behold, my bowels are filled with compassion towards you.
>
> Have ye any that are sick among you? Bring them hither. Have ye any that are lame, or blind, or halt, or maimed, or leprous, or that are withered, or that are deaf, or that are afflicted in any manner? Bring them hither and I will heal them, for I have compassion upon you; my bowels are filled with mercy . . . for I see that your faith is sufficient that I should heal you.

> And it came to pass that when he had thus spoken, all the multitude, with one accord, did go forth with their sick and their afflicted, and their lame, and with their blind, and with their dumb, and with all them that were afflicted in any manner; and he did heal them every one as they were brought forth unto him.

Alma taught his son Helaman that his (Alma's) faith in Jesus Christ had been a source of joy, a release from sorrow, and a support in time of trouble. After telling of his wayward past and an encounter he had had with an angel of God, Alma explained that he had been in deepest despair until he called upon Jesus for help. He then was filled with joy:

> And oh, what joy, and what marvelous light I did behold; yea, my soul was filled with joy as exceeding as was my pain!
>
> Yea, I say unto you, my son, that there could be nothing so exquisite and so bitter as were my pains. Yea, and again I say unto you, my son, that on the other hand, there can be nothing so exquisite and sweet as was my joy.
>
> Yea, methought I saw, even as our father Lehi saw, God sitting upon his throne, surrounded with numberless concourses of angels, in the attitude of singing and praising their God; yea, and my soul did long to be there (Alma 36:20-22).

In addition to the things we have covered in this chapter, the Book of Mormon tells us many other things about Jesus, such as the facts that he teaches prayer, he knows all things, he is interested in complete and accurate records, and he cares for mankind.

A Testimony

We first became acquainted with the Lord Jesus Christ in the premortal life and have come into mortality to gain experience and to get a physical body and to make spiritual progress. I believe, and the Book of Mormon teaches, that left to ourselves, to our own resources, to our own strength and wisdom, none of us—nor all of us collectively—could steer a course that would take us back into the presence of God. We need a Savior, a Redeemer, an Advocate, a Messiah. No wonder angels sang and the heavens rejoiced at the birth of Christ. No wonder there was a night as bright as day. Jesus, the Son of God, has come to earth, he has paid for the fall of Adam unconditionally and for our individual sins on conditions of our faith, repentance, baptism, and continued obedience. The word *gospel* means "the good news." What is that good news? That there is a Redeemer, and his name is Jesus Christ. He is the Way, the Truth, the Light, the Law, the King, the Creator, the Savior, the Example, the Judge. He is the Advocate, the Mediator, the Lawgiver, the Resurrection, and the Life–a name that is above every other name. All this and more is what I have found the Book of Mormon tells us about Jesus, and I know that what I have found is the truth.

The Ministry of the Father and the Son 3

Robert L. Millet

The Prophet Joseph Smith identified the Book of Mormon as the "most correct of any book on earth."[1] A modern Apostle has observed, "As far as learning the gospel and teaching the gospel are concerned, the Book of Mormon, by all odds, is the most important of the standard works, because in simplicity and in plainness it sets forth in a definitive manner the doctrines of the gospel."[2] The Book of Mormon is that "portion of the word" given in our day to declare and prove the truthfulness of the Restoration. It also establishes a theological foundation in the Church and, in conjunction with the Bible, aids men in "confounding . . . false doctrines and laying down of contentions, and establishing peace" among those who will give heed to its words (2 Nephi 3:12).

"And They Are One God"

Joseph Smith taught in 1844, "I have always declared God to be a distinct personage, Jesus Christ a separate and distinct personage from God the Father, and that the Holy Ghost was a distinct personage and a Spirit: and these three constitute three distinct personages and three Gods."[3] Here was sound and solid doctrine, doctrine which the

Robert L. Millet is assistant professor of Ancient Scripture at BYU.

Prophet assures us he had always taught, doctrine which was consistent and in harmony with the teachings of the Book of Mormon. Neither Joseph Smith nor the prophets in the Book of Mormon taught "trinitarian" doctrines,[4] for such were false and a part of those religious creeds which the Lord himself declared to be "an abomination in his sight" (JS–H 1:19).

From the time of the First Vision on, Joseph the Prophet knew that the Father and Son were separate individuals. Whether he understood from that experience in the Sacred Grove that the Father had a body of flesh and bones is uncertain; we do know that the Saints were teaching the materiality of God as early as 1836.[5] Regarding the nature of God, Joseph Smith instructed the School of the Prophets (in the winter of 1834-35): "God is the only supreme governor and independent being in whom all fullness and perfection dwell; who is omnipotent, omnipresent and omniscient; without beginning of days or end of life; and that in him every good gift and every good principle dwell; and that he is the Father of lights."[6] In April of 1843 Joseph the Prophet gave a simple explanation which has profound theological implications: "The Father has a body of flesh and bones as tangible as man's; the Son also; but the Holy Ghost has not a body of flesh and bones, but is a personage of Spirit" (D&C 130:22). By 1844 the Prophet was able to deliver the crowning pronouncements of his ministry regarding the person and nature of God. In the famous King Follett Discourse, Joseph Smith taught: "God himself was once as we are now, and is an exalted man, and sits enthroned in yonder heavens! That is the great secret." Continuing: "It is the first principle of the Gospel to know for a certainty the Character of God, and to know that we may converse with him as one man converses with another, and that he was once a man like us; yea, that God himself, the Father of us all, dwelt on an earth, the same as Jesus Christ himself did."[7]

In this paper we will refer to the two central characters of the Godhead as *Elohim*, "the literal Parent of our Lord and Savior Jesus Christ, and of the spirits of the human race,"[8] and *Jehovah*, the premortal God of Abraham, Isaac, and Jacob who became the mortal Messiah, Jesus

Christ. President Joseph Fielding Smith has given the following insightful information regarding the ministries of Elohim and Jehovah:

> After Adam's transgression he was shut out of the presence of the Father who has remained hidden from his children to this day, with few exceptions wherein righteous men have been privileged with the glorious privilege of seeing him. The withdrawal of the Father did not break the communication between men and God, for another means of approach was instituted and that is through the ministry of his Beloved Son, Jesus Christ.[9]

President Smith has further explained: "All revelation since the fall has come through Jesus Christ, who is the Jehovah of the Old Testament. In all of the scriptures, where God is mentioned and where he has appeared, it was Jehovah. . . . The Father has never dealt with man directly and personally since the fall, and he has never appeared except to introduce and bear record of the Son."[10]

It is very clear from the scriptures that while Jehovah-Christ is the God who deals directly with man, Elohim, the Eternal Father, is the ultimate object of man's worship. A modern revelation at the time of the organization of the Restored Church explained:

> By these things [specifically the teachings of the Book of Mormon and modern revelations] we know that there is a God in heaven, who is infinite and eternal, from everlasting to everlasting the same unchangeable God, the framer of heaven and earth, and all things which are in them;
>
> And that he created man, male and female, after his own image and in his own likeness, created he them;
>
> And gave unto them commandments that they should love and serve him, the only living and true God, and that he should be the only being whom they should worship (D&C 20:17-19; cf. JST, John 4:25-26).

That Elohim is our Father in Heaven and thus the God of Jesus Christ is particularly clear in the Book of Mormon. Lehi spoke of God the Eternal Father as the "Lord God" who would raise up a Messiah among the Jews, even a Savior of the world (1 Nephi 10:4). Nearly fifty years later, Nephi spoke of the scattering and gathering of Israel, and especially the Jews:

> And after they have been scattered, and the *Lord God* hath scourged them by other nations for the space of many generations,

> yea, even down from generation to generation until they shall be persuaded to believe in Christ, the Son of God, and the atonement, which is infinite for all mankind—and when that day shall come that *they shall believe in Christ, and worship the Father in his name*, . . . the Lord will set his hand again the second time to restore his people from their lost and fallen state. Wherefore, he will proceed to do a marvelous work and a wonder among the children of men (2 Nephi 25:16-17; emphasis added).

Indeed, the Book of Mormon record is replete with references regarding the distinct personalities of Elohim the Father and Jehovah or Jesus Christ the Son (see, for example, 2 Nephi 30:2; 31:7-21; 32:9; 33:12; Jacob 4:5; Alma 5:48; 12:33-34; Moroni 4:3; 5:2; 7:22-27, 32, 48).

The Book of Mormon prophets most often made reference to "God" or "the Lord" without any indication of whether Elohim or Jehovah was intended. Elder Bruce R. McConkie has observed:

> Most scriptures that speak of God or of the Lord do not even bother to distinguish the Father from the Son, simply because it doesn't make any difference which God is involved. They are one. The words or deeds of either of them would be the words and deeds of the other in the same circumstance.
>
> Further, if a revelation comes from, or by the power of the Holy Ghost, ordinarily the words will be those of the Son, though what the Son says will be what the Father would say, and the words may thus be considered as the Father's.[11]

Sometimes in our zeal to declare and establish the distinction between the two personages, we overlook the fact that Elohim and Jehovah are infinitely more one than they are separate! In the words of the risen Lord to the Nephites: "Ye shall be even as I am, and I am even as the Father; and the Father and I are one" (3 Nephi 28:10; cf. 11:27, 36).

Jesus Christ: The Eternal God

On the title page of the Book of Mormon we learn of the major purposes of the sacred volume. Moroni explained that the records had been kept and preserved "to show unto the remnant of the House of Israel what great things the Lord hath done for their fathers; and that they may know the covenants of the Lord that they are not cast off forever—And also to the convincing of the Jew and Gentile that Jesus is the Christ, the Eternal God, manifesting himself unto all nations." The Book of Mormon is obviously another testament of Jesus Christ: it establishes the historical veracity of Jesus of Nazareth, bears witness of his divine Sonship, and serves as an accompanying testament with the Bible that he "hath abolished death, and hath brought life and immortality to light through the gospel" (2 Timothy 1:10). The Book of Mormon helps, of course, to sustain and reinforce the messianic testimonies of the New Testament prophets and apostles. But it does more than this. Nephi explained, "And as I spake concerning the convincing of the Jews, that Jesus is the very Christ, it must needs be that the Gentiles be convinced also that Jesus is the Christ, the Eternal God" (2 Nephi 26:12). The Book of Mormon prophets certify that Jesus Christ is the Eternal God. That is, the Book of Mormon is a witness to the fact that Christ is God, the Eternal One, that he is the Jehovah of the Old Testament, the God of the ancient patriarchs, the Holy One of Israel. Had we access to all of the records of all the prophets who knew God from the beginning, undoubtedly we would see in their experiences and in their writings the unmistakable witness that Christ was and is the Eternal God. The Book of Mormon has come to us untainted and unhampered, and thus we find within its covers this repeated announcement. In stressing the importance of Latter-day Saints viewing Christ for who and what he really is, Elder Bruce R. McConkie has written:

> Christ-Messiah is God!
>
> Such is the plain and pure pronouncement of all the prophets of all the ages. In our desire to avoid the false and absurd conclusions contained in the creeds of Christendom, we are wont to shy away from this pure and unadorned verity; we go to great lengths to use language that shows there is both a Father and a Son, that they are separate Persons and are not somehow mystically intertwined as an essence or spirit that is everywhere present. Such an approach is perhaps essential in reasoning with the Gentiles of sectarianism; it helps to overthrow the fallacies formulated in their creeds.
>
> But having so done, if we are to envision our Lord's true status and glory, we must come back to the pronouncement of pronouncements, the doctrine of doctrines, the message of messages, which is that Christ is God. And if it were not so, he could not save us.[12]

One of the strongest sections of the Book of Mormon with regard to the role of Christ as the Eternal God is 1 Nephi 11. Nephi's pondering and prayer in response to his father's dream resulted in a remarkable vision (1 Nephi 11-14). In chapter 11 Nephi's divinely sent guide began the explanation of the tree which Lehi had seen. Nephi was caught away into vision: "And it came to pass that I looked and beheld the great city of Jerusalem, and also other cities. And I beheld the city of Nazareth; and in the city of Nazareth I beheld a virgin, and she was exceedingly fair and white" (1 Nephi 11:13). Nephi was asked by the angel, "Knowest thou the condescension of God?" He answered, "I know that he loveth his children; nevertheless, I do not know the meaning of all things" (1 Nephi 11:16-17). Nephi seemed to grasp the fact that the great God has love and compassion for his earthly children, that he condescends in the sense that he who is infinite and perfect has tender regard for those who are so very finite and imperfect. But the angel had much more in mind. "And he said unto me: Behold, the virgin whom thou seest is *the mother of God*, after the manner of the flesh." Nephi witnessed as Mary was "carried away in the Spirit." "And I looked and beheld the virgin again, bearing a child in her arms. And the angel said unto me: Behold the Lamb of God, yea, even *the Eternal Father*!" (See 1 Nephi 11:13-21, 1830 edition; emphasis added).[13] Nephi observed while the Eternal One–Jehovah, who would come to be known as Jesus Christ–went forth among the children of men "ministering unto the people, in power and great glory; and the multitudes were gathered together to hear him; and I beheld that they cast him out from among them." Nephi thereafter bore witness of the irony of the ages–the greatest contradiction of eternity:[14] "And I looked and beheld the Lamb of God, that he was taken by the people; yea, *the Everlasting God* was judged of the world; and I saw and bear record. And I, Nephi, saw that he was lifted up upon the cross and slain for the sins of the world" (1830 edition, 1 Nephi, chapter 3, p. 26; emphasis added. Compare with 1981 edition, 1 Nephi 11:32-33).

Jacob bore a similar testimony: "I know that ye

know that in the body he [Christ] shall show himself unto those at Jerusalem, from whence we came; for it is expedient that it should be among them; for it behooveth the great Creator that he suffereth himself to become subject unto man in the flesh, and die for all men, that all men might become subject unto him" (2 Nephi 9:5). In similar fashion an angel explained to King Benjamin concerning the condescension of God:

> For behold, the time cometh, and is not far distant, that with power, *the Lord Omnipotent* who reigneth, who was, and is from all eternity to all eternity, shall come down from heaven among the children of men, and *shall dwell in a tabernacle of clay*. . . .
>
> And lo, he shall suffer temptations, and pain of body, hunger, thirst, and fatigue, *even more than man can suffer*, except it be unto death; for behold, blood cometh from every pore, so great shall be his anguish for the wickedness and the abominations of his people.
>
> And lo, he cometh unto his own, that salvation might come unto the children of men even through faith on his name; and even after all this *they shall consider him a man*, and say that he hath a devil, and shall scourge him, and shall crucify him (Mosiah 3:5, 7, 9; emphasis added; cf. 1 Nephi 19:7-10; 2 Nephi 1:10).[15]

Indeed, nothing is more plain in the Book of Mormon than the fact that the God of ancient Israel, the God of the Fathers, would come to earth as the mortal Messiah, would "descend from his throne divine" ("I Stand All Amazed," *Hymns of The Church of Jesus Christ of Latter-day Saints* [Salt Lake City, 1985], p. 193) to rescue rebellious souls and thus make salvation available to the penitent.[16]

The confrontation between Amulek and Zeezrom provides invaluable insights into the role of Jehovah as premortal God and mortal Savior. Zeezrom, crafty and skilled in his rhetorical devices, sought to cross and embarrass Amulek "that he might destroy that which was good." Zeezrom asked, "Thou sayest there is a true and living God?" to which Amulek responded, "Yea, there is a true and living God." Zeezrom followed up: "Is there more than one God?" to which the Nephite missionary answered simply, "No." Amulek had answered correctly on two counts. There is only *one Godhead*, as this inspired spokesman would shortly observe: "Every thing shall be restored to its perfect frame, as it is now, or in the body, and shall be brought and be arraigned before the bar of *Christ the Son, and God the Father and the Holy Spirit, which is one Eternal God*, to be judged according to their works." At the same time, *Jehovah* is the one true God–the God known to men from the beginning. Zeezrom, anxious to trap the servant of the Lord, asked: "Who is he that shall come? Is it the Son of God?" Amulek appropriately replied, "Yea." His answer was perfect, and perfectly understandable to those with eyes of faith: Christ-Jehovah is both God and Son of God, and, as we shall note shortly, both Father and Son. The deceptive lawyer's questions simply provided a forum for the truth, an occasion for the declaration of deep and penetrating doctrine. Jehovah is the one true and living God, "the very Eternal Father of heaven and of earth." This God would come down to earth, take a body of flesh and bones, and offer salvation from sin to the truly repentant (Alma 11:21-44; emphasis added).[17]

Because men must believe this dimension of the "doctrine of Christ" to be saved–the doctrine that the premortal Lord Omnipotent would take a mortal and then an immortal body in working out the infinite and eternal atonement–Satan has labored incessantly to deny and stamp out the true message with regard to the coming of the Messiah. And so it is that in the Nephite record we find repeatedly the haughty assertion of the anti-Christ: "There shall be no Christ!" Sherem (Jacob 7), Nehor (Alma 1), and Korihor (Alma 30) were among the most vocal and visible of the anti-Christs in the Book of Mormon. Skilled orators like Sherem and Korihor contended that things of the future (and essentially things of the Spirit) *could not be known* (Jacob 7:1-9; Alma 30:13-15, 24-26, 48). There was also another group of anti-Christs who proved to be particularly interesting: the Zoramites. The Zoramites had, as a result of their false traditions and idolatry, rejected the law of Moses and the ordinances of the true church. Alma and his missionary companions discovered that these people had "built synagogues, and that they did gather themselves together on one day of the week." The Nephite missionaries noted also that the Zoramites "had a place built up in the center of their synagogue, a place for standing" where each person would utter the same prayer (Alma 31:1, 8-14). The words of the prayer are most instructive in assessing the extent of their apostasy:

> Holy, holy God; we believe that thou art God, and we believe that thou art holy, and that thou wast a spirit, and that thou art a spirit, and that *thou wilt be a spirit forever.*
>
> Holy God, we believe that thou hast separated us from our brethren; and we do not believe in the tradition of our brethren, which was handed down to them by the childishness of their fathers; but we believe that thou hast elected us to be thy holy children; and also *thou hast made it known unto us that there shall be no Christ* (Alma 31:15-16; emphasis added).

This group of apostates seemed to be caught up in a type of predestination, a doctrine of unconditional election and reprobation. Most interesting for the purposes of this discussion, however, is the fact that they had come to deny the coming Messiah by denying the coming condescension and incarnation of Jehovah; stated simply, to say that their God would always be a spirit was equivalent to saying that there would be no Christ.

The belief that the Eternal God would come to earth as a mortal Messiah was often very unpopular among those who needed a Messiah most. Lehi bore witness to the people of Jerusalem of the need for repentance, and of the impending doom should spiritual change not take place. He also spoke of "the coming of a Messiah, and also the redemption of the world." Note the reaction of the people: "And when the Jews heard these things they were angry with him; yea, even as with the prophets of old, whom they had cast out, and stoned, and slain; and *they also sought his life*, that they might take it away" (1 Nephi 1:20; emphasis added; cf. Alma 21:9-10).[18] Limhi explained to Ammon concerning the wickedness of King Noah and the atrocities committed during his abominable reign:

> And a prophet of the Lord [Abinadi] have they slain; yea, a chosen man of God, who told them of their wickedness and abominations, and prophesied of many things which are to come, yea, even the coming of Christ.
>
> *And because he said unto them that Christ was the God, the Father of all things, and said that he should take upon him the*

> *image of man, and it should be the image after which man was created in the beginning; or in other words, he said that man was created after the image of God, and that God should come down among the children of men, and take upon him flesh and blood, and go forth upon the face of the earth—*
>
> And now, because he said this, they did put him to death (Mosiah 7:26-28; emphasis added; cf. 17:7-8).

In summary, Christ was and is THE ETERNAL GOD. The Lamb of God is also the one true Shepherd over all the earth, the Eternal Father, and the Savior of the world (1830 edition, 1 Nephi, chapter 3, p. 32; cf. 1 Nephi 13:40-41). In the words of Nephi: "And my soul delighteth in proving unto my people that save Christ should come all men must perish. For *if there be no Christ there be no God*; and if there be no God we are not, for there could have been no creation. But *there is a God and he is Christ*, and he cometh in the fulness of his own time" (2 Nephi 11:6-7; emphasis added).[19]

The Name of Christ Known Anciently

One of the greatest contributions of modern revelation (and in this category we include the Book of Mormon) is an insight into the nature of Christ's eternal gospel, the revelation to the Church and to the world that Christian doctrine and Christian ordinances have been taught by Christian prophets since the days of Adam. The Book of Mormon is a powerful witness of the fact that the ancient prophets eagerly anticipated the coming of Jesus Christ and worshipped the Father in the name of the Son, as they had been commanded from the beginning (see Moses 5:7-8). At the time of the confusion of tongues, the brother of Jared penetrated the veil and entered the realm of divine experience. He beheld the spirit body of the Lord, received the assurance that he was redeemed from the Fall, and heard the following from the mouth of Jehovah: "Behold, I am he who was prepared from the foundation of the world to redeem my people. Behold, *I am Jesus Christ. I am the Father and the Son.* In me shall all mankind have life, and that eternally, even they who shall believe on my name" (Ether 3:14; emphasis added; cf. 4:7-8).[20]

While Nephi was in the midst of his remarkable vision, the angel began to explain the various meanings of objects in Lehi's dream, such as the fountain of filthy water and the mists of darkness. Then the angel spoke: "And the large and spacious building, which thy father saw, is vain imaginations and the pride of the children of men. And a great and a terrible gulf divideth them; yea, even the word of the justice of the Eternal God, *and Jesus Christ which is the Lamb of God* of whom the Holy Ghost beareth record" (1830 ed., 1 Nephi, chapter 3, p. 28; emphasis added; cf. 1 Nephi 12:18).[21] Jacob, the brother of Nephi, rejoiced in the assurance which he had that his posterity would eventually come to "the true knowledge of their Redeemer." "Wherefore," he continued, "as I said unto you, it must needs be expedient that *Christ–for in the last night the angel spake unto me that this should be his name* –should come among the Jews, among those who are the more wicked part of the world" (2 Nephi 10:2-3; emphasis added). It is difficult to know exactly what Jacob had in mind in the preceding statement. Did he mean that this was the first occasion whereby he came to know that the name of the Holy One of Israel, the Messiah, would be Christ? Did he mean that the angel had simply confirmed in his mind the specific name of the Messiah, something which he already knew? The question here is largely one of language: *we* know the Lord Jehovah as Jesus Christ, names which literally mean "the Lord is salvation" and "the Messiah or anointed one," respectively. The exact name by which Christ was known to other peoples of the past (and of different languages) is unknown to us. Elder Theodore M. Burton has written by way of explanation:

> We do not know the language or the exact words used by the Book of Mormon prophets. Certainly they did not speak English. A good translator translates meanings and not just words. The reader of the translation must be able to understand the thought expressed in the original work and understand the meaning thereof. If Joseph Smith, in translating the words actually used, had written down the original words, no one would have understood what was meant. Even if he had used the English equivalents and had written "the Redeemer, the Anointed," not everyone would have understood whom he referred to. But when he translated those words as *Jesus Christ*, everyone understood, and that very quickly. It is a good translation. . . .

> Thus, the ancient Book of Mormon prophets and the prophets of the Old Testament were all speaking of the same person, though they used the words their people would understand. They referred to the same person we refer to as "Jesus Christ, the Son of God." Regardless of the language they used, the meaning is clear. Joseph Smith, in translating the Book of Mormon, used the words "Jesus Christ" because they gave a clear-cut understanding of what was written by the original scribe.[22]

Nephi similarly spoke of the coming of the anointed one, bearing a confirmatory witness (of that of his prophetic predecessors and of the word of angels): "For according to the words of the prophets, the Messiah cometh in six hundred years from the time that my father left Jerusalem; and *according to the words of the prophets, and also the word of the angel of God, his name shall be Jesus Christ, the Son of God*" (2 Nephi 25:19; emphasis added). An angel also explained to King Benjamin concerning the condescension of God, and attested to his infinite anguish and suffering. The angel then taught, "And *he shall be called Jesus Christ, the Son of God*, . . . and his mother shall be called Mary" (Mosiah 3:8; emphasis added). Even as Adam was counseled by an angel to do all that he did in the name of the Son (Moses 5:8), so the Nephite prophets affirmed that "as the Lord God liveth, there is none other name given under heaven save it be this Jesus Christ, of which [has been] spoken, whereby man can be saved" (2 Nephi 25:20; cf. 31:21; Mosiah 3:17; Moses 6:52; Acts 4:12).

Jesus Christ: Father by Creation

As indicated earlier, Elohim is the Father of the spirits of all men, including Jesus Christ (Hebrews 12:9; Numbers 16:22), and is thus the ultimate object of our worship. "True worshipers," Jesus taught the woman at the well in Samaria, "shall worship the Father in spirit and in truth; for the Father seeketh such to worship him" (JST, John 4:25). Elohim is our Father because he gave us life—provided a spirit birth for each of us. Jesus Christ is also known by the title of *Father*, and is so designated in scripture.[23] We shall consider the ways in which the Lord Jehovah—Jesus the Christ—is called Father, and shall specifically note the contribution of the Book of Mormon to our understanding of these matters.

Jesus Christ is known as Father by virtue of his role as Creator. Eons before he ever became mortal he was directly involved in creation. "While yet in the premortal existence Jehovah advanced and progressed until he became like unto God. Under the direction of the Father he became the Creator of worlds without number, and thus was himself the Lord Omnipotent."[24] Enoch expressed the grandeur of the Lord's creative enterprise when he exclaimed: "Were it possible that man could number the particles of the earth, yea, millions of earths like this, it would not be a beginning to the number of thy creations" (Moses 7:30). To Moses the Lord explained how it was that he had created the world: "For mine own purpose have I made these things. Here is wisdom and it remaineth in me. And *by the word of my power, have I created them, which is mine Only Begotten Son*, who is full of grace and truth. And worlds without number have I created; and I also created them for mine own purpose; and *by the Son I created them, which is mine Only Begotten*" (Moses 1:31-33; emphasis added; cf. Hebrews 1:1-3).

Because Jehovah-Christ created the heavens and the earth, he is appropriately known in the Book of Mormon as "the Father of heaven and of earth." The Nephite and Jaredite prophets came to know full well that the Messiah, the Only Begotten Son of the Father in the flesh, was the same being who had created all things (see 2 Nephi 25:12). The angel explained to King Benjamin that "he shall be called Jesus Christ, the Son of God, *the Father of heaven and earth, the Creator of all things from the beginning*" (Mosiah 3:8; emphasis added). Zeezrom asked Amulek: "Is the Son of God the very Eternal Father?" "And Amulek said unto him: Yea, he is the very Eternal Father of heaven and of earth, and all things which in them are; he is the beginning and the end, the first and the last" (Alma 11:38-39). Finally, the words and testimony of the Lord himself seem appropriate in this regard. Just prior to his ministry to the Nephites, and immediately following the destruction in the New World, Jehovah spoke: "Behold, I am Jesus Christ the Son of God. I created the heavens and the earth, and all things that in them are. I was with the Father from the beginning. I am in the Father, and the Father in me; and in me hath the Father glorified his name" (3 Nephi 9:15).

Jesus Christ: Father through Spiritual Rebirth

In the premortal world, Jehovah became the chief advocate of the plan of the Eternal Father (Moses 4:2), a plan which called for redemption to be made available through the shedding of the blood of an innocent and Only Begotten Son. As the Savior and foreordained Messiah, Jesus Christ thus became "the author of eternal salvation unto all them that obey him" (Hebrews 5:9), and the Father's gospel became his by adoption–the gospel of Jesus Christ. Jesus became the advocate and intercessor for fallen man, the way to the Father (John 14:6). Under the Almighty Elohim, Jehovah became the Father of salvation, the Father of eternal life (see Ether 3:14).

Things on earth are patterned after that which is in heaven. God dwells in the family unit, and so the order of heaven is patriarchal. Those on earth who accept the gospel of Jesus Christ enter the family of Jesus Christ, take upon them the family name, and thus become inheritors of family obligations and family privileges. Inasmuch as one was not originally a member of the family of the Lord Jesus prior to the time of accountability (or conversion), he must be adopted into that family; one must "subscribe the articles of adoption"–have faith in Christ, repent of all sins, be baptized by immersion by a legal administrator, and receive and enjoy the gift of the Holy Ghost–meet the legal requirements of the kingdom of God to properly qualify and be received into the new family relationship.[25]

Spiritual rebirth is an absolute necessity for one who aspires to the celestial kingdom. Even as one may enter mortality only through mortal birth, so also may one qualify for life in the spiritual realm–eternal life–only after spiritual rebirth, through being born again as to things of righteousness. The Lord commanded Adam to teach these things freely unto his children, saying "that by reason of transgression cometh the fall, which fall bringeth death, and inasmuch as ye were born into the world by water, and blood, and the spirit, which I have made, and so became of dust a living soul, even so ye must be born again into the kingdom of heaven, of water, and of the Spirit, and be cleansed by blood, even the blood of mine Only Begotten; that ye might be sanctified from all sin, and enjoy the words of eternal life in this world, and eternal life in the world to come, even immortal glory" (Moses 6:59). Jesus Christ becomes the Covenant Father of all who receive and abide by the terms and conditions of his new and everlasting covenant, the fulness of his gospel (D&C 66:2; 133:57). That person who enters the gospel covenant and strives thereafter to live worthy of the directions and purifying powers of the Spirit is born again into this new family relationship; he "becometh as a child" in the sense of becoming "submissive, meek, humble, patient, full of love, willing to submit to all things which the Lord seeth fit to inflict upon him, even as a child doth submit to his father" (Mosiah 3:19). As it is with the physical creation of the heavens and the earth, so it is with the human character and personality: Christ is the Father of creation, and through applying his atoning blood men and women become "new creations," "new creatures of Christ" through the medium of the Holy Ghost.

After a stirring and inspiring sermon by their noble king and spiritual leader, Benjamin, the Nephites were overcome by the Spirit of the Lord, such that they had "no more disposition to do evil, but to do good continually" (Mosiah 5:2). Further, they entered into a sacred covenant to keep the commandments of God all the remainder of their days. King Benjamin was delighted by the people's response and added, "And now, *because of the covenant which ye have made ye shall be called the children of Christ, his sons and his daughters*; for behold, this day he hath spiritually begotten you; for ye say that your hearts are changed through faith on his name; *therefore, ye are born of him and have become his sons and his daughters*." King Benjamin then enjoined upon his people the responsibility to take upon them the family name—the name of Christ—that they might know both the voice and the name by which the Lord could eventually call them home (Mosiah 5:1-15; emphasis added).

The "new creation" associated with spiritual rebirth generally involves the gradual crucifixion and death of the "old man of sin" and the birth of the new person. Occasionally that rebirth entails a sudden and dramatic renovation of character, as in the case of Alma the Younger. Described as "a very wicked and an idolatrous man" (Mosiah 27:8), a member of a group characterized as "the very vilest of sinners" (Mosiah 28:4), Alma rebelled against the teachings of his righteous father; he and the sons of Mosiah became a significant stumbling block to the growth of the Church. But the fasting and prayers of a righteous father and concerned members of the Church availed much, and an angel was sent to Alma to awaken his immortal soul from the sleep of spiritual death and open his eyes to the truth. Rising from three days of bitterness associated with pain and sorrow and repentance, a new Alma stood before the Church, bade them "to be of good comfort," and said: "I have repented of my sins, and have been redeemed of the Lord; behold *I am born of the Spirit*. And the Lord said unto me: Marvel not that *all mankind*, yea, men and women, all nations, kindreds, tongues and people, *must be born again*; yea, born of God, *changed from their carnal and fallen state, to a state of righteousness, being redeemed of God, becoming his sons and daughters*; and thus they become new creatures; and unless they do this, they can in nowise inherit the kingdom of God" (Mosiah 27:8-26; emphasis added). This same Alma would later ask the people of Zarahemla: "And now behold, I ask of you, my brethren of the church, *have ye spiritually been born of God? Have ye received his image in your countenances? Have ye experienced this mighty change in your hearts*?" (Alma 5:14; emphasis added).

Abinadi challenged the life-styles of wicked King Noah and his priests. In the process of delivering a scathing denunciation, he also delivered a penetrating commentary on Isaiah's greatest Messianic utterance (Isaiah 53). Isaiah had said of the coming Messiah, "When thou shalt make his soul an offering for sin, he shall see his seed" (Isaiah 53:10). Abinadi explained:

> Behold I say unto you, that *whosoever has heard the words of the prophets*, yea, all the holy prophets who have prophesied

> concerning the coming of the Lord—I say unto you, that *all those who have hearkened unto their words*, and believed that the Lord would redeem his people, and have looked forward to that day for a remission of their sins, I say unto you, that *these are his seed, or they are the heirs of the kingdom of God.*
>
> For these are they whose sins he has borne; these are they for whom he has died, to redeem them from their transgressions. And now, are they not his seed? (Mosiah 15:11-12; emphasis added).

When he had finished his work on Calvary, the Lord of the living and the dead entered the world of spirits. Having made his soul "an offering for sin" in Gethsemane and on the cross, the Master was greeted in the spirit world by his seed, "an innumerable company of the spirits of the just," the righteous dead from the days of Adam to the meridian of time. To these persons—his seed—he taught the principles of his gospel and prepared them to come forth in a glorious resurrection (See D&C 138:12-19).[26]

Finally, let us consider the words of Christ himself to the Nephites prior to his visit to America: "I came unto my own, and my own received me not. And the scriptures concerning my coming are fulfilled. And *as many as have received me, to them have I given to become the sons of God*; and even so will I to as many as shall believe on my name, for behold, by me redemption cometh, and in me is the law of Moses fulfilled" (3 Nephi 9:16-17; emphasis added; cf. Ether 3:14).[27]

Jesus Christ: Father by Divine Investiture of Authority

Jesus Christ explained to a group during his Palestinian ministry, "I am come in my Father's name" (John 5:43). Our Lord acted and spoke on behalf of Elohim, such that he could proclaim, "My doctrine is not mine, but his that sent me" (John 7:16). Christ is therefore known as Father "by divine investiture of authority,"[28] meaning that "the Father, Elohim, has placed his name upon the Son, has given him his own power and authority, and has authorized him to speak in the first person as though he were the original or primal Father."[29]

There are numerous instances throughout the standard works wherein we can see this principle in operation. "And [Jehovah] called upon our father Adam by his own voice, saying: I am God; I made the world, and men before they were in the flesh. And he also said unto him: If thou wilt turn unto me, and hearken unto my voice, and believe, and repent of all thy transgressions, and be baptized, even in water, *in the name of mine Only Begotten Son*, who is full of grace and truth, *which is Jesus Christ*, the only name which shall be given under heaven, whereby salvation shall come unto the children of men, ye shall receive the gift of the Holy Ghost" (Moses 6:51-52; emphasis added). To Enoch the Lord spoke: "And *That* which I have chosen [the Savior] hath pled before my face. Wherefore, he suffereth for their sins; inasmuch as they will repent in the day that *my Chosen* shall return unto me, and until that day they [those in "prison" in the spirit world] shall be in torment; Wherefore, for this shall the heavens weep, yea, and all the workmanship of mine hands" (Moses 7:39-40; emphasis added). Another dramatic occasion wherein the premortal Christ spoke on behalf of his Father is found in the experience of Moses on an unnamed mountain. Jehovah said, "My works are without end, and also my words, for they never cease." And then he continued: "And I have a work for thee, Moses, my son; and thou art in the similitude of mine Only Begotten; and mine Only Begotten is and shall be the Savior, for he is full of grace and truth" (Moses 1:4, 6; cf. vv. 32-33).[30]

We find the principle of divine investiture of authority particularly prevalent in the Doctrine and Covenants. In fact, there were a number of occasions on which the Lord chose to speak as both Christ and Elohim in the same revelation. For example, in section 29 of the Doctrine and Covenants we read the following verse: "Listen to *the voice of Jesus Christ, your Redeemer, the Great I AM*, whose arm of mercy hath atoned for your sins" (D&C 29:1; emphasis added). But now note verse 42 of the same section: "I, the Lord God, gave unto Adam and unto his seed, that they should not die as to the temporal death, until I, the Lord God, should send forth angels to declare unto them repentance and redemption, *through faith on the name of mine Only Begotten Son*" (emphasis added). In Doctrine and Covenants 49 the same principle is at work, this time in an opposite sequence. "Thus saith the Lord; for I am God, and have sent *mine Only Begotten Son* into the world for the redemption of the world" (v. 5; emphasis added). Now note the last verse of the revelation: "Behold, *I am Jesus Christ*, and I come quickly" (D&C 49:28; emphasis added). What better way is there to establish firmly in the minds of the Saints that the words of Jehovah are the very same words as those of Elohim; that they have the same mind and thoughts; that they are totally and completely *one*?[31]

The Book of Mormon demonstrates investiture of authority in yet other ways than those we have considered so far. One of the powerful witnesses of the Nephite and Jaredite records is that Jesus Christ is Father because Elohim has literally *invested* his Son with his own attributes and powers; in this sense, Christ is Father *by inheritance*. In the words of Elder Bruce R. McConkie: "How is our Lord the Father? It is because of the atonement, because he received power from his Father to do that which is infinite and eternal. This is a matter of his Eternal Parent investing him with power from on high so that he becomes the Father because he exercises the power of that Eternal Being."[32] In like manner, President John Taylor wrote that Christ "is also called the Very Eternal Father. Does not this mean that in Him were the attributes and power of the very Eternal Father?"[33]

One of the grandest messianic sermons ever delivered was Abinadi's defense before King Noah and his wicked priests. The doctrine of this sermon is deep and profound. Abinadi had just quoted from Isaiah's great messianic prophecy (Isaiah 53).

> And now Abinadi said unto them: I would that ye should understand that God himself shall come down among the children of men, and shall redeem his people.
>
> And because he dwelleth in flesh he shall be called the Son of God, and having subjected the flesh to the will of the Father, being the Father and the Son—
>
> The Father, because he was conceived by the power of God; and the Son, because of the flesh; thus becoming the Father and the Son—
>
> And they are one God, yea, the very Eternal Father of heaven and of earth.

> And thus the flesh becoming subject to the Spirit, or the Son to the Father, being one God, suffereth temptation, and yieldeth not to the temptation, but suffereth himself to be mocked, and scourged and cast out, and disowned by his people (Mosiah 15: 1-5).

A number of key doctrinal matters are given in the foregoing text:

1. God himself—Jehovah, the God of ancient Israel—would come to earth, take a body of flesh and bones, and accomplish the work of redemption for all mankind.

2. Because Jehovah-Christ would have a physical body and dwell in the *flesh*—like every other mortal son and daughter of God—he would be known as the *Son* of God. At the same time, because he would be conceived by the power of God, and would thus have within him the powers of the *Spirit*, he would be known as the *Father*. In a modern revelation given in 1833, the Savior explained to the Prophet Joseph Smith that he is "the Father because he [Elohim] gave me of his fulness, and the Son because I was in the world and made flesh my tabernacle, and dwelt among the sons of men." Christ is thus known as the Son of God because in mortality his growth and development—like that of all the sons of God—were gradual, taking place line upon line and precept upon precept. That is, he received "grace for grace" and continued "from grace to grace" until he eventually received in the resurrection a fulness of the glory of the Father. "And thus he was called the Son of God, because he received not of the fulness at the first" (D&C 93:4, 12-14).

3. The will of the Son was to be swallowed up in the will of the Father. That is, the *flesh* would become subject to the *Spirit*, the mortal subject to the immortal. "I seek not mine own will," Jesus explained, "but the will of the Father which hath sent me" (John 5:30). Also, "I came down from heaven, not to do mine own will, but the will of

him that sent me" (John 6:38). In short, Jesus would do what Elohim would have him do. And since the will of Elohim was also the will of the premortal Jehovah, Jesus Christ the mortal would carry out the will of Jehovah the immortal. In 3 Nephi 1:13-14 Nephi received comfort the night before Jesus was to be born. Note the unusual use of words to refer to the will of the Father and the will of the Son: "Behold, I come unto my own, to fulfil all things which I have made known unto the children of men from the foundation of the world, and *to do the will, both of the Father and of the Son–of the Father because of me, and of the Son because of my flesh.* And behold, the time is at hand, and this night shall the sign be given" (3 Nephi 1:14; emphasis added).[34] A related passage is to be found in the book of Ether. In conversing with the Brother of Jared, the Lord said: "And whatsoever thing persuadeth men to do good is of me; for good cometh of none save it be of me. I am the same that leadeth men to all good; he that will not believe my words will not believe me–that I am; and he that will not believe me will not believe *the Father who sent me*. For behold, *I am the Father*, I am the light and the life, and the truth of the world" (Ether 4:12; emphasis added). Again, the mortal Jesus would carry out the designs of the premortal Jehovah; Christ would carry out to the full extent the terms and conditions of the plan of Elohim, of which he (Christ) was the chief advocate and proponent in premortality.[35]

4. Thus Christ would be both the Father and the Son. He would be called the Father because he was conceived by the power of God, and inherited all of the divine endowments, particularly immortality, from his exalted sire. He would be called the Son because of his flesh–his mortal inheritance from his mother, Mary. Therefore, Christ would be both *flesh* and *spirit*, both *man* and *God*, both *Son* and *Father* (cf. Alma 7:12-13). And they–the Father

> and the Son, the man and the God, the flesh and the spirit—are to be blended wondrously in one being, Jesus Christ, "the very Eternal Father of heaven and of earth." Indeed, the Book of Mormon is an additional witness of the fact that in Christ "dwelleth all the fulness of the Godhead bodily" (Colossians 2:9).

A final matter which might be mentioned briefly in this regard is the manner in which Christ spoke repeatedly of Elohim the Father during his Nephite ministry. This is a most interesting example of divine investiture of authority: on these occasions Jesus ascribed his words to Elohim, which, as we have noted already, are also the words and feelings of Jehovah. He spoke of the doctrine of the Father (3 Nephi 11:31-32); the law and commandments of the Father (3 Nephi 12:19); the Father granting the land of America as an inheritance (3 Nephi 15:13; 16:16); the Father making covenants with Abraham and the house of Israel (3 Nephi 16:5; 20:27); the mercies and judgments of the Father (3 Nephi 16:9); and the words given by the Father to Malachi (3 Nephi 24:1). Christ here showed deference and total commitment to Elohim, for the Lord Jesus also made clear to the Nephites that he (Christ) was the God of ancient Israel, the God who made covenant with Abraham, the God who gave the law of Moses, the God of the whole earth (3 Nephi 11:14; 15:5). As we have sought to establish, the words of one (Jehovah-Christ) are the words of the other (Elohim), and thus reference to *the Father* will frequently include (and intend) reference to both Elohim and the premortal Jesus Christ.

Conclusion

Less than two months before his death, Joseph Smith said to the Saints in Nauvoo: "The Savior has the words of eternal life. Nothing else can profit us." He then counseled his people, "I advise all to go on to perfection, and search deeper and deeper into the mysteries of Godliness."[36] One of the greatest mysteries in the Christian world is the matter of the Godhead, the relationship of the Father and the Son. If it is truly life eternal to know God and his Son

(John 17:3; D&C 132:24), then surely God does not seek to remain unknown, nor to have his children glory in the mystery of his incomprehensibility. As the modern seer taught in 1844, "It is the first principle of the gospel to know for a certainty the character of God."[37] Thus, we conclude that the first principle of revealed religion focuses on God—who he is, how he is related to Jesus Christ, and what we must do to know and be like them.

Joseph Smith taught us that a man could "get nearer to God by abiding by" the precepts of the Book of Mormon than by adhering to the teachings of any other book.[38] This is certainly true because of the sublime spirit which accompanies the reading of the Book of Mormon, as well as the marvelous lessons on life which flow from the pages of this ancient but timely record. But a person can also get nearer to God by a prayerful search of the Book of Mormon because the Book of Mormon is a book about God, a sacred volume kept and preserved by a people who had come to know him. Through diligently searching the Book of Mormon we are able to grasp the essential reality that Elohim is the Father of Jesus Christ and of all men, and is thus the ultimate object of our worship. Further, we come to sense the scriptural verity that Jesus is the Christ, the Eternal God, and that he manifests himself to those who will receive the words of his appointed servants. We learn that Jesus Christ is called *Father*, being so designated because of his creative labors, his work of renewing and regenerating souls, and his ability to speak for and in behalf of the Almighty Elohim. Christ is Father because he has inherited through conception the powers and attributes of his exalted parent.[39] But we also learn from the Book of Mormon that these two beings who "constitute the great, matchless, governing and supreme power over all things"[40] are *one*; Jesus Christ represents the Father, the Man of Holiness, and Elohim "is the Father in every sense in which Jesus Christ is so designated, and distinctively He is the Father of spirits."[41]

God has revealed himself anew in our day. But the "restitution of all things" is still under way, and the doctrinal restoration (certainly including many more truths concerning God and his nature) will continue into the Millennium.[42]

> God shall give unto you knowledge by his Holy Spirit, yea, by the unspeakable gift of the Holy Ghost, that has not been revealed since the world was until now;
>
> Which our forefathers have awaited with anxious expectation to be revealed in the last times, which their minds were pointed to by the angels, as held in reserve for the fulness of their glory;
>
> A time to come in the which nothing shall be withheld, whether there be one God or many gods, they shall be manifest.
>
> All thrones and dominions, principalities and powers, shall be revealed and set forth upon all who have endured valiantly for the gospel of Jesus Christ (D&C 121:26-29).

Until that glorious day, we have available to us a priceless volume of scripture which contains a veritable flood of intelligence regarding the nature of God and particularly the ministry of the Father and the Son. If one is sincere in his efforts to know God and embrace his gospel truths, then surely he must make the study of the Book of Mormon a lifetime pursuit. "And now," the prophet Moroni beckoned, "I would commend you to seek this Jesus of whom the prophets and apostles have written, that the grace of God the Father, and also the Lord Jesus Christ, and the Holy Ghost, which beareth record of them, may be and abide in you forever. Amen" (Ether 12:41).

Notes

1. *Teachings of the Prophet Joseph Smith*, comp. Joseph Fielding Smith (Salt Lake City: Deseret Book Co., 1976), p. 194.

2. Bruce R. McConkie, "The Foolishness of Teaching," Address to LDS Church Educational System (Salt Lake City: The Church of Jesus Christ of Latter-day Saints, 1981), p. 6.

3. *Teachings of the Prophet Joseph Smith,* p. 370.

4. For statements that Joseph Smith's "early theology" (including the teachings of the Book of Mormon) reflect trinitarian doctrine, see Thomas G. Alexander, "The Reconstruction of Mormon Doctrine: From Joseph Smith to Progressive Theology," *Sunstone* 5 (July-August 1980):25; Boyd Kirkland, "Jehovah as the Father," *Sunstone* 9 (Autumn 1984):37; Jan Shipps, *Mormonism: The Story of a New Religious Tradition* (Urbana/Chicago: University of Illinois Press, 1985), p. 80. See also Van Hale, "Defining the Mormon Doctrine of Deity," *Sunstone* 10 (1985): 27, for an argument that Mormon doctrine has never been trinitarian.

5. One of the statements most often used as an evidence that

Joseph Smith did not understand the corporeality of God during the pre-1835 era is from the *Lectures on Faith*. Note the following: "There are two personages who constitute the great, matchless, governing, and supreme power over all things, by whom all things were created and made. . . . They are the Father and the Son—*the Father being a personage of spirit, glory, and power*, possessing all perfection and fullness, the Son, who was in the bosom of the Father, *a personage of tabernacle*, made or fashioned like unto man, or being in the form and likeness of man" (*Lectures on Faith* 5:2; emphasis added). It is always difficult for us to read the minds of prophets and thus to conclude *now* what they had in mind or understood *then*. A modern Apostle has written concerning the Father and Son: "Each is a personage of spirit; each is a personage of tabernacle. Both of them have bodies, tangible bodies of flesh and bones. They are resurrected beings." Further: "A personage of spirit, as here used [in *Lectures on Faith*] and as distinguished from the spirit children of the Father, is a resurrected personage. Resurrected bodies, as contrasted with mortal bodies, are in fact spiritual bodies." (Bruce R. McConkie, *A New Witness for the Articles of Faith* [Salt Lake City: Deseret Book Co., 1985], pp. 72, 73.)

The Reverend Truman Coe, a Presbyterian minister who had lived among the Saints in Kirtland for four years, published the following regarding the Mormons in the 11 August 1836 *Ohio Observer*: "They contend that the God worshipped by the Presbyterians and all other sectarians is no better than a wooden god. They believe that the true God is a material being, composed of body and parts; and that when the Creator formed Adam in his own image, he made him about the size and shape of God himself." (See Milton V. Backman, Jr., "Truman Coe's 1836 Description of Mormonism," *Brigham Young University Studies* 17 [Spring 1977]: 347, 354.)

6. *Lectures on Faith* 2:2.

7. *Teachings of the Prophet Joseph Smith*, pp. 345-46.

8. See "The Father and the Son: A Doctrinal Exposition by the First Presidency and the Twelve," 30 June 1916; cited in James E. Talmage, *The Articles of Faith* (Salt Lake City: Deseret Book Co., 1975), pp. 465-73; quotation on p. 466.

9. *Man: His Origin and Destiny* (Salt Lake City: Deseret Book Co., 1954), p. 304.

10. *Doctrines of Salvation*, comp. Bruce R. McConkie, 3 vols. (Salt Lake City: Bookcraft, 1954-56), 1:27; see also Joseph Fielding Smith, *Answers to Gospel Questions*, ed. Joseph Fielding Smith, Jr., 5 vols. (Salt Lake City: Deseret Book Co., 1957-66), 1:13-21; 3:58.

11. "Our Relationship with the Lord," in *Brigham Young University 1981-82 Fireside and Devotional Speeches* (Provo: Brigham Young University Publications, 1982), p. 101.

12. *The Promised Messiah* (Salt Lake City: Deseret Book Co., 1978), p. 98.

13. In the 1837 and 1840 editions of the Book of Mormon, the

Prophet Joseph Smith altered 1 Nephi 11:18, 21, 32 to read "the mother of *the Son of* God," "the *Son of* the Eternal Father," and "*the Son of* the Everlasting God," respectively. In the same editions, 1 Nephi 13:40 was likewise altered to read "*the Son of* the Eternal Father, and the Savior of the world." The most recent printings of the Book of Mormon (1981) follow the 1840 readings. One careful student of the text of the Book of Mormon has suggested that the Prophet made the change in 11:18 "as a clarification possibly to avoid the Catholic-sounding formula mother of God, that had been objected to by early critics of the Book of Mormon." (Stanley R. Larson, "A Study of Some Textual Variations in the Book of Mormon Comparing the Original and the Printer's Manuscripts and the 1830, the 1837, and the 1840 Editions" [Master's thesis, Brigham Young University, 1974], p. 269; Larson cites Oliver Cowdery, "Trouble in the West," *Latter Day Saints' Messenger and Advocate* 1 (April 1835): 105, to show the prevalence of anti-Catholic sentiment at the time.)

14. Joseph Smith taught that Christ had "descended in suffering below that which man can suffer; or, in other words, suffered greater sufferings, and was exposed to more powerful contradictions [cf. Hebrews 12:3] than any man can be" (*Lectures on Faith* 5:2).

15. Note also the teaching of Amulek regarding the "infinite atonement" of Christ: "For it is expedient that there should be a great and last sacrifice; yea, *not a sacrifice of man*, neither of beast, neither of any manner of fowl; for *it shall not be a human sacrifice;* but it must be an infinite and eternal sacrifice." Amulek further explained that the atonement is infinite because the Atoner himself is an infinite being: "This is the whole meaning of the law [of Moses], every whit pointing to that great and last sacrifice; and that great and last sacrifice will be *the Son of God, yea, infinite and eternal*" (Alma 34:10, 14; emphasis added).

16. Elder Bruce R. McConkie has described the condescension of God as a dual matter: (1) the condescension of God the Father–Elohim; and (2) the condescension of God the Son–Christ (see *The Promised Messiah*, p. 367; cf. *The Mortal Messiah*, 4 vols. (Salt Lake City: Deseret Book Co., 1979-81), 1:314-15; *Mormon Doctrine*, 2d ed. (Salt Lake City: Bookcraft, 1966), p. 155.

17. See a brief but excellent discussion of the nature of the Godhead in the Book of Mormon (and specific reference to the encounter in Alma 11) in Roy W. Doxey, "I Have a Question," *Ensign*, August 1985, pp. 11-13.

18. Note in Alma 33:14-17 that the prophet Zenock was martyred because he had "testified of the Son of God, and because the people would not understand his words." See also Helaman 8:13-23.

19. For a discussion of "Why Messiah Became Mortal," see McConkie, *The Promised Messiah*, chapter 25.

20. One of the most interesting verses in the Book of Mormon is Ether 3:15. The Lord said to the Brother of Jared, "And never have I showed myself unto man whom I have created, for never has a man believed in me as thou hast." Both Joseph Fielding Smith and Bruce R.

McConkie have suggested that this verse refers to the fact that the Lord had never yet revealed himself to man in such a total and complete manner (*Doctrines of Salvation* 1:37; *The Promised Messiah*, pp. 47, 599-600). For additional explanations see Sidney B. Sperry, *Problems of the Book of Mormon* (Salt Lake City: Bookcraft, 1964), pp. 49-51; *Book of Mormon Compendium* (Salt Lake City: Bookcraft, 1968), pp. 467-68; Daniel H. Ludlow, *A Companion to Your Study of the Book of Mormon* (Salt Lake City: Deseret Book Co., 1976), pp. 317-19. Perhaps one other possibility could exist with regard to Ether 3:15. Could it be that this appearance of the Lord Jehovah was the first occasion (it seems to be the first, at least according to the scriptural records we now possess) when Jehovah manifested himself unto man in the role of *Jesus Christ, the Son of God*? It appears that every other scriptural account that we have of theophanies before this experience involve such prophetic personalities as Adam, Enoch, and Noah encountering the Lord in the role of *Father*, wherein the Lord always speaks (by divine investiture of authority—to be discussed hereafter) of the coming of his "Only Begotten Son."

21. Subsequent editions of the Book of Mormon (1837, 1840 to 1981) read, "Yea, even the word of the justice of the Eternal God, and *the Messiah*, who is the Lamb of God, of whom the Holy Ghost beareth record." Why the Prophet Joseph Smith made this alteration is unknown.

22. *God's Greatest Gift* (Salt Lake City: Deseret Book Co., 1976), pp. 153, 155; emphasis in original. These are Elder Burton's conclusions after consultation with Professor Hugh W. Nibley.

23. See "The Father and the Son," in Talmage, *Articles of Faith*, pp. 465-73.

24. From Bruce R. McConkie, "The Mystery of Godliness," *Brigham Young University Devotional and Fireside Speeches* (Provo, Utah: Brigham Young University, 1985), p. 52.

25. See *Teachings of the Prophet Joseph Smith*, p. 328; Orson Pratt, "The Kingdom of God," in *Orson Pratt's Works* (Salt Lake City: Parker Pratt Robinson, 1965), pp. 46-48.

26. See McConkie, *The Promised Messiah*, pp. 360-61.

27. We join the true Church through baptism and thereafter receive the gift of the Holy Ghost. By enjoying the influences and gifts of the Spirit we are born again into the family of Jesus Christ and thus become the children of Christ. But it was never intended that we remain children forever—even the children of Christ. Through proving worthy of the ordinances of the holy temple and thereby entering the patriarchal order through celestial marriage, we get on a higher path which may lead us eventually (via worthiness) to become "gods, even the sons of God" (D&C 76:58; cf. 132:19-20). Having so attained, we become co-inheritors, "joint heirs" with Christ to all that the Father has; we are sons and daughters of God, meaning the Father. (See Bruce R. McConkie, *Doctrinal New Testament Commentary*, 3 vols. [Salt Lake City: Bookcraft, 1966-73], 2:261, 471-75; see also *A New Witness for the Articles of Faith*, p. 284.)

28. See "The Father and the Son," in Talmage, *Articles of Faith*, pp. 470-72.

29. McConkie, *The Promised Messiah*, p. 63; see also *A New Witness for the Articles of Faith*, p. 69.

30. For additional confirmation that the being on the mount was Jehovah and not Elohim (in support of the principle taught in notes 11 and 12), see James R. Clark, comp., *Messages of the First Presidency*, 6 vols. (Salt Lake City: Bookcraft, 1965-75), 4:269-71; McConkie, *The Promised Messiah*, p. 443.

31. Divine investiture of authority operates in circumstances other than those where the Savior speaks on behalf of the Father. For example, the Holy Ghost speaks on behalf of Christ (Moses 5:9) and angels speak in behalf of the Lord (Revelation 22:8-13). It may well be that the words spoken to Nephi the night before the Savior was to be born (3 Nephi 1:13-14) were spoken by the Spirit or an angel in behalf of Christ. (See McConkie, *The Mortal Messiah* 1:349, note 1.)

32. *The Promised Messiah*, p. 371.

33. *The Mediation and Atonement of our Lord and Savior Jesus Christ* (Salt Lake City: Deseret News Co., 1882), p. 138.

34. See McConkie, *The Promised Messiah*, pp. 371-72 for a discussion of this verse.

35. The author has been careful in this paper to make fairly sharp distinctions between Elohim and Jehovah, emphasizing at the same time their infinite unanimity. This has been done based on the clarifying instructions in the 30 June 1916 doctrinal exposition of the First Presidency and the Twelve as well as on subsequent doctrinal pronouncements. It appears, however, that some of the early leaders of this dispensation may not have drawn such fine lines between the Gods. For example, Joseph Smith wrote in August of 1842: "There are many souls whom I have loved stronger than death. To them I have proved faithful–to them I am determined to prove faithful, until God calls me to resign up my breath. O Thou, who seest and knowest the hearts of all men–Thou eternal, omnipotent, omniscient, and omnipresent *Jehovah–God–Thou Eloheim*, that sittest, as saith the Psalmist, 'enthroned in heaven,' look down upon Thy servant Joseph at this time; and let faith on the name of *Thy Son Jesus Christ* to a greater degree than Thy servant ever yet has enjoyed, be conferred upon him, even the faith of Elijah; and let the lamp of eternal life be lit up in his heart, never to be taken away." Further: "As the dews upon Mount Hermon, may the distillations of Thy divine grace, glory, and honor, in the plenitude of Thy mercy, and power, and goodness, be poured down upon the head of Thy servant. O Lord, God, *my heavenly Father*, shall it be in vain, that Thy servant must needs be exiled from the midst of his friends . . . ? Oh, no; Thou wilt hear me . . . and mine enemies shall not prevail." (*History of The Church of Jesus Christ of Latter-day Saints*, ed. B. H. Roberts, 7 vols. [Salt Lake City: The Church of Jesus Christ of Latter-day Saints, 1957], 5:127-28; emphasis

added; cf. also the "Proclamation of the Twelve Apostles of the Church of Jesus Christ of Latter-day Saints," 6 April 1845, in *Messages of the First Presidency* 1:252-53.

Note also the following from President John Taylor regarding the atonement of Jesus Christ: "As He in His own person bore the sins of all, and atoned for them by the sacrifice of Himself, so there came upon Him the weight and agony of ages and generations. . . . Hence His profound grief, His indescribable anguish, His overpowering torture, *all experienced in the submission to the eternal fiat of Jehovah* and the requirements of an inexorable law." (*Mediation and Atonement*, pp. 149-50; emphasis added; cf. pp. 127, 151). Similarly, Elder Franklin D. Richards taught: "The Savior said He could call to His help more than twelve legions of angels; more than the Roman hosts; *but He knowing the great purposes of Jehovah* could go like a lamb to the slaughter. He understood those purposes, could curb His powers, control His feelings, and could make a manly fight for righteousness and truth, and carry out the decrees of heaven." (*Journal of Discourses*, 26 vols. [London: Latter-day Saints' Book Depot, 1855-86], 26:172.

36. *Teachings of the Prophet Joseph Smith*, p. 364.

37. Ibid, p. 345.

38. Ibid., p. 194.

39. There are, of course, a number of places in scripture where Christ is called Father in an unspecified sense (e.g. Isaiah 9:6; Mosiah 16: 15; Mormon 9:12). "In these cases there is no impropriety in interpreting the prophetic statements as applying to any or all of the senses in which our Lord carries his Father's name" (McConkie, *The Promised Messiah*, p. 371).

40. See *Lectures on Faith* 5:2.

41. "The Father and the Son," in Talmage, *Articles of Faith*, p. 466.

42. See Bruce R. McConkie, "The Doctrinal Restoration," in *The Joseph Smith Translation: The Restoration of Plain and Precious Things*, ed. Monte S. Nyman and Robert L. Millet (Provo, Utah: Religious Studies Center, Brigham Young University, 1985), pp. 1-22.

A Comparison of Book of Mormon, Bible, and Traditional Teachings on the Doctrines of Salvation 4

Joseph F. McConkie

This paper will compare the teachings of the Book of Mormon, the Bible, and Christian tradition on doctrines essential to salvation. It will contrast the completeness and clarity with which these doctrines are taught in the Stick of Judah and the Stick of Joseph. Conclusions will then be drawn as to the most effective sources from which these doctrines ought to be learned and taught.

Jesus As the Son of God

No doctrine is more fundamental to true Christianity than that of the divine sonship of Christ. On this matter the Old Testament is silent[1] and the New Testament confusing. Matthew twice records that Jesus is the son of the Holy Ghost (Matthew 1:18-20), while Luke tells us that although Mary would be overshadowed by the Holy Ghost,

Joseph F. McConkie is associate professor of Ancient Scripture at BYU.

the child conceived in her womb would be the "Son of the Highest" and was to be called "the Son of God" (Luke 1:32, 35). It is the Book of Mormon that resolves the matter. In vision, Nephi sees Mary "carried away in the Spirit" to the presence of God. Thus the Son of God is conceived, as Nephi tells us, "after the manner of the flesh," and Nephi testifies that he is "the Son of the Eternal Father" (1 Nephi 11:16-21). Prophesying of the same event, Alma describes Mary as "a precious and chosen vessel, who shall be overshadowed and conceive by the power of the Holy Ghost, and bring forth a son, yea, even the Son of God" (Alma 7:10). Similarly, King Benjamin told his people that the "Lord Omnipotent" would come down from heaven and take upon himself a "tabernacle of clay." "He shall be called Jesus Christ," he said, "the Son of God, the Father of heaven and earth, the Creator of all things from the beginning; and his mother shall be called Mary" (Mosiah 3:5-8).

We depend on the testimony of Book of Mormon prophets for our understanding of the doctrine of the divine sonship of Christ. As we presently have it, the Old Testament makes no reference to the Messiah's being the Son of God; the Book of Mormon, from the writings of Nephi to those of Moroni, does so consistently. To establish this doctrine among the Zoramites, Alma quoted texts from Zenos and Zenock (see Alma 33:13-18), thus illustrating that the doctrine was once a part of the scriptures of the Old World and that the Nephites had brought it with them.

The importance of a God who is a personal being siring a Son of the flesh cannot be overstated, for it determines the very nature of the Atonement. A God of spirit essence cannot shed his blood in an atoning sacrifice, nor could such a one father a child in the flesh. Neither could an exalted, resurrected, and glorified being undergo a blood sacrifice himself, since the bodies of such beings do not contain the corruptible element of blood. Only the offspring of the union of an immortal being, one from whom the gift to live endlessly could be inherited, with a mortal personage of flesh and blood, could say of his own life: "No man taketh it from me, but I lay it down of myself [having obtained such capacity from my mortal mother]. I have power to lay it down, and I have power to take it again [which I inherited from my immortal Father]" (John 10:18).

Jesus As the Christ

We observe with some interest that critics of the Book of Mormon are offended by the book, not because it fails to teach and testify of Christ, but rather because it is so Christ-centered. Krister Stendahl, a Lutheran scholar, compares the Sermon on the Mount with the same discourse delivered by Christ in 3 Nephi. He observes that the Book of Mormon places a much stronger emphasis on the commissioning of the Twelve and the necessity of both baptism and belief in the words of Christ than the Gospel of Matthew does. He notes that "in the Matthean Sermon on the Mount, Jesus is pictured rather as a teacher of righteousness, basing his teaching on the law and the prophets, scolding the superficiality and foibles of the religionists of his time, proclaiming the will of God and not the glories of himself. Nor does the Sermon on the Mount specifically speak of 'being saved.' "[2]

Stendahl expresses concern about the doctrinal emphasis on the authority of Christ in the Book of Mormon account. The absence of such authority, he feels, strengthens rather than weakens "true revelation." He suggests that the beauty of the sermon is in its ambiguity, and that one characteristic of cults is the constant desire for additional answers. He likens the seeking of continuous revelation to putting "too much glitter in the Christmas tree."[3]

I was once involved in a formal debate with representatives of the Church of Christ in Issaquah, Washington. Their primary objection to the Book of Mormon, they told me, was its constant reference to Christ and his church prior to the meridian of time. "And the disciples were called Christians first in Antioch" (Acts 11:26), I was told, and none knew of Christ or his church before the time of his mortal ministry. The strength of this argument rests in the fact that neither the name *Christ* nor the word *church* appears in any modern translation of the Old Testament, whereas the contemporary portion of the Book of Mormon contains over two hundred references to the Savior by the name *Christ* and almost as many references to his church. Representative of such passages is the testimony of Nephi:

> Notwithstanding we believe in Christ, we keep the law of Moses, and look forward with steadfastness unto Christ, until the law shall be fulfilled. For, for this end was the law given; wherefore the law hath become dead unto us, and we are made alive in Christ because of our faith; yet we keep the law because of the commandments. And we talk of Christ, we rejoice in Christ, we preach of Christ, we prophesy of Christ, and we write according to our prophecies, that our children may know to what source they may look for a remission of their sins (2 Nephi 25:24-26).

Such, we are told, were "called to the church of God, or the church of Christ" (Mosiah 18:17).

It is an interesting paradox that those so anxious to label us a non-Christian cult are offended by the Book of Mormon because it is so Christ-centered–in their view, anachronistically so (on this latter issue, see the essay of Kent P. Jackson in this volume).

Christ As the Promised Messiah

Among Christians it is generally agreed that Isaiah 53 is the greatest of the Old Testament messianic prophecies. The prophecy has been variously interpreted as referring to Isaiah, the Jewish people, and Christ. No such ambiguity exists in the messianic prophecies of the Book of Mormon. Reference has already been made to the prophecy of Christ's birth to the beautiful virgin girl of Nazareth (1 Nephi 11:13-18) and to the angel's announcement that her name would be Mary (Mosiah 3:8). The angel also declared that Christ would work miracles, "such as healing the sick, raising the dead, causing the lame to walk, the blind to receive their sight, and the deaf to hear, and curing all manner of diseases. And he shall cast out devils, or the evil spirits which dwell in the hearts of the children of men. And lo, he shall suffer temptations, and pain of body, hunger, thirst, and fatigue, even more than man can suffer, except it be unto death; for behold, blood cometh from every pore, so great shall be his anguish for the wickedness and the abominations of his people." The Nephite King Benjamin also foretold the manner in which the Savior would be rejected, called a devil, scourged, and crucified, and he further promised that three days after his death he would rise again (Mosiah 3:5-10). Nothing in the Old Testament matches these prophecies for detail and plainness.

Nor was King Benjamin alone in making such prophecies. Alma also detailed the birth of the Son of God to a virgin named Mary, whom he described as "a precious and chosen vessel." This son of Mary, Alma tells us, was to "go forth, suffering pains and afflictions and temptations of every kind; and this that the word might be fulfilled which saith he will take upon him the pains and the sicknesses of his people. And he will take upon him death, that he may loose the bands of death which bind his people; and he will take upon him their infirmities, that his bowels may be filled with mercy, according to the flesh, that he may know according to the flesh how to succor his people according to their infirmities" (Alma 7:10-12).

The Book of Mormon is replete with messianic prophecies that are as detailed and plain as the accounts of his ministry given by the Gospel writers. There are no Old Testament prophecies that can match them in plainness.

The Fall of Adam

The Book of Genesis records the story of the creation and the subsequent fall of man, the most perfect account of which is found in the Joseph Smith Translation of the Bible. There is no indication that the Book of Mormon peoples had an independent revelation on this matter. In teaching about the Fall, Book of Mormon prophets quoted the account inscribed on the brass plates, which they had brought with them from Jerusalem (see 2 Nephi 2:17).

The Bible is superior to the Book of Mormon in telling the story of the Fall. Yet it is one thing to tell the story and quite another to understand the story that has been told. The Bible contributes relatively little to our understanding of the Fall. No more evidence is needed of this than the confusion on the matter in the Christian world.

The Book of Mormon prophets, however, are plain and instructive. For instance, Lehi explains that if Adam had not fallen by partaking of the forbidden fruit, he and Eve would have remained endlessly in the Garden of Eden and all created things would have "remained in the same state in which they were after they were created" (2 Nephi 2:22). There would have been an endless state in which there was no change: no aging, no separation of the body and spirit in death, no reunion of the same in resurrection, no rewards for righteousness, no punishments for wickedness, no celestial kingdom, no doctrine of heirship, no obtaining of exaltation, no endless continuation of the family unit. Nor is this all, for Adam and Eve would have remained incapable of having seed of their own. Thus, as Lehi so eloquently stated, "Adam fell that men might be; and men are, that they might have joy" (2 Nephi 2:25). Such is the eternal plan of our Heavenly Father.

From Alma we learn that Adam passed through a period of time in which he could have negated the effects of the Fall. He explained that "if Adam had put forth his hand immediately [after having partaken of the fruit], and partaken of the tree of life, he would have lived forever, according to the word of God, having no space for repentance; yea, and also the word of God would have been void, and the great plan of salvation would have been frustrated" (Alma 42:5).

The Plan of Salvation

From the Book of Mormon we gain the concept of a "plan of salvation." This phrase is not a part of the vocabulary or theology of those who believe the Bible alone, for it is not found in their Bibles. We know that it should be because it appears in the Book of Moses (Moses 6:62); but the Bible as we have it today does not contain this or any equivalent phrase. For that matter, neither does the Doctrine and Covenants. It is in the Book of Mormon that we repeatedly read such phrases as "the merciful plan of the great Creator" (2 Nephi 9:6), "the plan of our God" (2 Nephi 9:13), the "eternal plan of deliverance" (2 Nephi 11:5), "the plan of redemption" (Alma 12:25), "the great plan of the Eternal God" (Alma 34:9), the "plan of happiness" (Alma 42:8), "the plan of mercy" (Alma 42:15), and, of course, the "plan of salvation" (Jarom 1:2; Alma 24:14; 42:5).

The Bible and the Book of Mormon both testify of a God of order. Yet only the Book of Mormon teaches of an ordered, eternal plan for the salvation of men, a plan requiring a fall from the immortal or bloodless state to a mortal state in which men would have the corruptible element of blood flowing in their veins, a blood fall that required a blood atonement.

The Atonement

"Nothing in the entire plan of salvation compares in any way in importance with that most transcendent of all events, the atoning sacrifice of our Lord. It is the most important single thing that has ever occurred in the entire history of created things; it is the rock foundation upon which the gospel and all other things rest."[4] Indeed, "all other things which pertain to our religion are only appendages to it."[5] Without the Atonement, the whole plan of salvation would have been frustrated: there would be no Savior, no gospel of salvation, no saving purpose in gospel rituals, no forgiveness of sins, no righteousness, no resurrection, no judgment, no eternal rewards, and no degrees of glory. Yet as basic as the doctrine is, we have no clear explanation of it in the Old Testament. Judaism, which maintains a zealous love for the principles of the Old Testament, espouses no such doctrine. On this matter their theology is much more consistent than that of much of the Christian world. Judaism rejects the idea that there was a fall and hence recognizes nothing from which man needs to be saved; thus, they profess no need for a savior.

Many Christians, on the other hand, maintain a verbal allegiance to the doctrine of an atonement while labeling the Fall a myth. The Atonement, as seen by such, centers in the suffering of Christ and a reconciliation between God and man which is independent of Old Testament doctrine and priesthood. Old Testament ritual is seen as a prophetic type of New Testament events, but it is not believed that the Old Testament peoples understood its prophetic implications. Such views see no kinship between temple sacrifices, the payment of money, the burning of incense, or even prayers and the grace spoken of by Paul. The essence of their doctrine is that accepting Christ is all that is necessary to obtaining a remission of sins and the assurance of salvation in the world to come.

In contrast, the Book of Mormon maintains a consistency of doctrine between the Old and New Testament periods. Moroni, for instance, explained that God created Adam, that Adam in turn brought about the Fall, and that Christ came as a result of the Fall. He testified:

> Because of the redemption of man, which came by Jesus Christ, they are brought back into the presence of the Lord; yea, this is wherein all men are redeemed, because the death of Christ bringeth to pass the resurrection, which bringeth to pass a redemption from an endless sleep, from which sleep all men shall be awakened by the power of God when the trump shall sound; and they shall come forth, both small and great, and all shall stand before his bar, being redeemed and loosed from this eternal band of death, which death is a temporal death. And then cometh the judgment of the Holy One upon them; and then cometh the time that he that is filthy shall be filthy still; and he that is righteous shall be righteous still; he that is happy shall be happy still; and he that is unhappy shall be unhappy still (Mormon 9:13-14).

This brief excerpt from the Book of Mormon, representative of many passages, is without peer in the Bible.

Though we have but briefly touched on this doctrine of unsurpassed importance, what we have said is sufficient to establish the fact that Latter-day Saint understanding of the Atonement comes from the Book of Mormon. Although the Bible is admittedly superior to the Book of Mormon in describing events that led to Christ's suffering and death, we must turn to the Book of Mormon to find the more important matter of why he suffered.

The Resurrection

One may search the Bible from cover to cover in hopes of finding a definition of the word *resurrection*, but the effort will be in vain. The Old Testament does not even mention the word, and the closest we can come in the

New Testament is Paul's statement in 1 Corinthians 15:44 that we are "raised a spiritual body," which has led many to conclude that the resurrection is not corporeal. The Book of Mormon, by contrast, plainly teaches the nature of the resurrection. Amulek defined it thus: "This mortal body is raised to an immortal body, that is from death, even from the first death unto life, that they can die no more; their spirits uniting with their bodies, never to be divided; thus the whole becoming spiritual and immortal, that they can no more see corruption" (Alma 11:45). Alma described the resurrection in this language: "The soul shall be restored to the body, and the body to the soul; yea, and every limb and joint shall be restored to its body; yea, even a hair of the head shall not be lost; but all things shall be restored to their proper and perfect frame" (Alma 40:23). Prior to the recent addition of Joseph F. Smith's "Vision of the Redemption of the Dead" to the Doctrine and Covenants, even that compilation of revelations did not contain a definition of resurrection. Clearly our doctrine is founded on the Book of Mormon.

The Spirit World

Our comparison here is very simple. The Bible says nothing on the matter, except inferentially.[6] We turn to Alma to learn about the world of the spirits. Knowing that death is the separation of the body and the spirit and that resurrection is the inseparable reunion of the same, Alma was in a position to ask a question that those having no idea about the true nature of the Resurrection are unable to ask. "I would inquire," he said, "what becometh of the souls of men from this time of death to the time appointed for the resurrection?" At the feet of an angel he had learned that at death the righteous are received into a state of rest and peace, "where they shall rest from all their troubles and from all care, and sorrow." This state is called *paradise*. The wicked, those having "no part nor portion of the Spirit of the Lord," Alma learned, are consigned to a portion of the spirit world called "outer darkness." Among the wicked there is "weeping, and wailing, and gnashing of teeth, and this because of their own iniquity, being led captive by the will of the devil" (Alma 40:7, 12-13).

As one cannot understand the Atonement without understanding the Fall, so one cannot understand the nature of the spirit world without a proper understanding of the nature of the Resurrection. If a theology does not admit a physical resurrection, then biblical references or allusions to the "spirit world" would naturally be confused with heaven because that term is used to describe the Saints' eternal home.

The Necessity of Ordinances

If the Bible is clear on the necessity of ordinances, there is no evidence of it among those professing an allegiance to it. Let us consider baptism as an illustration. The word *baptism* is not found in the Old Testament, and most refuse to acknowledge its existence in Old Testament times. Christian denominations are divided as to the necessity of the ordinance. Among those that acknowledge its necessity, ritual history has witnessed a remarkable diversity of practices, ranging from the daily immersions of the Essenes to the practice of sprinkling infants.

The Book of Mormon is most explicit on this matter. Baptism is essential to salvation. Nephi tells us that Christ himself, though he was without sin, could not be saved without it (see 2 Nephi 31:5-9). For Latter-day Saints, what Nephi says about the necessity of baptism is equally true of all ordinances of salvation. Thus Joseph Smith said: "If a man gets a fullness of the priesthood of God he has to get it in the same way that Jesus Christ obtained it, and that was by keeping all the commandments and obeying all the ordinances of the house of the Lord."[7]

Justification: By Grace or Works?

What must one do to stand justified before God? Does one seek God's favor through fasting, prayer, and rituals? Or are such to be eschewed in favor of the doctrine that "the just shall live by faith" (Romans 1:17)? Such was the issue over which the Roman Catholic Church and Martin Luther did battle. Of this struggle one noted scholar wrote: "This doctrine of justification by faith has divided the old unity of Christendom; has torn asunder Europe, and especially Germany; has made innumerable martyrs; has kindled the bloodiest and most terrible wars of the past; and has deeply affected European history and with it the history of humanity."[8]

And what does the Book of Mormon have to say on a matter of such doctrinal importance? No answer is more effective than Alma's instruction to Corianton. Burdened with sin, Corianton was greatly agitated over the requirements of salvation. His father Alma taught him the principle of "restoration," declaring that "it is requisite with the justice of God that men should be judged according to their works; and if their works were good in this life, and the desires of their hearts were good, that they should also, at the last day, be restored unto that which is good. And if their works are evil they shall be restored unto them for evil" (Alma 41:3-4). "The meaning of the word restoration," he said, "is to bring back again evil for evil, or carnal for carnal, or devilish for devilish—good for that which is good; righteous for that which is righteous; just for that which is just; merciful for that which is merciful" (Alma 41:13). The principle is immutable. Alma instructed his son to

> see that you are merciful unto your brethren; deal justly, judge righteously, and do good continually; and if ye do all these things then shall ye receive your reward; yea, ye shall have mercy restored unto you again; ye shall have justice restored unto you again; ye shall have a righteous judgment restored unto you again; and ye shall have good rewarded unto you again. For that which ye do send out shall return unto you again, and be restored; therefore, the word restoration more fully condemneth the sinner, and justifieth him not at all (Alma 41:14-15).

Martin Luther, during his notable career, became the author of one of history's most classic cases of proof-texting. Taking selected texts from Romans, Galatians, and Ephesians, Luther said that these three books—along with 1 Peter, John's Gospel, and 1 John—would "teach everything you need to know for your salvation, even if you were never to see or hear any other book or hear any other teaching."[9] As is apparent, this is a very selective viewpoint which requires that one read only a narrow band of works in the Bible to sustain this doctrine. Paul is quoted to that end; Christ is not. The Old Testament and its doctrines are disregarded, James is called a "straw book," and a host of other references to works in the New Testament, most of which come from Paul, are ignored. Again, on this matter the Book of Mormon is most plain.

The Gathering of Israel

The Book of Mormon and the Old Testament both have much to say on the subject of the scattering and gathering of Israel. New World prophets frequently quote the prophecies of their Old World counterparts on this subject. The Book of Mormon makes three distinctive contributions regarding the gathering of Israel. First, it emphasizes the fact that the people of Israel were scattered because they rejected the Holy One of Israel, namely Jesus Christ. The Book of Mormon teaches that Israel will not be gathered until her people accept the Christ. As wickedness preceded the scattering, so righteousness must precede the gathering. The gathering, according to the Book of Mormon, is always first to Christ through obedience to the laws and ordinances of the gospel, and only then to a geographic location. Jacob taught the principle thus:

> Because of priestcrafts and iniquities, they at Jerusalem will stiffen their necks against him, that he be crucified. Wherefore, because of their iniquities, destructions, famines, pestilences, and bloodshed shall come upon them; and they who shall not be destroyed shall be scattered among all nations. But behold, thus saith the Lord God: When the day cometh that they shall believe in me, that I am Christ, then have I covenanted with their fathers that they shall be restored in the flesh, upon the earth, unto the lands of their inheritance (2 Nephi 10:5-7).

Surely God is appreciably more concerned with how his people live than where they live.

The second matter is an extension of the first. The Book of Mormon tells us that one does not accept Christ without uniting with his Church, thereby obtaining citizenship in his kingdom (see 2 Nephi 9:2; 3 Nephi 21:22). The third distinctive contribution of the Book of Mormon is the expansion of the Lord's promise to return Israel not to a single land of promise, but to *lands* of promise (see 1 Nephi 22:12; 2 Nephi 6:11; 9:2; 10:7-8). The Americas, the Book of Mormon declares, have been promised to the tribe of Joseph. Other lands undoubtedly have been promised to others of Jacob's children.

Scriptural Inerrancy and Infallibility

Various camps of the so-called Bible-believing world have recently revived the struggle over the issue of biblical inerrancy and infallibility. Since the extent of our faith and trust in scripture is very directly associated with our understanding of the doctrines of salvation, let us address this matter from the perspective of the Book of Mormon. Joseph Smith said "that the Book of Mormon was the most correct of any book on earth" (Book of Mormon Introduction). The eighth article of faith states: "We believe the Bible to be the word of God as far as it is translated correctly; we also believe the Book of Mormon to be the word of God." Given such statements, are we as Latter-day Saints to argue for the inerrancy or infallibility of the Book of Mormon as the fundamentalists do for the Bible?

Significantly, Book of Mormon prophets responded to this issue, while Bible prophets are not recorded as having done so. For the Bible it can only be said that it offers no justification for the fundamentalist tenets of infallibility and inerrancy. The Bible makes no claim to either. One cannot fairly say that they are biblical doctrines. But what does the Book of Mormon say on this matter?

Book of Mormon prophets emphatically rejected the notion of infallible scripture. The title page to the Book of Mormon announces the book to be the result of "the spirit of prophecy and of revelation—written by way of commandment." In it, Mormon, who abridged the record, states that "if there are faults they are the mistakes of men." This says simply that inspired men, prophets of God, and men commissioned to write the word of God are not themselves infallible. Even in the inspiration of their office they may be hindered by frailties of the flesh. The weaknesses of the flesh have been the common lot of all the Lord's prophets and none have been more sensitive to those weaknesses than the prophets themselves.

Nephi wrote, "If I do err, even did they err of old; not that I would excuse myself because of other men, but because of the weakness which is in me, according to the flesh, I would excuse myself" (1 Nephi 19:6). His reference to "they . . . of old" would include such as Isaiah, Moses, and Abraham, none of whom made any pretense to perfection in their inspired writings. Of himself, Nephi said he was not "mighty in writing, like unto speaking; for when a man speaketh by the power of the Holy Ghost the power of the Holy Ghost carrieth it into the hearts of the children of men." That which he wrote in "weakness," he maintained, would have to be made strong, like his spoken words, by the power of the Holy Ghost (2 Nephi 33:1, 4). In other words, the lifeblood of proper understanding of the written or the spoken word must always be the spirit of revelation, or the Holy Ghost. Thus, infallibility is no more necessary in the written word than in the spoken word, for both are equally dependent on the spirit of revelation for understanding.

Moroni shared the concern of his fellow prophets when he wrote, "The Gentiles will mock at these things, because of our weakness in writing." We "stumble," he lamented, "because of the placing of our words," though he added that it is fools who mock (Ether 12:23-36). "If there be faults," he declared, "they be the faults of a man" (Mormon 8:17). Yet, in the spirit of prophecy he said: "I speak unto you as though I spake from the dead; for I know that ye shall have my words. Condemn me not because of mine imperfection, neither my father, because of his imperfection, neither them who have written before him; but rather give thanks unto God that he hath made manifest unto you our imperfections, that ye may learn to be more wise than we have been" (Mormon 9:30-31).

Revelation

The Bible evidences that whenever God had a people whom he acknowledged as his own, he guided them by revelation. The Book of Mormon affirms that God spoke to the scattered remnants of Israel anciently and testifies that he will continue speaking to those willing to hear his voice until the end of time. Indeed, the Book of Mormon sounds a solemn warning to any who deny the spirit of revelation:

> Wo be unto him that hearkeneth unto the precepts of men, and denieth the power of God, and the gift of the Holy Ghost! Yea, wo be unto him that saith: We have received, and we need no more! And in fine, wo unto all those who tremble, and are angry because of the truth of God! For behold, he that is built upon the rock receiveth it with gladness; and he that is built upon a sandy foundation trembleth lest he shall fall. Wo be unto him that shall say: We have received the word of God, and we need no more of the word of God, for we have enough! For behold, thus saith the Lord God: I will give unto the children of men line upon line, precept upon precept, here a little and there a little; and blessed are those who hearken unto my precepts, and lend an ear unto my counsel, for they shall learn wisdom; for unto him that receiveth I will give more; and from them that shall say, We have enough, from them shall be taken away even that which they have (2 Nephi 28:26-30).

Has God ceased to be a God of miracles? Have angels ceased to appear? Has God withheld the power of the Holy Ghost, the revelator, from the children of men? "Or will he, so long as time shall last, or the earth shall stand, or there shall be one man upon the face thereof to be saved?" (Moroni 7:36-37). The Book of Mormon answers with a most emphatic "No!"

Conclusion

A brief comparison of the Book of Mormon and the Bible on doctrines fundamental to salvation and the Christian message allows us to draw the following conclusions.

New Testament doctrines fundamental to the Christian message—the promised Messiah's being the Son of God; Jesus' being the Christ; the nature of the spirit world and resurrection; the plan of salvation; church organization; the ordinance of baptism; and the conferring of the Holy Ghost—often go unmentioned in the Old Testament as we now have it. But each of these doctrines is clearly taught in the Book of Mormon, which is largely contemporary with the Old Testament. In the Book of Mormon we find a doctrinal consistency not found in the Bible. Developing this principle, Nephi said of God:

> He is the same yesterday, today, and forever; and the way is prepared for all men from the foundation of the world, if it so be that they repent and come unto him. For he that diligently seeketh shall find; and the mysteries of God shall be unfolded unto them, by the power of the Holy Ghost, as well in these times as in times of old, and as well in times of old as in times to come; wherefore, the course of the Lord is one eternal round (1 Nephi 10:18-19).

The Book of Mormon is superior to the Bible in teaching each of the doctrines of salvation considered in this paper. While the Bible is superior to the Book of Mormon in detailing circumstances surrounding Adam's transgression and events that attended the atonement of Christ, yet it is to the Book of Mormon that we turn for understanding of the doctrinal implications of both. Affirming this principle, Elder Bruce R. McConkie observed "that Lehi and Jacob excel Paul in teaching the Atonement; that Alma's sermons on faith and on being born again surpass anything in the Bible; that Nephi makes a better exposition of the scattering and gathering of Israel than do Isaiah, Jeremiah, and Ezekiel combined; that Mormon's words about faith, hope, and charity have a clarity, a breadth, and a power of expression that even Paul did not attain; and so on and so on."[10]

The Book of Mormon and the Bible are not in disagreement on the doctrines under consideration. The Book of Mormon consistently goes beyond the Bible in its teachings, but is certainly in harmony with it.

In the case of each doctrine considered, it is the Book of Mormon and not the Bible that establishes the doctrinal position of The Church of Jesus Christ of Latter-day Saints. We are not dependent on the Bible for our knowledge of the doctrines of salvation.

On each of these doctrines there is considerable diversity of understanding in the Bible-believing world. When we as Latter-day Saints seek to justify our doctrinal beliefs through the Bible, we are clearly out of context. We did not obtain our understanding from the Bible, and if we had only the Bible, there is every reason to believe that our understanding would be similar to that of those whom we are attempting to persuade otherwise. Joseph Smith put it this way: "Take away the Book of Mormon and the revelations and where is our religion? We have none."[11]

When the Lord spoke to Joseph Smith saying, "This generation [meaning dispensation] shall have my word through you" (Doctrine and Covenants 5:10), the context of the revelation was the coming forth of the Book of Mormon. From the Book of Mormon we learn the basic doctrines by which salvation comes. The Book of Mormon is the source from which we are both to learn and to teach the doctrines of the kingdom to each other and to the world. Competent doctrinal understanding presupposes a mastery of the Book of Mormon. In the context of missionary work, no true conversion can take place until the Book of Mormon is accepted as the basic source of the doctrines of salvation.

Notes

1. The phrase "Son of God" in Daniel 3:25 is "angel" in verse 28. A better rendering of verse 25 would be "looks like a god" as in the New English Bible, or "looks like an angel" as in the James Moffatt translation.

2. Krister Stendahl, "The Sermon on the Mount and Third Nephi," in *Reflections on Mormonism: Judaeo-Christian Parallels,* ed. Truman G. Madsen (Provo, Utah: Brigham Young University, Religious Studies Center, 1978), pp. 143-44.

3. Ibid., p. 154.

4. Bruce R. McConkie, *Mormon Doctrine,* 2d ed. (Salt Lake City: Bookcraft, 1966), p. 60.

5. Joseph Smith, in Joseph Fielding Smith, comp., *Teachings of the Prophet Joseph Smith* (Salt Lake City: Deseret Book, 1975), p. 121.

6. For instance, from Genesis 37:35 it can be inferred that Jacob, who vowed to wear mourning clothes until his death, expected to be both recognized by his son Joseph and dressed in his mourning garments in the realm of the dead after being buried in them. See also Zechariah 3:1-5; 1 Peter 3:19-22; 4:6.

7. *Teachings*, p. 308.

8. Paul Tillich, *The Protestant Era* (Chicago: University of Chicago Press, 1948), p. 196, as cited in Sidney B. Sperry, *Paul's Life and Letters* (Salt Lake City: Bookcraft, 1955), p. 172.

9. As cited by Richard Lloyd Anderson, *Understanding Paul* (Salt Lake City: Deseret Book, 1983), p. 179.

10. Bruce R. McConkie, in Conference Report, October 1983, p. 106.

11. Joseph Smith, *History of The Church of Jesus Christ of Latter-day Saints,* 7 vols. (Salt Lake City: Deseret Book Company, 1978), 2:52.

The Beginnings of Christianity in the Book of Mormon 5

Kent P. Jackson

There is no question that the gospel of Jesus Christ is central to the Book of Mormon. The title page affirms that the book was written, among other reasons, "to the convincing of the Jew and Gentile that Jesus is the Christ, the Eternal God, manifesting himself unto all nations." This phrase identifies the Book of Mormon's two main teachings, or witnesses, that Jesus is indeed the Christ and that he is also the Eternal God. The Book of Mormon bears a powerful testimony to both.

One aspect of the significance of the Book of Mormon is the fact that it is a Christian testimony coming from a time when the knowledge of Christ was limited in the world. God has not always allowed a full understanding of gospel principles to be had among the people of the earth, even among those of the house of Israel. From the days of Moses to the days of Christ, Israel was denied priesthood and gospel blessings that are reserved for the faithful. Because of rebellion against God, the Israelites were restricted in their opportunities and in their knowledge (see D&C 84:23-27; JST, Exodus 34:1-2). Yet the Lord did not

Kent P. Jackson is associate professor of Ancient Scripture at BYU.

leave them without a measure of true religion; the law of Moses and its authority of the Aaronic Priesthood were given to the Israelites until they could live in accordance with the higher principles and blessings of the gospel of Christ. Alma taught: "He that will harden his heart, the same receiveth *the lesser portion of the word*; and he that will not harden his heart, to him is given *the greater portion of the word*, until it is given unto him to know the mysteries of God until he know them in full. And they that will harden their hearts, to them is given *the lesser portion of the word until they know nothing concerning his mysteries*" (Alma 12:10-11; emphasis added). Rebellion leads to loss of opportunities, and ancient Israel, through much of its history, suffered the consequences of its rebellious behavior by having much of the message of the gospel withdrawn.[1]

The Book of Mormon is a powerful witness of these principles. In it we follow the history of one family of Israelites which proved itself worthy to be blessed with great light and knowledge concerning Christ. Just as the passage quoted above from Alma teaches, when Lehi's descendants were righteous the heavens were opened to them and they learned of Christ. Even a superficial comparison of the content of the Book of Mormon with that of the Bible enables one to see that the level of understanding concerning sacred things was greater among Lehi's descendants than among the people from which they came.[2] With the separation of Lehi and his family from their native society came a revelation—perhaps more accurately a *restoration*—of gospel principles that were unknown to the mainstream of their countrymen. The records of Lehi, Nephi, and Jacob on the small plates of the Book of Mormon contain sufficient information to demonstrate that with the prophetic callings of Lehi and his sons a restoration of the gospel took place.[3]

In this study I shall examine some of the key passages and historical events that recount the revelation of Christianity to the family of Lehi.

The Call of Lehi

According to chapter 1 of 1 Nephi, when Lehi was preaching in Jerusalem his message followed the pattern familiar from Old Testament prophets of his time. The thrust of his message concerned the fact that Jerusalem would be destroyed soon and its inhabitants taken away because of their wickedness. According to Nephi, his father was one of "many" prophets in Jerusalem who preached the same message at that time.[4] In addition to that, Lehi saw in vision "God sitting upon his throne," "One descending out of the midst of heaven," and also "twelve others following him" (1 Nephi 1:8-10). The one sitting on the throne is identified as God, but the others–including the "One" who descends–are not identified in that chapter of Nephi's record. The first of those who descended gave Lehi a book, which he was commanded to read. Nephi made only brief observations regarding its content: Lehi read in it "concerning Jerusalem–that it should be destroyed, and the inhabitants thereof; many should perish by the sword, and many should be carried away captive into Babylon" (1 Nephi 1:13). This is typical of the writings of the other Judahite prophets in Lehi's generation.[5]

Nephi did not tell us more about the content of the book, but he mentioned that his father was greatly moved as he continued to read and see it in vision. He proclaimed the greatness of the Lord in not allowing those who would come unto God to perish (1 Nephi 1:14). Perhaps Lehi was making reference then to the fact that his own group would be saved from the coming destruction, or perhaps he spoke on a deeper level of God's power to save from sin. When Lehi preached to the Jews the message that he learned from his visions, he testified of two things: first, that the inhabitants of Jerusalem were wicked and would be destroyed, and second, in Nephi's words, "of the coming of *a Messiah*, and also the redemption of the world" (1 Nephi 1:19; emphasis added). For these pronouncements Lehi was persecuted, and the Jews attempted to kill him (1 Nephi 1:20).

Nephi's report of his father's first vision and its consequences is intriguing. He mentions "One descending out of the midst of heaven" as though his identity were unknown at the time. Latter-day Saints today would have no hesitation in identifying him as Christ. Since Nephi clearly knew much of Christ when the record was written, his ambiguity on the subject, or that of his father, must have been deliberate.[6] Perhaps Nephi was telling his readers that his father did not know at the time who the "One descending" was. This is not unlikely, since it is not until 1 Nephi 10 that Lehi began to instruct his children on the topic of Jesus' mission, giving them information that he had received in later revelations.

As Nephi further related the preaching of his father that followed his first vision, he mentioned that Lehi spoke plainly of one whom he called "a Messiah." The term *a Messiah*, without a definite article "the,"[7] is very uncharacteristic of the writing of Nephi, who later wrote of Christ with tremendous force, clarity, and directness. It seems reasonable that Nephi's writing was intended to convey Lehi's limited perspective at the time with regard to Christ, his mission, and his identity.

A Vision of Christ

First Nephi 10 paints for us a picture of the unfolding of the knowledge of Christ to Lehi and his people. In this chapter Lehi related to his group things that he had learned through revelation, particularly in the dream that is reported in chapter 8. Nephi's paraphrase of his father's teachings contains indefinite articles and in nonspecific references—as Lehi was revealing new and marvelous things to his children. Nephi's summary in verse 4 is instructive: "Yea, even six hundred years from the time that my father left Jerusalem, *a prophet* would the Lord God raise up among the Jews—even *a Messiah*, or, in other words, *a Savior* of the world" (1 Nephi 10:4; emphasis added). In the next verse Nephi mentioned Jesus again, using the following words: "*this Messiah*, of whom he had spoken, or *this Redeemer* of the world" (1 Nephi 10:5; emphasis added). The power of Christ's atonement is introduced in the next verse for the first time in the Book of Mormon: "Wherefore, all mankind were in a lost and in a fallen state, and ever would be save they should rely on *this Redeemer*" (1 Nephi 10:6; emphasis added).

Thus in recounting these early revelations, Nephi used such terms as "a Messiah," "this Messiah," "a prophet," "a Savior of the world," and "this Redeemer"—all in obvious reference to Christ. Nephi's reason for using such language is apparent. These are precisely the kinds of words that one uses with reference to an individual or a concept that is being introduced for the first time. It appears that such was the case with the knowledge of Jesus Christ and the nature of his mission, which were being revealed as new ideas to Lehi and his sons. Nephi, the careful and sensitive historian, preserved the integrity of the event with this kind of language, even though his report of it was written at least three decades later.

It was over forty years after Lehi left Jerusalem that Jacob was visited by an angel who told him that the Messiah's name would be "Christ" (2 Nephi 10:3; see also 2 Nephi 25:19)—the first reference to that name in the Book of Mormon. That name is used very frequently thereafter, for a total of 315 times in the Book of Mormon. The name "Jesus" is not introduced in the Book of Mormon until 2 Nephi 25:19, in a context more than forty years after Lehi's departure from Jerusalem. There Nephi taught that "according to the words of the prophets, and also the word of the angel of God, his name shall be Jesus Christ." Beginning with this first reference, the name "Jesus" is found in common use in the Book of Mormon, and it appears a total of 161 times.

In 1 Nephi 10:7, Nephi began the report of his father's teachings of the mortal works of the Savior, beginning with the ministry of John the Baptist, who would baptize the Messiah (1 Nephi 10:9). Lehi taught his children that the gospel would be preached to the Jews; they would slay "the Messiah, who should come," after which he would rise from the dead. Nephi himself pointed out that "the Messiah who should come" would be the Son of God, giving us the first reference to the paternity of Christ in the Book of Mormon (1 Nephi 10:17).[8]

The Testimony of Nephi

Because Nephi was anxious to see the same things that his father had seen in vision, a vision similar to that of his father was opened to him (1 Nephi 14:29). In addition to giving the interpretation of individual items in Lehi's dream, Nephi's report of his vision provided an expanded prophecy of the future and gave a fuller and deeper interpretation of what Lehi witnessed. The most important part of Nephi's vision was his testimony of the mission of Christ. Nephi's visionary witness of Jesus must have been of extreme significance for him and for his people in later generations. The information concerning the Savior that was revealed to him, Lehi, and Jacob during the early years of their ministries probably formed the foundation for later Nephite and Lamanite belief in Christ's mortal works. Unfortunately, as the subsequent history of their people attests, not all Book of Mormon people believed their message.[9]

Nephi's vision of Christ includes information concerning his mortal coming in Palestine and his glorified coming in the Americas. Adding to the things that had been made known by his father, Nephi taught the following concerning Christ: he would be the Son of God, born to Mary (1 Nephi 11:13-21); he would minister "in power and great glory," blessing the lives of others (1 Nephi 11:24, 28, 31); he would be followed by the Twelve Apostles (1 Nephi 11:29); he would be judged and slain by the Jews (1 Nephi 11:32-33); in the Americas there would be destruction preceding his coming (1 Nephi 12:4-5); he would then appear in glory (1 Nephi 12:6); twelve Nephite disciples would be called (1 Nephi 12:7-10); and three generations of righteousness would follow his appearance (1 Nephi 12:11-12). Because of these things that were revealed concerning Jesus, the Book of Mormon peoples who believed in him were really *Christians*. Their record, therefore, is "Another Testament of Jesus Christ."

The Testimony of the Prophets

As is apparent in several passages, Lehi's and Nephi's

sources of information concerning the mission of Christ were not restricted to revelation and visitations of angels. Lehi and his family members learned of Christ as well through reading the revelations of earlier prophets found on the brass plates. The prophet Zenos's record appears to have been a major written source for Nephi's knowledge of Christ.[10] From it Nephi learned the following: Christ would be buried in a sepulchre. There would be "three days of darkness, which should be a sign given of his death unto those who should inhabit the isles of the sea, more especially given unto those who are of the house of Israel" (1 Nephi 19:10). The Lord would "visit all the house of Israel at that day"—the righteous with his voice and the wicked with his vengeance (1 Nephi 19:11-12). The people of Jerusalem would be scattered because they crucified the Lord, only to be gathered again in the last days when they would accept him (1 Nephi 19:13-15). In the writings of Zenock, Nephi read that the Lord would be "lifted up," and in Neum's record it was foretold that Christ would be crucified (1 Nephi 19:10). But more fully to persuade his people "to believe in the Lord their Redeemer," Nephi read to them from the writings of Isaiah (1 Nephi 19:23), and he reproduced several chapters of Isaiah's words in his own record.

The Testimony of the Book of Mormon

Lehi and his descendants were separated from their Israelite brethren for a special mission, and the testimony which they left for us in their sacred record has blessed the lives of millions of people and will bless the lives of many millions more. The revelation of the gospel of Jesus Christ to Lehi and his sons was the revelation of the gospel to us in the last days. It is significant that the Lord began his latter-day work by bringing into the hands of Joseph Smith a ready-made volume of testimony for Christ. There is no greater testimony for the Lord Jesus Christ than the Book of Mormon. Not only does it bear testimony to the atoning mission of Jesus in mortality, but it also testifies that he is in fact "the Eternal God" (title page), "the God of our fathers, . . . the God of Abraham, and of Isaac, and the

God of Jacob" (1 Nephi 19:10), "the Lord Omnipotent who reigneth, who was, and is from all eternity to all eternity, . . . the Father of heaven and earth, the Creator of all things from the beginning" (Mosiah 3:5, 8), "the very Eternal Father of heaven and of earth, and all things which in them are; . . . the beginning and the end, the first and the last" (Alma 11:39).

Notes

1. For a summary of some of the evidence, see Kent P. Jackson, "The Law of Moses and the Atonement of Christ," in *Studies in Scripture, Volume 3: The Old Testament–Genesis to 2 Samuel*, ed. Kent P. Jackson and Robert L. Millet (Sandy, Utah: Randall Book Co., 1985), pp. 153-54, 156-59.

2. It is not unreasonable to conclude that the prophets in ancient Israel knew and understood the gospel. While Doctrine and Covenants 84: 23-27 tells us that the Melchizedek Priesthood was withdrawn from Israel in Moses' day, Joseph Smith taught that the *prophets* of Israel did hold it; see *Teachings of the Prophet Joseph Smith*, comp. Joseph Fielding Smith (Salt Lake City: Deseret Book Co., 1976), pp. 180-81. Ancient Israel's sacred record, written as it was in a time when gospel blessings were not available to all, offers only a few precious passages that speak of Christian doctrine as known in the Church today. Even the Joseph Smith Translation offers little evidence of a widespread or complete understanding of Christianity in the dispensation of Moses.

3. One major problem that one encounters in analyzing the gospel education that Lehi, Nephi, and Jacob received is the nature of the record in which our information is contained: the small plates of Nephi. Nephi wrote that he began his record keeping by making the large plates, which probably happened more than ten years after his family left Jerusalem. He reported that he wrote on them his father's record, their journeys in the wilderness, and his and his father's prophecies (1 Nephi 19:1). Thirty or forty years after the departure of Lehi's family, Nephi made the small plates and wrote on them the record that we have in 1 and 2 Nephi (see 2 Nephi 5:28-34). Our information concerning Lehi's and Nephi's early visions thus comes from a record written at least thirty years after many of the events that it describes. In writing his record on the small plates it is likely that Nephi drew from his memory of the events, his father's written record, his own earlier record on the large plates, and the inspiration of the Holy Ghost. And it is likely that Nephi's descriptions of those early events reflect his more mature, seasoned, and broadened perspective of later years. For a convenient summary of the sources and structure of the Book of Mormon, see Eldin Ricks, *Story of the Formation of the Book of*

Mormon Plates (Salt Lake City: Olympus Publishing Company, 1966), pp. 1-7.

4. We know of the following who were roughly contemporary with Lehi: Huldah (2 Kings 22:14-20), Jeremiah, Obadiah, Nahum, Habakkuk, and Zephaniah.

5. Compare, for example, Huldah in 2 Kings 22:15-17; Jeremiah in Jeremiah 5:1-10; Habakkuk in Habakkuk 1:1-10; and Zephaniah in Zephaniah 1:1-18.

6. For the nature of Nephi's report of his father's experiences, see S. Kent Brown, "Lehi's Personal Record: Quest for a Missing Source," *BYU Studies* 24(Winter 1984): 19-42.

7. In English the definite article is "the," and the indefinite articles are "a" and "an."

8. Brown, p. 36, n. 43.

9. See the arguments of Sherem in Jacob 7:1-21; Korihor in Alma 30:6-60; and the Zoramites in Alma 31:8-17.

10. For comments on Zenos's contributions, see Bruce R. McConkie, "The Doctrinal Restoration," in *The Joseph Smith Translation: The Restoration of Plain and Precious Things*, ed. Monte S. Nyman and Robert L. Millet (Provo, Utah: Religious Studies Center, Brigham Young University, 1985), pp. 17-18; *A New Witness for the Articles of Faith* (Salt Lake City: Deseret Book Co., 1985), pp. 558-59, 563.

The Three Nephite Churches of Christ

6

Rodney Turner

The earthly church of Jesus Christ in all ages is destined to become the celestial "church of the Firstborn" (D&C 76:67, 92-94). As we individually strive for perfection, so must the Church—the collective body of Christ—do the same. In this respect, the history of Christ's church in the Book of Mormon is an example, a challenge, and a warning to the Church in the latter days (3 Nephi 30; Mormon 9:28-31).

The word *church* literally means those called out of the world into the kingdom of God—a "peculiar people" (Deuteronomy 14:2; 1 Peter 2:9). In this sense, the Church has been found on the earth in every gospel dispensation since the days of Adam. Although it is always founded upon the keys and powers associated with the Melchizedek Priesthood, and always embodies certain basic doctrines and ordinances, its organizational structure reflects the times and circumstances in which it is established. Thus the Church of each dispensation has had a personality all its own.

Moreover, the word *church* has a number of connotations. It may refer to a given religion, denomination, congregation, place of worship, and so forth. For example,

---

Rodney Turner is professor of Ancient Scripture at BYU.

its first use in the Book of Mormon is in connection with Nephi's efforts to obtain the brass plates of Laban. Nephi's reference to "my elder brethren" (meaning Laman and Lemuel) was taken by Laban's servant to refer to "the brethren of the church" (1 Nephi 4:26), or, in other words, the Jewish synagogue or assembly of which Laban was a member.

In its broadest sense, the term connotes the powers of both good and of evil as in 1 Nephi 14:10 which states that in the final analysis there are "save two churches only; the one is the church of the Lamb of God, and the other is the church of the devil." In most instances in the Book of Mormon, the term refers to the organized body of believers in Christ or God. False or apostate churches are clearly identified as such.

Nephi's Church of Christ

The prophecy that young Nephi would become "a ruler and a teacher over [his] brethren" (1 Nephi 2:22) was initially fulfilled in a somewhat informal way (2 Nephi 5:19). But within thirty years of Lehi's departure from Jerusalem, and following a great schism within his colony (2 Nephi 5:3-14), Nephi consecrated his younger brothers, Jacob and Joseph, "priests and teachers over the land of my people" (2 Nephi 5:26; see Jacob 1:18).[1]

Since the gospel is viable only under the authority of the higher priesthood,[2] and since Nephi was not only a prophet but a seer as well (1 Nephi 10:17; 11:1-15:1), he undoubtedly possessed the fullness of the Melchizedek Priesthood and its associated ordinances. Although the Book of Mormon does not contain an account of either Lehi's or Nephi's ordination to the "holy order,"[3] their visions and prophetic ministries leave no doubt that such divine authority was conferred upon them. This same authority was held by those righteous prophet-kings who succeeded Nephi.

The precedent established by Nephi for the king to consecrate or set apart priests and teachers over the people was continued by his successors (Jarom 1:7). One of King Benjamin's last official acts was to appoint priests to teach those who, following his address, "had taken upon them the name of Christ" (Mosiah 6:1-3).

Thus, a Nephite theocracy was established with Nephi functioning as high priest[4] as well as being the first in a dynasty of kings who also bore his name (Jacob 1:11; Mosiah 25:13). This dynasty continued for almost five hundred years—from about 570 B.C. to 91 B.C. when it was replaced by a system of governors and judges (2 Nephi 5:18; Jacob 1:9-11; Mosiah 25:13; 29:41-47).

The Book of Mormon does not indicate the exact nature and extent of the Church, as such, among the early Nephites.[5] However, it does provide some vital information concerning their religious life. For instance, there were many prophets in addition to priests and teachers (Enos 1:22; Jarom 1:10; Words of Mormon 1:16). Their scripture was the brass plates of Laban containing the writings of Moses and the ancient prophets up to Jeremiah (1 Nephi 4:38). They observed the moral injunctions and ritual aspects of the law of Moses (1 Nephi 4:15-16; 2 Nephi 5:10; 25:24; Jarom 1:5). They built at least one temple patterned after that of Solomon (2 Nephi 5:16).[6] Most important, they knew of the Messiah and of the first principles and ordinances of the gospel (2 Nephi 9; 25:23-30; 31-32).[7]

Jarom (c. 475-362 B.C.)[8] writes of prophets, priests, and teachers laboring diligently in teaching the law of Moses in conjunction with faith in the future Messiah "as though he already was" (Jarom 1:11). Although many were spiritually dead, many had revelations and enjoyed "communion with the Holy Spirit" (Jarom 1:3-5).

The Passing of Nephi's Church

The passing of the first Nephite church accompanied the fall of the original Nephite nation in the third century B.C. The seeds of destruction for both were planted during the reign of Nephi's successor in the late sixth century (Jacob 1:15). Jacob, Nephi's brother, warned the people that if they did not repent the Lamanites would conquer the land of Nephi "and the Lord God will *lead away the righteous out from among you*" (Jacob 3:4; emphasis added).[9] The generations came and went as unnamed prophets and priests labored to persuade the vacillating populace to honor their covenants with God. This early period presents a mixed picture of zealous but fruitless missionary work among the Lamanites, combined with material prosperity and spiritual apathy.

Enos (c. 535-420 B.C.) wrote: "There was nothing save it was exceeding harshness, preaching and prophesying of wars, and contentions, and destructions, and continually reminding them of death, and the duration of eternity, and the judgments and the power of God . . . [that] would keep them from going down speedily to destruction" (Enos 1:23). Jarom, his son, in describing similar conditions in his day, wrote that the prophets "did threaten" the people, warning them that if they fell into transgression "they should be *destroyed from off the face of the land*" (Jarom 1:10; emphasis added). The fulfillment of this prophecy was temporarily forestalled because the prophets "did prick their hearts with the word, continually stirring them up unto repentance" (Jarom 1:12). But in the end, prophetic warnings were to no avail: the first Nephite civilization was self-doomed. Mosiah II's declaration that God's judgments came when a majority of the people chose iniquity (Mosiah 29:27) proved true with his grandfather's generation.

Armed conflict between the Nephites and Lamanites began in the reign of Nephi (Jacob 1:13-14) and continued in a sporadic, but increasingly intense, fashion throughout the following centuries. Fearful that the Nephites would be destroyed, Enos prayed that "the Lord God would preserve a record of my people" (Enos 1:13). Jarom ruefully observed that God "has not *as yet* swept them off from the face of the land" (Jarom 1:3; emphasis added).

Omni (c. 425-318 B.C.) wrote: "We had many seasons of peace; and we had many seasons of serious war and bloodshed" (Omni 1:3). According to Amaron, by 280 B.C. "the more wicked part of the Nephites were destroyed" (Omni 1:5). The judgments of God had taken their toll (Omni 1:7).

Abinadom, the nephew of Amaron, wrote the melancholy account of the twilight of the Nephite kingdom—a period in which revelation and prophecy had ceased (Omni

1:11). It only remained for Amaleki to write of its night. By revelation King Mosiah I–the "Moses" of the Book of Mormon–led those who "would hearken unto the voice of the Lord" in an exodus from the land of Nephi northward to the land of Zarahemla (Omni 1:12).[10] This exodus probably occurred around 270 B.C., just prior to the final destruction of the original Nephite nation.[11]

During the period between Mosiah's exodus from the land of Nephi and King Benjamin's discourse on Christ, the law of Moses figured prominently in the religious life of the newly formed Nephite-Mulekite confederation (Omni 1:19; Mosiah 1:10). Several factors account for its emphasis. First, the law of Moses was binding on the entire house of Israel until the death of Christ (2 Nephi 25:24; 3 Nephi 1:24-25). Second, the decimating Nephite-Lamanite wars left but a remnant of Nephites to join the numerically superior people of Zarahemla (Mosiah 25:2). Third, the original language of the people of Zarahemla had become so badly corrupted that the Nephites could not understand them. Having neither scriptures nor prophets to guide them, these "Mulekites" even denied the existence of God (Omni 1:17). Consequently, they had to be taught the Nephite tongue before they could be instructed in even the lesser law of Moses. Although the law of Christ was known to the Nephites,[12] the learning and the living of the preparatory gospel (D&C 84:26-27) was necessarily the initial preoccupation of Zarahemla's people (Mosiah 2:3).

However, of itself the Mosaic law had no saving power; it was a discipline designed to bring ancient Israel to Christ (Mosiah 3:14-15; Galatians 3:24). Eventually –because "*they have been a diligent people* in keeping the commandments of the Lord" (Mosiah 1:11; emphasis added)–these Nephites[13] became spiritually prepared for the greater blessings associated with the fulness of the gospel of Christ.[14] King Benjamin's last major duty was to bring about a spiritual transformation of his subjects.

He did this by testifying of the redeeming blood of the "Lord Omnipotent," thereby opening the way for his people to enter into a covenant with Christ, taking his name upon them, and obtaining a remission of their sins and that "peace of conscience" which only the Holy Ghost can bestow (Mosiah 4:2-3, 11; 5:2; 6:2).[15]

Alma's Church of Christ

Benjamin's people now enjoyed the spiritual blessings of the fulness of the gospel, but they did not have an organized church of Christ per se. Yet one had been established —not by King Benjamin, nor in the land of Zarahemla, but by a descendant of Nephi in the land of their father's first inheritance—the land of Nephi. His name was Alma—the founder of "the first church which was established among them *after their transgression*" (3 Nephi 5:12; emphasis added).[16]

Alma's church was an outgrowth of an expedition to the land of Nephi in the early second century B.C. Zeniff and "a considerable number" of Nephites obtained Lamanite permission to resettle the lands of Lehi-Nephi and Shilom (Omni 1:29; Mosiah 9:6-8). Appointed king by his people, Zeniff reigned over this southern colony during Benjamin's concurrent reign over the land of Zarahemla (Mosiah 7:9).[17]

Following precedent, Zeniff consecrated worthy men to serve as priests.[18] But his son and successor, Noah, practiced a corrupted form of the Mosaic law (Mosiah 11:5, 10-11).[19] He also replaced his father's priests with his own immoral supporters—the elder Alma being one of them (Mosiah 11:5; 17:1-2). Gross idolatry and immorality characterized Noah's Solomon-like reign, and his people succumbed to serious transgressions (Mosiah 7:24-25; 11:1-15).

Abinadi, one of Noah's subjects, fruitlessly preached repentance among the people until he had to flee because of threats against his life. Returning in disguise two years later, Abinadi delivered a final warning to Noah and his priests and also explained the relationship of Christ to the Mosaic law (Mosiah 12-16).[20] His powerful discourse was contemptuously rejected, with one critical exception: Alma—the sole defender and convert of the to-be-martyred prophet (Mosiah 17:2).[21]

Cast out, Alma fled for his life and then went about

privately teaching Abinadi's doctrines. Thereafter, "having authority from the Almighty God" (Mosiah 18:13; 23:10; Alma 5:3),[22] he proceeded to baptize 204 men and women and to ordain priests, commanding them to teach nothing save that which he taught or which could be found in the writings of the holy prophets (Mosiah 18:18-19; 25:21).[23]

Thus was the second Nephite church—"the church of God, or the church of Christ" established around 140 B.C. (Mosiah 18:17).[24] The administration of Alma, its founder and first presiding high priest, was to last about fifty years (Mosiah 23:16; 29:47).

Upon escaping to Zarahemla in about 120 B.C. (following the arrival of King Limhi's people), Alma was authorized by King Mosiah II to form branches of the church throughout all of the land. Mosiah also "gave him power to ordain priests and teachers over every church" (Mosiah 25:19-22).[25] Although Mosiah granted Alma the legal right—the keys—to do this, it is evident from the foregoing that Alma had not received his original authority from that prophet-king.

That that authority was centered in the Melchizedek Priesthood is clear from Alma the Younger's discourse on the "high priesthood" in Alma 13. His description of the ordination of others to this priesthood is doubtlessly a description of his own ordination as well: "Now they were ordained after this manner—being *called* with a holy calling, and *ordained* with a holy ordinance, and taking upon them the high priesthood of the holy order, which calling and ordinance, and high priesthood, is without beginning or end" (Alma 13:8; emphasis added).[26] In 91 B.C., Alma conferred the office of high priest upon his son Alma and gave him "charge concerning all the affairs of the church" (Mosiah 29:42; Alma 4:4).[27]

The first reference in the Book of Mormon to the office of elder—the basic office in the Melchizedek Priesthood—appears in connection with the branches of the Church established by Alma the Younger in the land of Zarahemla (Alma 4:7; 6:1). This suggests that the Church underwent an ecclesiastical development somewhat analogous to that of the later primitive-apostolic Church among the Jews or that of the restored Church in this day.

Because the religion of the Nephites (and of those Lamanites who later joined them) was a unique blend of the lesser law of Moses and the greater law of Christ, it was necessary that these two divine laws be administered under the authority of the Melchizedek order (see Hebrews 7:11-12).

The subsequent history of the Church is one of success and failure, dedication and apostasy. Priestcraft appeared for the first time in Alma's church in 91 B.C. (Alma 1:12, 16). Apostasy became so severe in 83 B.C. that Alma surrendered the chief judgeship to devote himself for the next eight years to "bearing down in pure testimony" against "all the pride and craftiness and all the contentions which were among his people" (Alma 4:18-20). A reform was effected, but it was short-lived. A few years of peace and stability would be followed by still another spiritual decline.

However, the remarkable ministries of the four sons of Mosiah produced the very first conversions–numbering in the thousands–among the Lamanites (Mosiah 27:34-37; 28:1-9; Alma 17-26). A Lamanite branch was established (Alma 19:35). These converts continued faithful, since they "never did fall away" (Alma 23:6). Rejecting the term Lamanites, they adopted the title Anti-Nephi-Lehies "and the curse of God did no more follow them" (Alma 23:16-18; see 2 Nephi 5:21-23).

Following eight years of civil and general warfare, the post-war period (60-53 B.C.) saw the first of several migrations by sea to the land northward where more temples, synagogues and sanctuaries were built (Alma 63:4-9; Helaman 3:14).[28] At the same time, the Church in the land of Zarahemla was inundated by blessings, so "that even the high priests and the teachers were themselves astonished beyond measure" (Helaman 3:25). "Tens of thousands" were baptized into the Church in 43 B.C. Even so, the familiar cycle of prosperity, pride, apostasy, judgments, and repentance was repeated between the years 41 and 30 B.C. The corruption of the laws of Mosiah II reflected the corruption of a majority of the people and "the church had begun to dwindle" (Helaman 4:23).

Abandoning his position as chief judge, Nephi (son of

Helaman II), with his brother Lehi, embarked on the widest-ranging mission in all Nephite history. They cried repentance from Bountiful on the north to the land of Nephi on the south. Many Nephite dissenters were reclaimed, and eight thousand Lamanites in the land of Zarahemla were baptized.

These successes were followed by the most remarkable conversion incident recorded in the Book of Mormon. A military garrison of three hundred Lamanites in the land of Nephi experienced an unprecedented manifestation of the baptism of fire and of the Holy Ghost—accompanied by the ministering of angels (Helaman 5:43-49; cf. 3 Nephi 9:20; Ether 12:14). They then went forth as a missionary force among their own people, testifying with such power that "the more part of the Lamanites were convinced of them" (Helaman 5:50). Weapons were laid down, hatreds abandoned, and Nephite lands returned.

Thus in 30 B.C. the centuries-old wars between the Nephites and Lamanites finally came to an end. They would not be resumed for 352 years! For the first time in history, the two peoples intermingled freely and without fear in all of their lands. And for the first time, Lamanite missionaries labored among the Nephites, including those who had migrated northward (Helaman 6:4-6). A world had turned upside down!

Unfortunately, the first Gadianton conspiracy, which was born in 52 B.C., continued to spread moral corruption and political turmoil among the Nephites whose spiritual decline was in marked contrast to the flowering of the Lamanites. While the Lamanites converted those of their people who belonged to the Gadianton band, the majority of the Nephites entered into covenants with that secret society (Helaman 6:21, 37). The result was chaotic. The period from 29 to 16 B.C. saw chief judges assassinated, the government overthrown, and fratricidal wars breaking out among the Nephites. These ended only because of a heaven-sent famine. Repentance followed.

But in 12 B.C. the second Gadianton band arose, composed of both Nephite and Lamanite dissenters. Like its predecessor, the band's pernicious influence spread moral corruption throughout most of the Nephite society. Apostasy reigned. In contrast, "the Lamanites did observe strictly to keep the commandments of God, according to the law of Moses" (Helaman 13:1; cf.15:5).

Such was the spiritual state of affairs when the Lamanite prophet Samuel came among the people of Zarahemla. In spite of his powerful warning of the eventual "utter destruction" of the entire Nephite nation, and his prophecies concerning the birth and death of Christ, Samuel's message was rejected by the majority of the people. Even many Lamanites lost faith. Only the most believing among them and their Nephite brothers stood firm as the time for Christ's birth drew near. While the miraculous signs attending that event resulted in a majority of the people repenting, within three years the Gadianton disease became virulent again. Due to "the wickedness of the rising generation," the faith of the Lamanites also declined (3 Nephi 1:30). The threat became so great in A.D. 13 that the Nephites and Lamanites joined forces "to maintain their rights, and the privileges of their church and of their worship, and their freedom and their liberty" (3 Nephi 2:12). The Gadianton band had become the common enemy, the moral opposition, of both peoples.

In spite of their general unworthiness, the two united peoples were led both politically and militarily by great prophets (3 Nephi 3:16, 18-19). It was this inspired leadership which brought about the utter defeat of the Gadianton band and another religious reformation among the people in A.D. 22 (3 Nephi 4:27-5:3; 6:6). The post-war years produced great material prosperity as cities were rebuilt, new highways were constructed, and commerce flourished. Mormon notes the presence of many merchants, lawyers, and officers (bureaucrats), and–for the first time–writes of the rise of a class system based on one's wealth and education (3 Nephi 6:10-12). "And thus there became a great inequality in all the land, insomuch that the church began to be broken up . . . save it were among a few of the Lamanites" (3 Nephi 6:14).

Once more prophets called for repentance and testified of the imminent death and resurrection of Christ. Corruption in high places–among the judges, high priests, and lawyers–resulted in the covert murders of these prophets. A new secret combination was formed in an effort to overthrow the state and establish an autocratic monarchy. In A.D. 30 the assassination of the chief judge, Lachoneus, brought down the government. It was replaced by independent tribal groups.[29] The voice of the people was no longer the voice of God: a majority chose evil. The most devastating divine judgments in all Book of Mormon history were soon to be unleashed.

The Church was shattered: "there were but few righteous men" left (3 Nephi 7:7). Reminiscent of Peter's later words, Mormon wrote, "And thus six years had not passed away since the more part of the people had turned from their righteousness, like the dog to his vomit, or like the sow to her wallowing in the mire" (3 Nephi 7:8; cf. 2 Peter 2:22). Such was "their quick return from righteousness unto their wickedness and abominations" (3 Nephi 7:15). And it was to be their last; the familiar cycle would not be repeated in that generation. For although prophets continued to cry repentance,[30] and many were baptized, the time for the Holy One of Israel to die had arrived. And when he died, the second rebellious Nephite nation died with him. As it was with that ancient people, so will it be with the world in these last days. No longer will the repentance of others save the wicked from the inescapable judgments of the Lord.

The first words that the resurrected Savior spoke to the surviving Nephites and Lamanites (see 3 Nephi 10:18) consisted of a summary of the awesome destructions that had befallen the house of Joseph in America (3 Nephi 8:5-9:12). However, God's justice was quickly tempered by his mercy as the risen Redeemer pled with the survivors who "were more righteous" than those who had perished to "repent of your sins, and be converted, that I may heal you" (3 Nephi 9:11, 13; 10:12). He then confirmed the words of his prophets: "By *me* redemption cometh, and in *me* is the law of Moses fulfilled" (3 Nephi 9:17; emphasis added).

The Perfected Church of Christ

The golden age of the ancient Church in America

began with the Father's witness of his descending Son: "Behold my Beloved Son, in whom I am well pleased, in whom I have glorified my name—hear ye him" (3 Nephi 11:7). Thus, at close of the year A.D. 34,[31] a more perfect order was established by the resurrected Christ in the presence of a "great multitude" gathered at the temple in the land Bountiful (3 Nephi 11:1).[32]

This church was to prove unique in several ways. First and foremost, its immediate architect and builder was not a mortal man, but the very Son of God. Then too, he established it upon the personal testimonies of those thousands of men and women who *experienced* the truth that he was the risen Lord, "the God of Israel." They "did *see* with their eyes and did *feel* with their hands, and did *know* of a surety and did *bear record*, that it was he, of whom it was written by the prophets, that should come" (3 Nephi 11:15; emphasis added). Such a "cloud of witnesses" is unprecedented in all known scripture.

Moreover, it was a post-Atonement, post-Resurrection church. Therefore, the heavy yoke of Moses' law (see Matthew 11:28; Acts 15:10)—with its onerous demands and daily sacrifices—was "done away," being replaced by the "easy" yoke of Christ and the offering of a broken heart and a contrite spirit (3 Nephi 9:19; 12:19). Now the people had but one law, the law of Christ; the "schoolmaster" (Galatians 3:24) had served its purpose. Blood sacrifice was immediately replaced by a new ordinance, one that Jesus introduced himself on this earth: the sacrament of bread and wine. Furthermore, the church was led by twelve disciples who, like the original Twelve in Jerusalem, were personally ordained by Jesus.[33]

In summarizing the Book of Mormon for John Wentworth, editor of the *Chicago Democrat*, the Prophet Joseph Smith wrote that the Savior, following his resurrection, "planted the Gospel here in all its fulness, and richness, and power, and blessing; . . . they had Apostles, Prophets, Pastors, Teachers, and Evangelists; the same order, the same priesthood, the same ordinances, gifts, powers, and blessings, as were enjoyed on the eastern continent."[34]

The Prophet's statement supports the view that such

a "fulness" did not exist among the Nephites prior to the Savior's resurrection. The "Elias" churches of Nephi and Alma prepared the way for that more perfect order established by the risen Christ himself.[35] For the time had come for Israel to receive a higher spiritual endowment than it had ever known. This endowment was to begin with a remnant of the house of Joseph in America.

In personally overseeing its organization, Jesus laid a firm foundation of doctrine and ordinances upon which his church was to be built.[36] There were to be no further "disputations . . . concerning the points of my doctrine" (3 Nephi 11:28). The multitude were eye- and ear-witnesses to almost all that transpired during the Savior's initial three-day ministry. The Church began in a unity of the faith. Its doctrines and ordinances were defined with unmistakable clarity by its divine Head and safeguarded by the inspired leadership of the twelve disciples—watchmen who saw eye to eye in that Zion-like age (see Isaiah 52:8; 3 Nephi 16:18). The Church was prepared to last. That it did so with perfect unity for 158 years is another factor which distinguished it from its unstable predecessors.

Then too, this church enjoyed a spiritual and temporal oneness never attained in all of Israel's history (4 Nephi 1:1-17). In addition to enjoying the Millennium-like state described in Fourth Nephi, the Church was blessed with a rich outpouring of knowledge from Christ himself. "He did expound all things unto them, both great and small" from the beginning of time to the final judgment (3 Nephi 26:1-4). In addition, this remnant of Joseph was the first and, to date, has been the *only* people to whom the glorious visions of the brother of Jared have been revealed (Ether 3:21-22; 4:1-2).[37]

In sum, the righteous remnant of American Israel was "added upon" with greater miracles, more splendid manifestations, and more excellent spiritual knowledge than any Israelite group had ever been granted. For as Jesus said, "So great faith have I never seen among all the Jews; wherefore I could not show unto them so great miracles, because of their unbelief" (3 Nephi 19:35).

In testifying of himself, in reconfirming the Sermon on the Mount, in declaring the principles and ordinances of life and salvation, and in explaining the relationship of latter-day Israel to the Gentiles, Jesus bound together the eastern and western churches in the common bonds of the fulness of the gospel. As the two churches were to be as one in the Lord, so were the members of the "body of Christ" to be as one in all things.

This unity in the pure love of Christ—which Jesus declared the hallmark of true discipleship (John 13:35)—was to be both symbolized and sustained by a new ordinance which he himself introduced in both the eastern and western churches: the sacrament. It not only memorializes the Atonement, it also symbolizes the gift of the Holy Ghost. One partakes of the former as a sign of, and as a means to, the latter. Thus Jesus promised to those who worthily partook of his flesh and blood that they should "never hunger nor thirst, but shall be *filled*" with the Holy Ghost (3 Nephi 20:8; 12:6; emphasis added).

In this respect, Mormon's description of the introduction of this ordinance is significant. The assembled Nephites did not simply "partake" of the sacrament, rather they ate and drank until they "were filled" (3 Nephi 18:4-5, 9).[38] Being physically "filled" with bread and wine betokened the glorious blessing which was to follow: being *filled* with the Holy Ghost (3 Nephi 20:8-9; 27:16). The importance of this spiritual endowment can hardly be overestimated.

The bestowal of the literally glorious baptism of fire and of the Holy Ghost was a vital aspect of the Savior's American ministry.[39] Whereas the twelve disciples were initially empowered to baptize the people in water, Jesus told the multitude: "*I will baptize you* with fire and with the Holy Ghost" (3 Nephi 12:1; emphasis added). He had promised this spiritual cleansing months before when he spoke out of the darkness following the terrible upheavals attendant on his own death (3 Nephi 9:20). Now the *light* of the world had come, and the promise was to be fulfilled.

The twelve disciples, who were to bear witness of Christ, were to experience the same glory-filled ordinance enjoyed by the three hundred Lamanite missionaries. Theirs had been a transcendently real experience: they were "encircled about, yea every soul, by a pillar of fire . . .

a flaming fire, yet it did harm them not" (Helaman 5:43-44).[40]

Following their *rebaptism* in water, the Nephite twelve were, in like manner, "filled with the Holy Ghost and with fire. And behold, they were encircled about as if it were by fire; and it came down from heaven" (3 Nephi 19:13-14, 20). It was a truly sanctifying washing of their spirits. Mormon writes, "They were as white as the countenance and also the garments of Jesus" (3 Nephi 19:25). Jesus prayed, "Father, I thank thee that thou hast *purified* those whom I have chosen" (3 Nephi 19:28; emphasis added). The disciples had received far more than a remission of past sins; they had been "sanctified in Christ by the grace of God," thus becoming "holy, without spot" (Moroni 10:33; cf. 3 Nephi 27:20). In other words, they had been "quickened by a portion of the celestial glory" (D&C 88:29). Such an endowment was needed, for Jesus told them: "Ye shall be judges of this people. . . . Therefore, what manner of men ought ye to be? Verily I say unto you, *even as I am*" (3 Nephi 27:27; emphasis added). They could not be what Jesus was if they did not possess the Spirit that he possessed (2 Nephi 31:12).

Subsequent to the Redeemer's ministry, the disciples went forth proclaiming the message of salvation "and as many as were baptized in the name of Jesus were filled with the Holy Ghost. And many of them saw and heard unspeakable things, which are not lawful to be written" (3 Nephi 26:17-18). Having received "the unspeakable gift of the Holy Ghost" (D&C 121:26), they were blessed with a knowledge of the mysteries of God.

While Mormon, under divine instructions, withheld much from his account that Jesus taught the people (3 Nephi 26:6-12), there is every reason to believe that all of those higher principles and ordinances of the gospel associated with a temple of the Melchizedek order were made known to and practiced by them.

The ministry of Christ (3 Nephi 26:13) was the magnificent culmination of all that had been achieved by those dedicated prophets, priests and teachers who had prepared the way for the coming of the Holy One of Israel to the house of Joseph. Branches of the Church were established in every land, and within two years "the people were all converted" (4 Nephi 1:2). A Millennium-like society arose in America which enjoyed unblemished peace, prosperity, equality, and happiness for more than a century and a half (4 Nephi 1:3-18).

The Passing of the Church

Tragically, after reaching its spiritual zenith through the Redeemer's personal ministry, the church of Christ was to experience its nadir within three centuries (3 Nephi 27:32). Indeed, in terms of sheer barbarity and unmitigated cruelty, nothing that had previously occurred would begin to equal that which was to come in the closing moments of Book of Mormon history.

The decline and fall of the Church and the nation must be briefly summarized. The heavenly unity of the Church became flawed in A.D. 194, when a "small part" of the people assumed the name Lamanites (4 Nephi 1:20). Unable to handle their unprecedented "prosperity in Christ," the third generation abandoned the principle of economic unity and no longer had all things in common (4 Nephi 1:23-24). The year 201 saw the emergence of class distinctions and spiritual disunity as apostate churches arose advocating various corrupt doctrines and practices (4 Nephi 1:26-29). Because of the influence of false prophets and priests, the Lord's disciples and the "people of Jesus" were subjected to physical persecution (4 Nephi 1:30-34).

In A.D. 231, these social and spiritual "disputations" produced the final great division of the once-united peoples into Nephites ("true believers in Christ") and Lamanites (willful apostates) (4 Nephi 1:35-38). History had repeated itself; it was Nephi versus Laman all over again. By 301, both groups had become "exceeding wicked one like unto another" (4 Nephi 1:45).

In 322, the first of the final series of wars between the two peoples began (Mormon 1:8). Soon thereafter, the three translated disciples were taken away, miracles ceased, gifts were lost, "and the Holy Ghost did not come upon any" (Mormon 1:13-14, 16; 8:10). The gifts of God were replaced by the counterfeits of Satan: it was a time of sorcery, witchcraft, and magic; "the power of the evil one was wrought upon all the face of the land" (Mormon 1:19; 2:10). The end was near. Mormon lamented, "I saw that the day of grace was passed with them, both temporally and spiritually" (Mormon 2:15). It was the year 344.

However, one last effort to redeem the Church was to be made. In 360 the Lord told Mormon, "Cry unto this people—Repent ye, and come unto me, and be ye baptized, and *build up again my church*, and ye shall be spared" (Mormon 3:2; emphasis added). Mormon did so, but to no avail. Describing their moral state, Mormon writes, "And there never had been so great wickedness among all the children of Lehi, nor even among all the house of Israel, according to the words of the Lord, as was among this people" (Mormon 4:12).[41] Much had been given; much had been betrayed (see D&C 82:3).

Church and nation were inextricably bound together; the fall of one was the fall of the other. Those few Nephites who survived the climactic battles associated with Cumorah were hunted down and killed unless they denied Christ (Moroni 1:2-3). When these martyrs died, the Church died with them. It had been born out of God's judgments upon the remnant of Israel in America, and had passed away in the chaos of a genocidal war that blotted out the glorious order Christ had established.

A heaven-like season of righteousness and peace had blessed the lives of three generations of Nephites and Lamanites. Now that season was over and a long night of spiritual darkness spread across the Western Hemisphere. Dawn would not break again for more than a thousand years. It would have to await the coming of another restorer, another Joseph, another gospel dispensation.

The Church in the Latter Days

The Book of Mormon was not written for ancient peoples. It was written for us (Mormon 8:35; Ether 12:23). From the standpoint of its prophets, we constitute the latter-day gentile church of Christ (1 Nephi 22:8; 3 Nephi 21:5-6). Nevertheless, the blood of Abraham, Isaac, and Jacob flows in our veins (D&C 86:8-10; 113:8; Abraham 2: 9-11). We are bound by lineage, by faith, and by covenant to the Israelites of the Book of Mormon. They knew of us, prophesied of us, prayed for us, and wrote to us. It is for us to learn—both as individuals and as a church—from their achievements and mistakes, and to receive their counsel, admonitions, warnings.

The churches of Nephi and Alma were churches of anticipation. They were admonished to look forward to the coming and redemptive mission of the Holy One in America (1 Nephi 12:6). But while their prophets and leaders were dedicated men of God, the general membership was often unstable, being prone to vacillate between fervent repentance and ungrateful apostasy—a fact which provoked Mormon's lamentation in Helaman 12. This is always the case when men fail to come to need God more than they need his gifts.

Although a degree of unity was achieved from time to time, it was imperfect and short-lived. Those people had the priesthood, the gospel, and inspired leadership, but the enlightening and sustaining power of the Holy Ghost seems to have been only relatively and inconsistently present. Being a mixture of wheat and tares, sheep and goats, these churches were doctrinally and authoritatively true but morally and spiritually imperfect. Not being really one in all things, they could not be wholly claimed by the Lord (D&C 38:27). A great sifting was needed, a refining fire was required. The unprecedented destructions at the time of Christ's crucifixion marked the beginning of that sifting and that fire.

The way was thus prepared for the Son of Man to descend from the heavens and establish his church in all of its power and perfection. His own prayer had—to a degree, and for a season—been answered: the Father's will was done on earth as it was done in heaven (Matthew 6:10; D&C 65:6).

The Church of Jesus Christ of Latter-day Saints is also a church of anticipation. It, too, anticipates additional revelation, the institution of higher principles, the establishment of Zion, the perfecting of the Saints, and the coming of the Son of Man.

Our leaders and many other faithful Saints are doing all in their power to further the Lord's purposes; however, we are yet to become truly one in all things (D&C 38:27; 101:6; 105:1-6). Such unity probably lies many years in the future. In the meantime the sheep and the goats, the wheat and the tares continue to dwell side by side. Consequently, we are not without some contention and dissension. Nor have we wholly escaped the plagues of selfishness, dishonesty, worldliness, immorality, family upheaval, and spiritual apathy that beset Babylon (Revelation 18:4; D&C 133:5). Thus, we comprise those wise and foolish virgins foretold by the Lord (Matthew 25:1-13; D&C 45:56-57; 133:10).

It seems that too many of us have overestimated our virtues by underestimating the Lord's standards. Therefore, the Bridegroom has yet to claim his bride—the Church. But he does not delay his coming; it is right on schedule. He has told his servants, "Be faithful, praying always, having your lamps trimmed and burning, and oil with you, *that you may be ready* at the coming of the Bridegroom" (D&C 33:17; emphasis added). Becoming "adorned as a bride" (D&C 109:74) worthy of her divine husband has been for the Church a long, painful process that is not yet over. But, as John saw in vision, it will be accomplished: "Let us be glad and rejoice, and give honor to him: for the marriage of the Lamb is come, and *his wife hath made herself ready*" (Revelation 19:7; emphasis added).[42]

Christ will have a pure people, a Zion people (D&C 82:14; 97:21; 100:16). Indeed, even now we observe an acceleration of the prophesied polarization of the forces of good and evil (D&C 1:35-36). This process will continue for some years until it reaches its climax at the Savior's coming.

The destructions which prepared the way for Christ's appearance to the Nephites and Lamanites will have their counterpart in these last days. In due time the Redeemer's wrath will be felt by all mankind. "And upon my house shall it begin, and from my house shall it go forth, saith the Lord" (D&C 112:23-26; 133:2). The eventual result will be "an entire separation of the righteous and the wicked"—both in the Church and in the world (D&C 63:54).

Prior to this total separation of the human family at his final coming, the Redeemer will manifest himself to his

Saints on several occasions (Isaiah 59:20; Daniel 7:13-14; D&C 133:2; 128:24).[43] Precious knowledge will be poured down upon his gathered peoples "by the unspeakable gift of the Holy Ghost" even as it was upon the ancient Nephites and Lamanites (D&C 121:26-33; 101:32-34). A time of spiritual unity and power like unto that enjoyed by ancient Enoch and his city lies ahead for the faithful (Moses 7:16-18; D&C 45:64-71). It will foreshadow the glorious millennial reign of earth's lawful King wherein the Saints will enjoy a sabbath of righteousness and peace of greater length and magnitude than has blessed any other dispensation since time began (D&C 45:59; Moses 7:65).

The perfected church of Christ in the Book of Mormon, blessed as it was with a truly glorious outpouring of the Holy Spirit, was a prophetic microcosm of the worldwide millennial kingdom of God which will come forth out of The Church of Jesus Christ of Latter-day Saints (D&C 65; JST, Revelation 12:1-3, 7).

But even as the "little millennium" of the ancient Church was followed by the most terrible apostasy in Book of Mormon history, so will the Lord's universal reign be followed, in that "little season" when Satan is loosed for the last time, by probably the greatest apostasy since the War in Heaven (Revelation 20:6-10; D&C 88:110-15). The centuries of spiritual darkness which followed the destruction of the Nephite nation in the fifth century A.D. was a portent of the final fate of Satan and his followers. They will be cast into the bottomless pit of the second death where darkness is absolute and from whence there is no known deliverance.

In 1832, the Lord called upon the Church to repent "and remember the new covenant, even the Book of Mormon and the former commandments which I have given them, not only to say, *but to do* according to that which I have written"(D&C 84:57; emphasis added). In this regard, the message of the Book of Mormon to the Saints in this dispensation is unmistakable: honor your solemn covenants, magnify the gift of the Holy Ghost which has been bestowed upon you, and become sanctified so that you might partake of the glory of the church of the Firstborn and dwell in his presence forever.

Notes

1. Jacob and Joseph were *consecrated* priests and teachers, but *ordained* to the "holy order" or greater priesthood (2 Nephi 6:2). Elder Joseph Fielding Smith explained that they were priests and teachers in the sense that they were given "a general assignment to teach, direct, and admonish the people" (*Answers to Gospel Questions,* ed. Joseph Fielding Smith, Jr., 5 vols. (Salt Lake City: Deseret Book Co., 1957-66), 1:124). Since there were no known descendants of the priestly tribe of Levi in Lehi's colony, the Nephites doubtless officiated in the duties of the Levitical Priesthood pertaining to the Mosaic law by virtue of the Melchizedek Priesthood which they held.

2. While the lesser (Levitical-Aaronic) priesthood pertains to the preparatory gospel (the law of Moses, etc.), the "greater priesthood administereth the [fulness of the] gospel and holdeth the key of the mysteries of the kingdom, even the key of the knowledge of God" (D&C 84:19-27). One evidence of the divine calling of Joseph Smith is that he did not presume to organize the Church of Christ before receiving the Melchizedek Priesthood.

3. Being from the non-priestly tribe of Manasseh (Alma 10:3), Lehi and Nephi were, like Jesus, technically ineligible to hold the Levitical Priesthood (see Hebrews 7:14.)

4. The text does not specifically refer to Nephi as a high priest. The term first appears in Mosiah 23:16 where it is applied to Alma the Elder. However, it is not inappropriate to apply it to Nephi who held the higher priesthood and who presided over those priests whom he had personally appointed.

5. Insofar as a Nephite organization is concerned, the word *church* does not appear in the Book of Mormon until Mosiah 18:27. While it is clear that Nephi and his successors taught the people of Christ, there is no textual evidence that the early Nephites had an ecclesiastical organization independent of that associated with the law of Moses.

6. Lacking literal descendants of Levi, the Nephites were obliged to assign holders of the Melchizedek Priesthood to perform the temple duties normally carried out by men of the Levitical order. While the Book of Mormon is silent as to those ordinances associated with the fulness of the gospel being performed in the temple, Nephi was almost surely acquainted with them.

7. It is apparent from Nephi's teachings on the need and purpose of baptism (2 Nephi 31-32) that baptism and the related ordinance of the laying on of hands for the gift of the Holy Ghost were practiced in the days of Nephi. However, the first recorded instance of actual baptisms is found in Mosiah 18:13-16. The first explicit instance of the baptism of fire and of the Holy Ghost involved a group of three hundred Lamanites and occurred about 30 B.C. (Helaman 5:43-45; compare 3 Nephi 9:20; Ether 12:14). It has been suggested that the baptism of the Holy Ghost is implied in connection with the "mighty change" experienced by King Benjamin's

people following his discourse on salvation through Christ (Mosiah 4:1-3, 11; 5:2, 7).

8. The dates given are rather rough approximations. It appears that the early Nephite prophets (except Nephi himself, who died in his seventies) lived a hundred years or more.

9. Jacob's prophecy of a future leading away of a remnant of righteous Nephites seems to have prompted him to laboriously engrave the long, convoluted allegory of Zenos (Jacob 5) concerning the various scatterings and gatherings of Israel throughout the world.

10. Nephi had fled to the land of Nephi ("the land of our fathers' first inheritance"—Mosiah 9:1) to escape his vengeful brothers (2 Nephi 5: 4-8). The migration of Mosiah I from that land was to the north, where he encountered the people of Zarahemla, the Jewish colony led by Mulek, the son of King Zedekiah, which fled Jerusalem about 587 B.C. (Omni 1:14-16).

11. Mormon implies that whatever formalized church there was came to an end in connection with the overthrow of the Nephite kingdom. Mosiah I was probably the last of the original Nephite kings. He subsequently reigned over the unified Nephite-Mulekite nation until his death in about 160 B.C., when his son, Benjamin, became king. We can only approximate some Book of Mormon dates. While the Jaredites seem to have lived to a good age (Coriantum lived to be 142; his wife died at 102 —Ether 9:24), the few Nephite ages given range from 63 to 82 (Mosiah 29: 45-46; 4 Nephi 1:20).

12. Although the people of Zarahemla had to be taught line upon line about Israel's God and his commandments, a clear understanding of Christ was had by the prophets who wrote on the small plates of Nephi. For example, Amaleki—the last writer on these plates—said, "I would that ye should come unto Christ, who is the Holy One of Israel, and partake of his salvation, and the power of his redemption" (Omni 1:26).

13. The term *Nephites* also includes the people of Zarahemla (Mosiah 25:13).

14. It is noteworthy that King Benjamin's testimony of Christ was preceded by a period in which false Christs and false prophets, preachers, and teachers caused much discord leading to the defection of many Nephites to the Lamanites. Only the sharp warnings of King Benjamin and other "holy men" brought peace to the land (Words of Mormon 1:15-18).

15. While it is true that the Nephites had been taught concerning the prophecies on the brass plates as well as "all that has been spoken by our fathers until now" (Mosiah 2:34-35), the relevance of these scriptures must have been overshadowed by the external demands of the Mosaic law. If these *obedient* people already enjoyed the *fulness* of the gospel, then presumably they had already taken Christ's name and received a remission of sins. Had such been the case, Benjamin's appeal, "I would that ye *should take* upon you the name of Christ" (Mosiah 5:8; emphasis added;

see also 6:1-3), and the people's plea for a remission of sins (Mosiah 4:2-3), appear anachronistic. It was *because* of their obedience that Benjamin gave them a unique name by which "they may be distinguished above *all the people*" who had come from Jerusalem (Mosiah 1:11; emphasis added; see also 5:11-12). Before bestowing that name, he revealed the "mysteries of God" to them (Mosiah 2:9). These mysteries—declared by an angel —concerned the identity of the "Lord Omnipotent" who was to come to earth and be crucified and resurrected so that all mankind might be saved *through his atoning blood* rather than through the relatively impotent law of Moses (Mosiah 3:2-19). None could plead innocent once they learned of Christ. Therefore the angel told Benjamin, "And even *at this time,* when thou *shalt have taught* thy people the things which the Lord thy God hath commanded thee, even *then* are they found *no more* blameless in the sight of God" (Mosiah 3:22; emphasis added; see 4:5-6, 11; 5:4; Alma 9:19-21). Convinced of the need for the Savior, the people then cried out for the "atoning blood of Christ" and received a remission of sins and spiritual rebirth, thus becoming, by covenant, "the children of Christ, his sons, and his daughters" (Mosiah 4:2-3, 11-12, 20, 26; 5:2-10). They had taken upon themselves a name they had not possessed before— "for behold, *this day* he hath spiritually begotten you" (Mosiah 5:7; emphasis added). The whole tenor of the account indicates that Benjamin did not simply reiterate doctrines already understood by the Nephites. He parted the veil and revealed the redemptive power of "Christ, the Lord God Omnipotent" (Mosiah 5:15).

16. I believe that the phrase "after their transgression" refers to the apostasy in the time of Mosiah I, which led to the destruction of the first Nephite nation (Jarom 1:10; Omni 1:12), rather than that of King Noah and his supporters as described in Zeniff's record (Mosiah 9-22). Had there been a functioning church of Christ in the land of Zarahemla, there would have been no need for Alma to organize a second church, nor for Mosiah to grant Alma permission to set up branches throughout that land. In addressing the Nephites in Zarahemla in 83 B.C., Alma the Younger said, "We were brought into this land, and here we *began* to establish *the* church of God throughout this land *also*" (Alma 5:5; emphasis added). Though it had many branches, at any given time there was but one authorized church of God (Mosiah 25:22).

17. See Omni 1:27-30. The account of this colony of Nephites in their ancient land of Nephi is found in Mosiah 7-22.

18. Prior to leaving Zarahemla, Zeniff very likely had been ordained a high priest of the Melchizedek order by King Benjamin.

19. It is very likely that Zeniff restored the temple originally built by Nephi in the sixth century B.C. (2 Nephi 5:16). King Noah seems to have remodeled this same temple on a grand scale, making it far more elaborate and costly than it previously had been (Mosiah 11:10). Like Herod the Great, who remodeled the second temple (that of Zerubbabel; Ezra 3), Noah's project was doubtless more a matter of personal vanity than genuine piety.

20. Zeniff's group left Zarahemla many years before King

Benjamin delivered his discourse on Christ in 124 B.C. (Omni 1:27-30). The extent to which Zeniff and his people had an understanding of the relationship of the law of Moses to Christ is conjectural. In any event, Noah and his priests seem to have been totally ignorant of that relationship, being steeped in idolatry and gross immorality (Mosiah 11:6-15; 12:27-32). Hence the need for the prophet Abinadi to declare essentially the same message to Noah (Mosiah 13:27-28), and especially to Alma, that Benjamin had delivered to his people.

21. There is no textual evidence that Alma ever conversed privately with Abinadi, or that he was ordained to the Melchizedek Priesthood by him. However, Abinadi's initial testimony may have been heard by Alma and may have served to prepare him for the prophet's final witness two years later.

22. The source of Alma's authority is not given. He may have been ordained by Abinadi, by an angel, or by some unknown person. His authority to establish the Church appears independent of any earlier ordination to the priesthood.

23. Lacking such authority, King Limhi made no attempt to organize a church or to perform baptisms (Mosiah 21:33-34).

24. This is the first specific reference in the Book of Mormon to an organized church of Christ.

25. The priesthood offices cited in the Book of Mormon are teacher, priest, elder, high priest and, in effect, presiding high priest. Prophets are frequently mentioned. The gift of seership is also cited in connection with Joseph Smith (2 Nephi 3:6-14) and Mosiah II (Mosiah 8:13-17; see 28:16).

26. Whereas all worthy males are entitled to hold an office in the priesthood in the LDS Church, in Book of Mormon times only selected men were so privileged. From all indications, there was no universal priesthood.

27. Alma the Younger is the only man in the Book of Mormon specifically spoken of as exercising the "high priesthood" (Alma 4:20).

28. The Nephite synagogue was "built after the manner of the Jews" (Alma 16:13)–an evidence that the Jews had synagogues before the Babylonian captivity. It was a place of assembly and a house of worship that served both the practical and the spiritual needs of the people (2 Nephi 26:26; Alma 21:16). The sanctuary may have been a portion of the synagogue reserved strictly for worship. The Nephites had synagogues throughout their history (3 Nephi 18:32; Moroni 7:1). The Lamanites also had temples, sanctuaries and synagogues (Alma 23:2; 26:29).

29. Jesus prophesied a similar condition immediately preceding his second coming. Nations as we know them will be no more (D&C 87:6), "and then shall all the *tribes* of the earth mourn" (Matthew 24:30; emphasis added).

30. The greatest of these was Nephi, the grandson of Helaman, of whom Mormon wrote, "He had greater power than they [his opponents],

for it were not possible that they could disbelieve his words" (3 Nephi 7: 18; emphasis added).

31. Third Nephi 10:18 is interpreted to mean that Christ appeared in America shortly after the widespread destructions ended. Yet, Mormon states that he came "in the *ending* of the thirty and fourth year" and the upheavals began on the fourth day of the first month of that year (3 Nephi 8:5). What he means by "ending" is not totally clear. A different interpretation might logically argue for a time sometime after the middle of the year. Whether from a spiritual, psychological, or practical standpoint, the survivors might have been too distraught and disoriented to receive the Lord immediately after his resurrection. They would have needed to make provision for the necessities of life and to rebuild their homes. All this would have taken time. Mormon's description of the people gathered at the temple in Bountiful discussing the physical changes that had occurred (Helaman 11:1-2), and "conversing about this Jesus Christ," suggests a settled rather than a chaotic situation. (See S. K. Brown, "Jesus Among the Nephites: When Did It Happen?" in *A Symposium on the New Testament* [Salt Lake City: Church Educational System, 1984], pp. 74-77). Similarly, the worldwide upheavals associated with Armageddon (Revelation 16:16-21; D&C 45:47-53) will be followed by a period of comparative calm ending in the Savior's second coming (Ezekiel 39; JST, Matthew 24:44-49).

32. Following the Redeemer's subsequent calling of twelve Nephite disciples (3 Nephi 11:18-22; 12:1), they went forth and "formed a church of Christ in all the lands round about" (4 Nephi 1:1).

33. The office of Apostle was introduced for the first time in history by Jesus himself. Since Apostles are, above all things, special witnesses of the resurrected Lord, such a calling could hardly exist prior to his mortal ministry. The twelve Nephite disciples will be judged by the Twelve in Jerusalem (Mormon 3:19).

34. Joseph Smith, *History of The Church of Jesus Christ of Latter-day Saints,* ed. B. H. Roberts, 2d ed. rev., 7 vols. (Salt Lake City: The Church of Jesus Christ of Latter-day Saints, 1972-73), 4:538.

35. Alma's church seems to have been somewhat more fully organized than Nephi's. Even so, Mormon describes its ecclesiastical arrangement as consisting only of teachers, priests, and elders, presided over by a high priest. The doctrines and ordinances of Alma's church were correspondingly simple, consisting only of such first principles as faith, repentance, baptism, the Atonement, the Resurrection, the Judgment, and so forth. The primitive Church among the Jews was similarly limited both as to ecclesiastical development and doctrinal maturity. This is made clear when one contrasts the relevant material in the four Gospels with that found in the other books of the New Testament.

36. Moroni provides valuable information concerning the bestowal of the Holy Ghost, priesthood ordinations, the administration of the sacrament, baptism, and certain other Church procedures (Moroni 2-6).

37. Moroni wrote an account of the visions of the brother of Jared

on the plates of Mormon (Ether 4:4-5). These revelations constitute part, if not all, of the sealed portion of the material left untranslated by Joseph Smith. Most commentators believe that these revelations will not be had again until the millennial reign of Christ. However, Moroni wrote that they would be had by the "Gentiles"– meaning the Latter-day Saints –when they "become clean before the Lord" (Ether 4:6). I believe that this will be before the second, or world, coming of Christ.

38. Commenting on this verse, President George Q. Cannon wrote: "In our Church numerous instances have occurred where . . . bread and wine (or water) have been partaken of as a meal, and not, as is usual when the Sacrament is passed in our general meetings, in the shape of small pieces of bread and a little sip of water. . . . It seems from this that in partaking of this ordinance they satisfied their appetites– that is, they ate and drank until they were filled. This would be the proper manner to administer this ordinance now if circumstances permitted" ("Editorial Thoughts [Passing the Sacrament]," *The Juvenile Instructor* 32 [15 January 1897]:52-53). Philo Dibble told Oliver B. Huntington of an occasion in 1838 in Far West, Missouri, during which "the Prophet Joseph Smith gave the people a true pattern. A pattern of the true manner of Partaking of the sacrament. The people came together in the morning without their breakfast, to the bowery on the Public Square where there was prepared a plenty of good bread and a barrel of wine. The bread and wine was blessed, every person ate bread and drank wine as they wanted all day, when they wanted. . . . No one said 'less [let's] go and get a drink' but with solemnity they commemorated the death and sufferings of Jesus. . . . No one was intoxicated during the day" (*Diary of Oliver B. Huntington, 1847-1900*, part 2 [Provo, Utah: Brigham Young University Library, 1942], entry of 4 September 1887).

39. The baptism of fire and of the Holy Ghost was not bestowed upon any of Jesus' followers among the Jews until after he was resurrected: "The Holy Ghost was promised unto them who believe *after* that Jesus was glorified" (JST, John 7:39; see Acts 1:4-8; 2:1-4; emphasis added).

40. The same baptism of fire and the Holy Ghost was experienced by the Twelve in Jerusalem on the day of Pentecost (Acts 2:1-4). In all likelihood, the original Twelve received this ordinance *before* the Nephite twelve, who are answerable to them. This is a further evidence that the risen Savior did not visit America until the end of A.D. 34.

41. During this period, the Lamanites practiced idolatry, human sacrifice, and forced cannibalism (Mormon 4:14, 21; Moroni 9:8). The Nephites were guilty of torture, rape, and cannibalism (Moroni 9:9-10). Doctrinally, Mormon's polemic against the baptism of little children indicates that it was at least advocated by some Church members around the middle of the fourth century.

42. The Lord's use of the metaphor of an oriental marriage is very meaningful. The bride-to-be goes to her husband's house where she spends the day being dressed and adorned by her attendants (the virgins) for her marriage. Late in the evening, about eleven o'clock, the bridegroom leads

a torchlight procession to his house. As he approaches, the shout is heard, "The bridegroom is coming!" The bride's attendants go to meet him with their lighted lamps and escort him into his house and to his waiting bride. The spiritual "adorning" of the Saints *in his house* precedes the Lord's coming. It is now under way.

43. See also Brigham Young in *Journal of Discourses*, 26 vols. (London: Latter-day Saints' Book Depot, 1855-86), 7:142.

Fasting in the Book of Mormon and the Bible

7

Stephen D. Ricks

For Latter-day Saints, a natural part of every month is fast Sunday, when they abstain from food and drink for two meals, contribute a fast offering from the money saved by fasting (if not contributing more than that), and join with others in worship and in bearing witness to the truth. On other occasions, special needs will also warrant fasting: an illness, preparation for giving or receiving a priesthood blessing, a vital decision, or a persistent dilemma. The practice of fasting, so significant and cherished a part of the Latter-day Saint religious life, is also abundantly attested in ancient Israel and in the Book of Mormon.

Fasts may be individual and private or communal and public; they may be periodic and institutionalized (e.g., in our own practice, fast Sunday) or spontaneous (i.e., fasts which are not explicitly prescribed). Among the ancient Israelites and the Nephites, all of these types of fasting are attested, and will be considered in this paper.

Stephen D. Ricks is assistant professor of Hebrew at BYU.

Periodic and Institutionalized Fasts

1. *Day of Atonement Fasting.* The only periodic fast prescribed for the Israelites in the Pentateuch (the five books of Moses) occurs on the Day of Atonement, "the tenth day of the seventh month" of the ancient Jewish calendar (the first month of the current Jewish calendar), when the Lord commanded the Israelites to meet together to "afflict [their] souls" (i.e., to fast) and to "offer an offering made by fire unto the Lord" (Leviticus 23:27ff.; see also 16:29, 31; Numbers 29:7-10). There are no references to this festival in the Old Testament outside of the books of Moses, although Isaiah 58:3-7 may refer to abuses of the fast associated with the Day of Atonement.

   The observance of the Day of Atonement fast is never explicitly mentioned in the Book of Mormon. However, its observance may be implied in Alma 30:2, where fasting, mourning, and prayer are referred to, and in Alma 45:1, where fasting, rejoicing, and prayer are mentioned as taking place at the beginning of the year, at the time when the Day of Atonement rites were probably observed among the Nephites. This presumption that these two fasts reflect observances associated with the Pentateuch is, I think, strengthened by the observation in Alma 30:3 (following the mention of fasting and associated rites) that "the people did observe to keep the commandments of the Lord; and they were strict in observing the ordinances of God, according to the law of Moses; for they were taught to keep the law of Moses until it should be fulfilled."[1]

2. *Other Periodic Fasts.* Four periodic fasts commemorating events surrounding or immediately following the destruction of the kingdom of Judah by the Babylonians are mentioned in Zechariah 7:5 and 8:19: (1) the fast that was held to observe the beginning of the siege of Jerusalem by Nebuchadnezzar on the tenth day of the tenth

month (Tebet) in the ninth year of the reign of Zedekiah (cf. 2 Kings 25:1; Jeremiah 39:1); (2) the fast commemorating the breach of the wall of Jerusalem on the ninth day of the fourth month (Tammuz) in the eleventh year of Zedekiah's reign (Jeremiah 39:2, 52:6-7); (3) the fast memorializing the destruction of the temple on the tenth day of the fifth month (Ab) in the nineteenth year of Nebuchadnezzar's rule (cf. Jeremiah 52:12-13; 2 Kings 25:8-9); (4) the fast commemorating the murder of the Babylonian puppet Gedaliah on the third day of the seventh month (Tishri; cf. 2 Kings 25:24-25; Jeremiah 41:1). Since all of these fasts commemorate events during the Babylonian conquest, the destruction of Jerusalem and afterwards (i.e., in the period immediately following the departure of Lehi's family from Jerusalem), they are, understandably, without parallels in the Book of Mormon.

Spontaneous Fasts

1. *Fasting Following a Death.* Both the Bible and the Book of Mormon record instances of fasting as a sign of mourning following a death. After the defeat and death of Saul and his sons, the men of Jabesh Gilead fasted seven days (1 Samuel 31:13; 1 Chronicles 10:12), as did David and his companions (2 Samuel 1:12). Similarly, public fasting occurs in the Book of Mormon in conjunction with prayer and mourning after the murder of the chief judge Seezoram (Helaman 9:10). No specific reason is mentioned in the Book of Mormon for these prayers, but they may have been to obtain solace for the living rather than mercy for the dead. Individual fasting following a death is also attested in ancient Israel (2 Samuel 3:35).

The practice of fasting as a sign of mourning following a death appears to have been a customary feature of pre-exilic Israelite religion (cf. 1 Samuel 31:13; 2 Samuel 1:12; 3:35; 1 Chronicles 10:

12). However, the practice is not recorded for the post-exilic period or in the New Testament. It is also of importance that fasting as a sign of mourning is recorded in the Book of Mormon only in pre-Easter passages (so Helaman 9:10), but never following the appearance of the risen Christ to the Nephites.

2. *Petitionary Fasting.* Spontaneous fasting, both in public and in private, for a specific purpose, is attested several times in the Book of Mormon and in the Old Testament. When Alma the Younger lay speechless and paralyzed, his father assembled the priests "to fast, and to pray to the Lord their God that he would open the mouth of Alma, that he might speak" (Mosiah 27:22-23; see also Alma 10:7). Similarly, David "fasted, and went in, and lay all night upon the earth" as he prayed to the Lord to spare the life of his first son by Bathsheba (2 Samuel 12:16ff.; for other examples of petitionary fasting see Nehemiah 1:4; Psalms 35:13; 69:10; 109:24; Daniel 6:18; 9:3). Esther 4:16 provides an instance of communal petitionary fasting, and accounts of public petitionary fasting are found in Judges 20:26; 2 Chronicles 20:3; Ezra 8:21, 23; Jeremiah 14:12; 36:6, 9.

3. *Preparatory Fasting.* Fasting as an act preparatory to seeking the gifts of the Spirit can be seen in the account of the sons of Mosiah, who had given themselves "to much prayer, and fasting; therefore they had the spirit of prophecy, and the spirit of revelation" (Alma 17:3, 9; see also Alma 5:46, 8:26). In a slightly different vein, Moses fasted on the mountain for forty days when receiving the Ten Commandments (see Exodus 34:28; Deuteronomy 9:9), Saul fasted before visiting the witch of Endor (1 Samuel 28:20), and Ahab and Jezebel proclaimed a public fast in anticipation of the trial of Naboth (1 Kings 21:9,12).

4. *Fasting As a Religious Exercise.* Fasting for no explicit reason is not attested in the Old Testament

before the Babylonian exile. However, this practice burst into full bloom during the early pre-Christian centuries, and is frequently mentioned in the intertestamental literature and in the New Testament (cf. Testament of Joseph 3:4; 9:2; Judith 6:8; Luke 2:36-38). It was probably against hypocritical fasting of this sort that Jesus inveighed: "Moreover when ye fast, be not, as the hypocrites, of a sad countenance: for they disfigure their faces, that they may appear unto men to fast. . . . When thou fastest, anoint thine head, and wash thy face, that thou appear not unto men to fast, but unto thy Father which is in secret" (Matthew 6:16-18). (This does not, I believe, represent a rejection of fasting as such, but rather a condemnation of its improper practice.) To an extent, this fasting had itself become somewhat institutionalized, and was observed on a regular basis by the Pharisees and possibly also by the disciples of John the Baptist. The Pharisee in Jesus' parable was probably referring to such a practice when he boasted, "I fast twice in the week" (Luke 18:12). Both later Jewish and Christian traditions agree in identifying these two days as Monday and Thursday.[2] The New Testament makes no specific mention of fasts regularly observed by the primitive Christian community. However, the Didache, or TEACHING OF THE TWELVE APOSTLES, dating from about A.D. 100 and giving one of the earliest post-New Testament glimpses of the life of the Church, provides for two fasts each week, on Wednesday and Friday, and not on Monday and Thursday "with the hypocrites" (i.e., the Pharisees, or possibly the Jews in general).[3] The pre-Easter portions of the Book of Mormon contain three references to such a practice among the Nephites (Omni 1:26; Alma 6:6; Helaman 3:35), the last two in conjunction with communal worship. After the appearance of the risen Christ to the Nephites, the only mention of fasting in the Book of Mormon is as a devotional exercise in the worship of the Christian community (3 Nephi 27:1; 4 Nephi 1:12; Moroni 6:5).

There are several types of fasting mentioned in the Bible which are not attested in the Book of Mormon, including penitential fasting (Deuteronomy 9:18; 1 Samuel 7:6; 1 Kings 21:27; Ezra 9:1; Joel 1:14, 2:12-17; Jonah 3:5-9), fasting following a misfortune besides death (Joshua 7:6; 1 Samuel 1:17, 20:34; 1 Kings 21:4; Esther 4:1, 3) and fasting in preparation for battle (1 Samuel 14:24).

There are several references in the Old Testament (but, again, none in the New Testament) to the practice of penitential fasting. After commanding the Israelites to "put away the strange gods and Ashtaroth from among [them]," Samuel ordered them to gather at Mizpeh. "And they gathered together to Mizpeh, and drew water, and poured it out before the Lord, and fasted on that day, and said there, We have sinned against the Lord" (1 Samuel 7:3-6). Even Ahab, when he heard the prophecy of doom pronounced against him by Elijah, "rent his clothes, and put sackcloth upon his flesh, and fasted, and lay in sackcloth, and went softly" (1 Kings 21:27). In response to these evidences of penitence, the Lord told Elijah: "I will not bring the evil in his [Ahab's] days: but in his son's days will I bring the evil upon his house" (1 Kings 21:28-29; cf. also Deuteronomy 9:18; Ezra 10:6; Nehemiah 9:1; Joel 1:14, 2:12-17; Jonah 3:5-9).

Fasting as a sign of mourning following a calamity besides death is attested in ancient Israel but is not found in the Book of Mormon. When Saul threw a javelin at his son Jonathan for having defended David, "Jonathan arose from the table in fierce anger and did eat no meat the second day of the month: for he was grieved for David, because his father had done him shame" (1 Samuel 20:34). Similarly, following the unexpected discomfiture of the Israelites by the people of Ai, Joshua and the elders of Israel fasted and lay prostrate before the ark of the Lord until evening (see Joshua 7:6).

In preparation for a battle against the Philistines, Saul forbade his soldiers to eat until evening "that I may be avenged on mine enemies" (1 Samuel 14:24). Jonathan disobeyed his father's directive at his peril.

In the Bible, other ritual acts are frequently associated with fasting: donning sackcloth (1 Kings 21:27; Nehemiah 9:1; Psalm 69:11; Isaiah 58:5; Daniel 9:3; Jonah 3:5), strewing ashes on oneself (Esther 4:1, 3; Isaiah 58:5; Daniel 9:3; Jonah 3:5), weeping (2 Samuel 1:12, 12:21-23; Nehemiah 1:4; Joel 2:12-17), prayer (Nehemiah 1:4; Daniel 9:3), mourning (2 Samuel 1:12; Nehemiah 1:4; Joel 2:12-17), making a libation of water (1 Samuel 7:6), anointing and washing oneself (2 Samuel 12:20), and offering peace and burnt offerings (Judges 20:26). In the Book of Mormon, the number of recorded acts connected with fasting is smaller: mourning is recorded twice (Alma 30:2; Helaman 9:10–though the exact manner of mourning is not more explicitly stated) and anointing and washing oneself is mentioned once (3 Nephi 13:17), while prayer is frequently mentioned (Omni 1:26; Mosiah 27:22, 23; Alma 5:46, 6:6, 17:3, 9, 28:6, 30:2, 45:1; Helaman 3:35; 3 Nephi 13:17, 27:1; 4 Nephi 1:12; Moroni 6:5).

In summary, recorded instances of fasting in the Old Testament and in the pre-Easter sections of the Book of Mormon show numerous sources of motivation, but communal fasting as a religious act plays a relatively minor role. By the time of Christ, however, religious devotion had become a major motive for fasting, and remained so both in the primitive Church in Palestine and in the Christian community in the New World.

APPENDIX

Fasting in the Old Testament

Type of Fasting	Reference	Participants	Concomitant Ritual Actions
Day of Atonement Fast	Lev. 16:29, 31	Public	"Do no work"
	Lev. 23:27-32	Public	"Offer an offering made by fire unto the Lord"; "do no work"
	Num. 29:7-10	Public	No work, sacrificial offerings
	Isa. 58:3, 5, 10	Public	
Fasting Following a Death	1 Sam. 31:13	Public	"Fasted seven days"
	2 Sam. 1:12	Individual	Rent clothes, mourned, wept
	2 Sam. 3:35	Individual	
	1 Chr. 10:12	Public	
Petitionary Fasting	Judg. 20:26	Public	Offered peace offerings and burnt offerings
	2 Sam. 12:16, 21, 22, 23	Individual	
	2 Chr. 20:3	Public	
	Ezra 8:21, 23	Public	
	Neh. 1:4	Individual	Wept, mourned, prayed
	Esth. 4:16	Communal	
	Ps. 35:13	Individual	"My clothing was sackcloth"
	Ps. 69:11	Individual	"I made sackcloth also my garment"
	Ps. 109:24	Individual	
	Jer. 14:12	Public	Crying out to the Lord
	Jer. 36:6, 9	Public	
	Dan. 6:18	Individual	
	Dan. 9:3	Individual	Prayer, supplication, sackcloth, ashes
Preparatory Fasting	Ex. 34:28	Individual	
	Deut. 9:9	Individual	
	1 Sam. 28:20	Individual	
	1 Kgs. 21:9, 12	Public	

Fasting in the Old Testament (Continued)

Type of Fasting	Reference	Participants	Concomitant Ritual Actions
Penitential Fasting	Deut. 9:18	Individual	
	1 Sam. 7:6	Public	Drew water and poured it out before the lord
	1 Kgs. 21:27	Individual	Put on sackcloth
	Ezra 10:6	Individual	
	Neh. 9:1	Public	"Sackclothes and earth upon them"
	Joel 1:14	Public	"Call a solemn assembly"
	Joel 2:12-17	Public	Weeping, mourning, solemn assembly
	Jonah 3:5-9	Public	Sackcloth and ashes
Fasting Following Misfortune Besides Death	Josh. 7:6	Private	"Joshua rent his clothes, and fell to the earth. . . and put dust upon [his head]."
	1 Sam. 1:7	Individual	
	1 Sam. 20:34	Individual	
	1 Kgs. 21:4	Individual	
	Esth. 4:1, 3	Individual	Tore clothes, sackcloth, ashes; cried out
War Fasting	1 Sam. 14:24	Public	
"Zechariah" Fasts	Zech. 7:3, 5; 8:19	Public	

Fasting in the Book of Mormon

Type of Fasting	Reference	Participants	Concomitant Ritual Actions
Day of Atonement Fast	Alma 28:6	Public	Prayer
	Alma 30:2	Public	Mourning, prayer
	Alma 45:1	Public	Prayer
Fasting Following a Death	Hel. 9:10	Public	Mourning
Petitionary Fasting	Mosiah 27:22, 23	Private	Prayer
	Alma 10:7	Individual	
Preparatory Fasting	Alma 5:46	Individual	Prayer
	Alma 8:26	Individual	
	Alma 17:3	Private	Prayer
	Alma 17:9	Private	Prayer
Fasting As a Pious Exercise	Omni 1:26	Communal	Prayer
	Alma 6:6	Communal	Prayer
	Hel. 3:35	Communal	Prayer
	3 Ne. 13:16-18	Individual	Anointing and washing
	3 Ne. 27:1	Communal	Prayer
	4 Ne. 1:12	Communal	Prayer
	Moro. 6:5	Communal	Prayer

Notes

1. I owe this insight to my friend Gordon Thomasson who deals with this and related subjects in his unpublished paper "Expanding Approaches to the Book of Mormon: Pre-Exilic Israelite Religious Patterns."

2. Mishnah Taᶜanit 2:9; Didache 8:1; Apostolic Constitutions 7:23; Epiphanius, Adversus Haereses 16:1.

3. Didache 8:1.

Faith, Hope, Charity 8

Larry E. Dahl

As part of his final appeal to his future readers to come unto Christ and be perfected in him, Moroni testified:

> Wheretofore, there must be faith; and if there must be faith there must also be hope; and if there must be hope there must also be charity. And except ye have charity ye can in nowise be saved in the kingdom of God; neither can ye be saved in the kingdom of God if ye have not faith; neither can ye if ye have no hope (Moroni 10:20-21).

Faith, hope, and charity are familiar terms often spoken of together, and nearly always in the same order. Paul indicates that the order has significance, charity being the last and also the greatest of the three (see 1 Corinthians 13:13). A perusal of Church manuals and magazines shows that faith is discussed the most, charity next, and hope the least. In fact, it has been my experience that hope, which is as necessary to our salvation as faith or charity, is rarely discussed as a gospel principle. Furthermore, treatment of faith and charity is often limited to simply reading the words of Paul or Alma or Moroni without a careful analysis of what these apostles and prophets said or what their intended meaning was. To add to our understanding, in

Larry E. Dahl is director of Doctrine and Covenants in the Religious Studies Center and associate professor of Church History and Doctrine at BYU.

this chapter we will explore some of the teachings of the Book of Mormon concerning faith, hope, and charity—their meanings, their relationships to each other, how they are acquired, and what their fruits are.

Faith

The word *faith* appears some 260 times in the Book of Mormon. Except for perhaps a half dozen instances, such as Alma 32; 48:15-16; 57:26-27; and Ether 12:6, the writers use the word without defining or describing it, apparently assuming that the reader understands its meaning.

The word *faith* is used in several contexts. At least 16 times it refers to one's system of belief, the Church, or the gospel, as in "He had hope to shake me from the faith" (Jacob 7:5); "This judge was after the order and faith of Nehor" (Alma 14:16); and "A few of the Lamanites who were converted unto the true faith" (3 Nephi 6:14). At least 6 references deal with one's having strong faith. For example, Ammon rejoiced over the Lamanite queen, saying, "Blessed art thou because of thy exceeding faith; I say unto thee, woman, there has not been such great faith among all the people of the Nephites" (Alma 19:10). And concerning the Nephite multitude to whom the Savior appeared after his resurrection, he told his disciples, "So great faith have I never seen among all the Jews" (3 Nephi 19:35). In at least 19 instances, the Book of Mormon peoples and the reader are encouraged or charged to acquire or exercise faith. At least 27 times, the word refers to someone's spiritual status. For instance, the Lamanite converts known as the people of Ammon are described as being "firm in the faith of Christ" (Alma 27:27), and Jarom records, "Our kings and our leaders were mighty men in the faith of the Lord" (Jarom 1:7). These are a few of the contexts in which the word *faith* appears in the Book of Mormon.

The rest of the 260 references to faith testify to the fruits of faith and the great blessings that flow from acquiring, retaining, and exercising it. Faith brings the power of the Holy Ghost to reveal truths, change hearts, remit sins, and sanctify (see Jarom 1:4; Mosiah 4:3; 5:4-7; Alma 9:20;

3 Nephi 27:19). Only through faith can miracles take place (see Ether 12:16, 18). Through faith, confining cords are broken (see 1 Nephi 7:12; Alma 14:26-28), prison walls tumble (Ether 12:13), military victories are won (Alma 57:21), mountains move (Jacob 4:6; Mormon 8:24; Ether 12:30), ancient records come forth (2 Nephi 3:19-21; Ether 12:22), and angels manifest themselves (Moroni 7:30). Exceeding faith allows some to see Christ and have all things revealed to them (see Ether 3:9; 4:7; 12:8, 19, 20, 31). Ultimately, the Savior "claimeth all those who have faith in him; and they who have faith in him will cleave unto every good thing" (Moroni 7:28), and he grants them eternal life (see Helaman 8:15). The list goes on and on. We are reminded several times that "the Lord is able to do all things according to his will, for the children of men, if it so be that they exercise faith in him" (1 Nephi 7:12; see also 2 Nephi 1:10; Moroni 10:23). It seems that the inspired writers of the Book of Mormon longed for later readers to understand clearly that the fruits of faith are both precious and possible.

How to Acquire Faith

The Book of Mormon also contains several passages about how one acquires faith. Consider the following in the order in which they appear.

Alma recorded that the keeping of the law of Moses by certain converted Lamanites served to "strengthen their faith in Christ" (Alma 25:15-16). He also taught a group of Zoramites that faith comes and is increased by experimenting with the word of God, by planting the word in one's heart, then by nourishing it with diligence and patience (Alma 32-33). When his listeners asked how to do that, Alma admonished them to search the scriptures and cry unto the Lord through prayer, to soften their hearts and to "begin to believe in the Son of God" (Alma 33:22).

Amulek added his plea to those same Zoramites "that ye may begin to exercise your faith unto repentance, that ye begin to call upon his holy name." He also reminded them that such prayer is vain unless it is accompanied by active concern for others (Alma 34:17, 28-29).

Growing in faith is tied to fasting and praying "oft" (Helaman 3:35). "You must repent, and cry unto the voice, even until ye shall have faith in Christ" (Helaman 5:41). Nephi, the son of Helaman, was similarly told that he would be made mighty in faith because of his unwearyingness in declaring the gospel, in seeking the Lord's will instead of his own, and in keeping the commandments (see Helaman 10:4-5).

The Lamanite prophet Samuel reminded the Nephites that coming to a knowledge of the truth and to a belief in the holy scriptures leads to faith (Helaman 15:7).

Mormon testified that "the Lord God prepareth the way that the residue of men may have faith in Christ" by sending angels to minister unto the children of men, by declaring by his own mouth to prophets that Christ should come, by manifesting things in divers ways unto the children of men, and by angels "declaring the word of Christ unto the chosen vessels of the Lord, that they may bear testimony of him" (Moroni 7:21-25, 28-32).

It seems clear from these verses that faith is a gift bestowed by God, and that a person can, and indeed must, qualify him or herself to receive that gift by learning of Christ through studying the scriptures, and listening to the prophets; by having honest, humble, and persistent prayer; by patiently obeying the commandments he or she has been given; and by fasting. Gaining faith is assured with such an approach.

Defining Faith

Undoubtedly it is much more important to know how to acquire faith and to experience its fruits than to be able to give a technical definition of it. However, many minds ache to understand clearly and to be able to explain principles precisely. What help, then, does the Book of Mormon give us in defining faith?

Alma 32 contains pertinent information. Three times Alma tells us what faith is not. He says, "Faith is not to have a perfect knowledge," for "if a man knoweth a thing he hath no cause to believe, for he knoweth it" (see 17-18, 21, 26). As both evidence and explanation of this notion,

Alma gives the example of planting a seed and observing it sprout. When a person has actually experienced the sprouting, Alma says his knowledge is perfect and his faith is dormant in that thing (v. 34). The phrase "in that thing" is an important key, for Alma is quick to remind us that our knowledge is not perfect in *all* things, but only in *that thing*, that is, that the seed is good. He adds, "Neither must ye lay aside your faith, for ye have only exercised your faith to plant the seed that ye might try the experiment to know if the seed was good" (v. 36).

This explanation helps us to understand Ether 3:19 better, which says that after the brother of Jared saw the finger of the Lord, "he had faith no longer, for he knew, nothing doubting." This does not mean that he no longer had need for faith and that he knew all things, but he did know specifically that Christ lived and had a spirit body. "In that thing" his knowledge was perfect and his faith dormant. However, he still needed to have faith concerning a myriad of other things he had not yet seen or experienced. Hence, whatever else it is, faith is an element of anticipation of unseen reality. It is oriented toward the future.

What other elements does faith possess besides anticipation? The following three passages about the two thousand stripling warriors are illuminating. First, after explaining that the Nephites were taught to defend themselves but never to be aggressors, the record states:

> And this was their faith, that by so doing God would prosper them in the land, or in other words, if they were faithful in keeping the commandments of God that he would prosper them in the land; yea, warn them to flee, or to prepare for war, according to their danger; and also, that God would make it known unto them whither they should go to defend themselves against their enemies, and by so doing, the Lord would deliver them; and this was the faith of Moroni (Alma 48:15-16).

Then, concerning the fact that all survived a vicious battle, Helaman explains,

> And now, their preservation was astonishing to our whole army, yea, that they should be spared while there was a thousand of our brethren who were slain. And we do justly ascribe it to the miraculous power of God, because of their exceeding faith in that which they had been taught to believe—that there was a just God, and whosoever did not doubt, that they should be preserved by his

> marvelous power. Now this was the faith of these of whom I have spoken; they are young, and their minds are firm, and they do put their trust in God continually (Alma 57:26-27).

Finally, in response to fervent prayers for strength against their enemies, the righteous Nephites received this welcomed answer:

> Yea, it came to pass that the Lord our God did visit us with assurances that he would deliver us; yea, insomuch that he did speak peace to our souls, and did grant unto us great faith, and did cause us that we should hope for our deliverance in him (Alma 58:11).

The sense of the word *faith* in these instances is that of assurance, trust, lack of doubt, and confidence. Also, in every instance, doing or a sense of obeying is present. "And thus they went forth" (Alma 48:20); "and they did obey and observe to perform every word of command with exactness" (Alma 57:21); "and we did take courage . . . and were fixed with a determination. . . . And thus we did go forth with all our might" (Alma 58:12-13). Thus the Book of Mormon teaches that faith is an assurance, confidence, and trust in unseen reality that impels one to act.

What of Alma 32:21, which says, "If ye have faith ye hope for things which are not seen, which are true"? Is this not a definition of faith? I suggest that it is more a statement of what follows faith than it is a definition of faith. If we define "faith" solely with the word "hope," then they are the same. But it is clear from many other passages in the Book of Mormon that hope is something different from, even beyond, faith. If one views Alma 32:21 as a statement that hope follows faith, then that view is consistent with other passages which treat hope as distinct from faith.

Hope

The word *hope* is used 50 times in the Book of Mormon. It is used in two senses: (1) a general one, consistent with common usage and meaning a "desire accompanied by expectation of fulfillment," or wanting or longing for something that may be a possibility, or a kind of wishing and wondering; and (2) a specific, theological sense, meaning a state of mind, heart, and spirit necessary for salvation, a gift of God given through the Holy Ghost.

Some examples of the general use of the word *hope* are found in Jacob and 3 Nephi. Jacob said that Sherem "had hope to shake me from the faith" (Jacob 7:5), and Giddianhi wrote to Lachoneus, "I hope that ye will deliver up your lands and your possessions, without the shedding of blood" (3 Nephi 3:10). Likewise, by gathering into one body and having provisions for seven years, the Nephites "did hope to destroy the robbers from off the face of the land" (3 Nephi 4:4).

These examples speak of a different hope from the second type: that which one must have in order to be saved (see Moroni 10:21), the hope that "cometh of faith, [and] maketh an anchor to the souls of men," making them "sure and steadfast, always abounding in good works" (Ether 12:4).

What does the Book of Mormon say about this saving hope? Saving hope follows, comes from and grows out of faith, as Moroni states: "Whoso believeth in God might with surety hope for a better world, yea, even a place at the right hand of God, which hope *cometh of faith*" (Ether 12:4; emphasis added). "Wherefore, ye may also have hope, and be partakers of the gift, if ye will but have faith" (Ether 12:9).

> And again, my beloved brethren, I would speak unto you concerning hope. How is it that ye can attain unto faith, save ye shall have hope? And what is it that ye shall hope for? Behold I say unto you that ye shall have hope through the atonement of Christ and the power of his resurrection, to be raised unto life eternal, and this because of your faith in him according to the promise. Wherefore, if a man have faith he must needs have hope; for without faith there cannot be any hope (Moroni 7:40-42).

A casual reading of these verses can lead to some confusion, however. Does verse 40 say that one must have hope before faith? What, then, does verse 42 mean, which states that without faith there cannot be any hope? The intended meaning, I submit, is that if one exercises faith, hope must follow, which hope is the sure and natural consequence of faith. The sense of verse 40 would then be, "How is it that ye can attain unto faith, save ye shall *then* [naturally, automatically, as an outgrowth and reward of your faith] have hope?" If one takes such a view, Moroni 7:40-42 is consistent internally and also with other Book of Mormon passages that speak of the sequence relationship of faith and hope.

Others have taken a somewhat different view. They speak of faith and hope as having reciprocal relationships at various levels. Applying such an understanding to Moroni 7:40-42 would suggest that verse 40 refers to one level of hope which leads to faith, which in turn leads to a second level of hope noted in verses 41 and 42. This pattern then repeats itself in an upward cycle. A careful examination of the scriptural record, however, shows reasons in favor of the idea that saving hope is a result, not an initial cause, of faith.

Taking the sequential view that faith precedes hope does not deny that something must precede faith. If it is not hope, what is it? Alma called it a "desire to believe" (Alma 32:27). Perhaps this could be thought of as a type of hope, relating to a general "wishing and wondering." But it is not the saving hope that I believe Mormon and Moroni refer to in Moroni 7:40-42. Saving hope *follows* faith.

In addition to teaching that saving hope comes as a result of faith, the Book of Mormon supports the idea that saving hope is a desire, a longing, a hungering and thirsting after righteousness with a full expectation of eventual fulfillment. Consider the following. The prophet Ether explained that hope "maketh an anchor to the souls of men, which would make them sure and steadfast, always abounding in good works, being led to glorify god" (Ether 12:4), and the Lamanite prophet Samuel taught that those who experience a change of heart "are firm and steadfast in the faith" (Helaman 15:7-8).

If "hope" makes men steadfast, and those who have experienced a "change of heart" are steadfast, can we not then link hope with a change of heart? It is interesting to examine the Book of Mormon references to a convert's change of heart in relation to the idea that hope consists of a desire for righteousness. After hearing King Benjamin's great address, his people testified: "We believe all the words which thou hast spoken unto us; and also, we know of their surety and truth, because of the Spirit of the Lord Omnipotent, which has wrought a mighty change in us, or in our hearts, that we have no more disposition to do evil, but to do good continually" (Mosiah 5:2). We learn from Mosiah 4:3 and 5:7 that this change of heart came as a result of their being "spiritually begotten" including having their sins remitted, which brought them peace of conscience and great joy. The same testimony comes from King Lamoni and his people at their conversion: "And they did all declare unto the people the self-same thing —that their hearts had been changed; that they had no more desire to do evil" (Alma 19:33).

It is clear that such a change is required of all who are to inherit the kingdom of God, for the voice of the Lord said to Alma at the time of his spiritual awakening: "Marvel not that all mankind, yea, men and women, all nations, kindreds, tongues and people, must be born again; yea, born of God, changed from their carnal and fallen state, to a state of righteousness, being redeemed of God, becoming his sons and daughters" (Mosiah 27:25). Before his conversion Alma desired to destroy the church of God (see Alma 36:6); after his conversion he longed to build his church and to be with God and angels (see Mosiah 28:3 and Alma 36:22, 24).

It all seems to fit. Faith (including prayer, repentance, and obedience) prepares a person to receive a spiritual rebirth, which brings a remission of sin and changes the heart so that it desires righteousness. This desire for righteousness is a primary ingredient of hope.

But there is more to hope than longing for righteousness. The Holy Ghost, who plays a major role in bringing about that desire, remains to fill the converted soul with staying power, a spiritual confidence, an assurance that his longings will be realized. Such confidence was reflected in King Benjamin's people when they said: "We . . . have great views of that which is to come; and were it expedient, we could prophesy of all things" (Mosiah 5:3). Similarly, Alma testified, "I know that he will raise me up at the last day, to dwell with him in glory; yea, and I will praise him forever" (Alma 36:28).

Heaven would not be heaven if we did not want to be there–if our hearts and our very natures were not in complete harmony with the righteousness that is there. Imagine the incongruity of someone struggling white-knuckle-like to keep what he regards as burdensome commandments in order to be saved in the kingdom of God, and once there to feel similarly burdened by the necessity of living those same principles eternally. Indeed, "ye can in nowise be saved in the kingdom of God . . . if ye have no hope" (Moroni 10:21).

Charity

Though spoken of explicitly the fewest number of times (27), *charity* is defined and explained in the Book of Mormon more directly and clearly than either faith or hope. Nephi said simply, "Charity is love" (2 Nephi 26:30). Mormon, as quoted by Moroni, expanded this definition to "Charity is the pure love of Christ" (Moroni 7:47). The verses that speak of charity indicate that if we are to be saved in the kingdom of God, we must experience charity in two dimensions, which I will call vertical and horizontal.

Vertical charity refers to the love of Christ has for us, which love motivated the Atonement. Moroni explained:

> And again, I remember that thou hast said that thou hast loved the world, even unto the laying down of thy life for the world, that thou mightest take it again to prepare a place for the children of men. And now I know that this love which thou hast had for the children of men is charity; wherefore, except men shall have charity they cannot inherit that place which thou hast prepared in the mansions of thy Father (Ether 12:33-34).

Horizontal charity refers to that love we must feel and extend to others of mankind. Nephi spoke of this dimension when he said: "I have charity for my people. . . . I have charity for the Jew. . . . I also have charity for the Gentiles" (2 Nephi 33:7-9). Mormon explained both dimensions of charity in these words: "Charity suffereth long, and is kind, and envieth not, and is not puffed up, seeketh not her own, is not easily provoked, thinketh no evil, and rejoiceth not in iniquity but rejoiceth in the truth, beareth all things, believeth all things, hopeth all things, endureth all things. . . . Charity never faileth" (Moroni 7:45-46).

When our hearts are filled with charity, we love as Christ loved, his goals become our goals, his work becomes our work, and ultimately his glory becomes our glory, for we will become "joint-heirs with Christ" (Romans 8:17) of "all that my Father hath" (D&C 84:38).

With this thought in mind, and thinking of charity in relationship to hope, it might be said that hope is a hungering and thirsting after righteousness for oneself, and charity is essentially a hungering and thirsting after righteousness for others. Not surprisingly, therefore, we find that Lehi, after tasting the fruit of the tree of life, "began to be desirous that [his] family should partake of it also" (1 Nephi 8:12), and that Nephi wrote, "I pray continually for [my people] by day, and mine eyes water my pillow by night, because of them" (2 Nephi 33:3).

Enos, after experiencing the joy of hearing his own sins were remitted, "pour[ed] out [his] whole soul unto God" for "the welfare of [his friends], the Nephites. And when he had obtained a promise of blessings for them, he then "prayed . . . with many long strugglings for [his enemies], the Lamanites" (Enos 1:9, 11). Following their conversion, Alma and the sons of Mosiah "were desirous that salvation should be declared to every creature, for they could not bear that any human soul should perish; yea, even the very thoughts that any soul should endure endless torment did cause them to quake and tremble" (Mosiah 28:3). This same commitment to serving to bless others is shown by all the prophet-leaders of the Book of Mormon.

Charity, like faith and hope before it, is bestowed by God upon those who prepare themselves to receive it. Mormon instructed members of the Church in his day, whom he described as "the peaceable followers of Christ, . . . that have obtained a sufficient hope by which ye can enter into the rest of the Lord" (Moroni 7:3), to "pray unto the Father with all the energy of heart, that ye may be filled with this love, which he hath bestowed upon all who are true followers of his Son, Jesus Christ" (7:48). Mormon's plea and his earlier explanation of the characteristics of charity (see Moroni 7:45) show that charity is an outgrowth of faith and hope that encompasses them both. How appropriate it is, then, to speak of these three principles in the order given—faith, leads to hope, and they develop into charity—charity being the "greatest" (1 Corinthians 13:13).

Line upon Line

It is worthwhile to ponder and discuss the gradually unfolding nature of faith, hope, and charity. Alma instructed Zeezrom that men are given a "lesser" or "greater" portion of the "word," and they enlarge or diminish that portion "according to the heed and diligence which they give unto" it. Those who obey will receive more and more until they know the mysteries of God "in full"; those who harden their hearts receive less and less "until they know nothing of his mysteries" (Alma 12:9-11). In this light, Book of Mormon phrases such as "a particle of faith" (Alma 32:27), "much faith" (Mosiah 27:14), "strong faith" (Alma 7:17), "exceeding faith" (Mosiah 4:3), and even "exceedingly great faith" (Moroni 10:11) are clearer and more meaningful.

Similarly, when we receive the baptism of fire that remits sin and brings hope, we do not suddenly vault into full spiritual maturity. In Peter's words, we are "newborn babes" in need of milk that we "may grow thereby" (1 Peter 2:2). In this connection, it is intriguing to consider the implications of the Savior's statement that certain Lamanites, "because of their faith in me at the time of their conversion, were baptized with fire and with the Holy Ghost, and they knew it not" (3 Nephi 9:20). Undoubtedly, they knew something had happened, for "they were encircled about, yea every soul, by a pillar of fire," and "they could speak forth marvelous words" (Helaman 5:43, 45), but their understanding of what they were experiencing may have come later.

There is no guarantee that the change of heart involved here will remain forever. Alma asks, "And now behold, I say unto you, my brethren, If ye have experienced a change of heart, and if ye have felt to sing the song of redeeming love, I would ask, can ye feel so now?" (Alma 5:26). We can lose the desire for righteousness. That desire comes from the companionship of the Holy Ghost, and when we become disobedient, or even casual about the gospel, we feel less and less of his power. On the other hand, awareness and obedience bring to us more and more of the power of the Spirit, intensifying our desire for righteousness. Hence we read of "sufficient hope" (Moroni 7:3), "firm hope" (Alma 34:41), "a more excellent hope" (Ether 12:32), and "a perfect brightness of hope" (2 Nephi 31:20).

I have not found specific evidence in the Book of Mormon that there are portions of charity. Obviously, vertical charity, Christ's love for us, is pure, full, perfect, consistent. However, I suspect that horizontal charity, our love for each other, functions on a continuum, as do faith and hope.

Faith, Hope, and Charity Must Be Centered in Christ

The Savior said: "I will show unto them that faith, hope and charity bringeth unto me–the fountain of all righteousness" (Ether 12:28). The first principle of the gospel is not just "faith," but "faith in the Lord Jesus Christ" (Article of Faith 4). Similarly, we must obtain not just hope, but a "hope in Christ" (Jacob 2:19), a "hope of his glory" (Jacob 4:4), and "we should hope for our deliverance in him" (Alma 58:11). Likewise, by simple definition, charity is not just "love," but "the pure love of Christ" (Moroni 7:47).

To say that true faith, hope, and charity must be centered in Christ may seem to be an unnecessary statement of the obvious. However, as with all other gospel principles, faith, hope and charity have their counterfeits. President Spencer W. Kimball has said: "Whatever thing a man sets his heart and his trust in most is his god; and if his god doesn't also happen to be the true and living God of Israel, that man is laboring in idolatry" (*Ensign*, June 1976, p. 4). There are many causes in the world to which men give their allegiance. They trust (have faith) in their chosen cause; they long for (hope for) the purposes of that cause to be fulfilled, and eagerly desire that others share their commitment and rewards (charity). Many of these causes are commendable, but all are ultimately inadequate to provide permanent solutions to the problems in this world, and salvation in the world to come. As the angel instructed King Benjamin, "There shall be no other name given nor any other way nor means whereby salvation can come unto the children of men, only in and through the name of Christ, the Lord Omnipotent" (Mosiah 3:17).

Conclusion

We began with Moroni's testimony that faith, hope, and charity are necessary for salvation. We close with Moroni's testimony that these gifts will always be available to those who believe. "And I would exhort you, my beloved brethren, that ye remember that he is the same yesterday, today, and forever, and that all these gifts of which I have spoken, which are spiritual, never will be done away, even as long as the world shall stand, only according to the unbelief of the children of men" (Moroni 10:19). May we have the good sense to believe and realize these marvelous gifts in our lives.

9

Love in the Book of Mormon

Gayle O. Brown

As we come to understand the gospel, we find that we are continually reminded of the principle of love. From the time we are very small, we are taught both to love God and to love one another. In actuality, we observe that some members of the Church seem to radiate and to demonstrate love very naturally. Others pass through a real struggle in order to display love. For these, loving constitutes a principle that requires understanding, nurturing, and work. While one's love generally increases with maturity, it is also possible to become less loving as one grows older. But most of us, it is to be hoped, use our lifetimes to assimilate the facets of love and to learn to be givers of love as well as recipients of God's love.

For those who desire and need to learn more about love, a study of the Book of Mormon can deepen their understanding and, I believe, enhance their ability to share that love. In this sacred book, we find examples of not only how we can be filled with love, but also what some results of love can be. In addition, it explains suitable and unsuitable objects of love. It further tells us whom God loves and whom we should love, and deals in depth with the aspects of charity, or the love of Christ. But before

Gayle O. Brown is an Arabic translator.

turning to a general discussion of these features of the message of the Book of Mormon, let me draw attention to three important aspects of love which are highlighted only briefly.

First, a point is made that love can have a consuming effect. We all recall Nephi's stirring lamentation in which, as he bemoans his own weaknesses, he exclaims, "O wretched man that I am!" (2 Nephi 4:17). Then, almost as a response to his despair, he recalls God's support in the past and declares, "[The Lord] hath filled me with his love, even unto the consuming of my flesh" (v. 21). From what Nephi says, it appears that the love of the Lord had come to him as a totally overwhelming feeling. Such, Nephi learned, was the *power* of love.

The second concise principle is described as a feasting, or banqueting, on the love of the Lord. In this connection, we read Jacob's brief but teeming statement that the pure in heart may feast upon the love of God if their minds are firm forever (see Jacob 3:2). Note that being allowed to partake of love in this manner requires not only that the participant be pure in heart but also possess a firm resolve to remain so. To such, the love of God is abundantly available.

Third, the Book of Mormon tells us that love can dispel all fear. One can think of few promises in modern life that are more welcome. It is in Mormon's important letter to his son Moroni that he affirms that he does not fear what man can do, for "perfect love casteth out all fear" (Moroni 8:16). In this connection, one is struck by a similar concept in 1 John 4:18 which states: "There is no fear in love; but perfect love casteth out fear: because fear hath torment. He that feareth is not made perfect in love."

It is clear from these impressive cameos that love can feel like a consuming of one's flesh, is available to the pure and steadfast of heart, and drives out fear. But the Book of Mormon has much more to say about love.

In introducing the topics which the Book of Mormon discusses at length, I want to observe that at times we are faced with trying to love someone who is difficult to love. Perhaps it is a child who has caused many problems. Perhaps it is a teacher who is unfair. It may be someone who has cheated us or harmed us in some way. We can all think of examples in our lives of people who are difficult to love. Nephi had faith in the Lord when he said, "I will go and do the things which the Lord hath commanded, for I know that the Lord giveth no commandments unto the children of men, save he shall prepare a way for them that they may accomplish the thing which he commandeth them" (1 Nephi 3:7). Because the Lord has commanded us to love, he will prepare a way for us to learn to love. Some of the ways are explained in the Book of Mormon in scriptures which refer to being "filled with love."

King Benjamin taught his people "to *keep the commandments of God*, that they might rejoice and be *filled with love* towards God and all men" (Mosiah 2:4; emphasis added). It appears that to be filled with love entails keeping the commandments of God. When we keep the commandments, it is easier to love God, ourselves, and all mankind.

He further stated that "the natural man is an enemy to God . . . unless he yields to the enticings of the Holy Spirit . . . and becometh as a child, submissive, meek, humble, patient, *full of love,* willing to submit to all things which the Lord seeth fit to inflict upon him, even as a child doth submit to his father" (Mosiah 3:19; emphasis added). This tells us, then, that if we do not become full of love we are, in reality, enemies to God.

Alma instructed his brethren to *humble themselves before the Lord*, *to pray continually* about temptation, and be *led by the Holy Spirit*. And if they did these three things, they would become "humble, meek, submissive, patient, *full of love* and all long-suffering" (Alma 13:28; emphasis added). In sum, basically, Alma instructs us to humble ourselves, to pray, and then to listen as we are led by the Holy Spirit. Following these three steps will assist us in acquiring the ability to become full of love.

Alma later spoke to his son Shiblon about love, counseling him to bridle his passions so that he could be filled with love (see Alma 38:12). We need to control those passions that are not conducive to loving others.

Mormon urged his people to "*pray unto the Father* with all the energy of heart, that ye may be *filled with this love,* which he hath bestowed upon all who are *true followers* of his Son, Jesus Christ" (Moroni 7:48; emphasis added). Note that both Alma and Moroni coupled prayer with the gaining of love. Could it be that the reason we may not feel love for others is that we have not really prayed for it—or, if we have, it has not been a prayer with all "energy of heart"? The latter part of the passage just quoted mentions love as something that is bestowed upon the "true followers" of Jesus Christ. If we do not feel the whole power of love, perhaps we have not prayed enough for it or are not yet true followers of Jesus Christ.

Mormon further discoursed on love in Moroni 8:26: "And the *remission of sins* bringeth meekness, and lowliness of heart; and because of meekness and lowliness of heart cometh the visitation of the Holy Ghost, which Comforter *filleth with hope and perfect love*, which love endureth by *diligence unto prayer*, until the end shall come, when all the saints shall dwell with God." Here another aspect of love is highlighted: the remission of sins. Through the remission of sins we are given qualities that make us people whom the Holy Ghost can visit and fill with perfect love. The qualities that lead to this are meekness and lowliness of heart.

Thus we glean from the pages of the Book of Mormon that, if we desire to become filled with love, we must keep the commandments of God (Mosiah 2:4), pray continually (Alma 13:28), bridle our passions (Alma 38:12), become true followers of Jesus Christ (Moroni 7:48), and meekly be led by the Holy Ghost (Moroni 8:26).

We can also find in the Book of Mormon specific mention of the results of love. It appears that, in part, Christ was able to endure persecution because of his loving kindness. We read in 1 Nephi 19:9, "Yea, they spit upon him, and he suffereth it, because of his loving kindness and his long-suffering towards the children of men." It is apparent that his suffering could be borne because of loving kindness. They scourged him and he suffered it, they struck him and he suffered it, they crucified him and he said, "Father, forgive them; for they know not what they do" (Luke 23:34).

On the other hand, God naturally shows mercy to

those who love him. Abinadi taught the people of King Noah that the Lord is merciful to those who love him, "showing mercy unto thousands of them that love me and keep my commandments" (Mosiah 13:14).

In another vein, Alma taught the people that "every man should love his neighbor as himself, that there should be no contention among them" (Mosiah 23:15). Naturally, if every man were to love his neighbor, there would be no contention.

In recounting his missionary experiences, Ammon attributed great love to those Lamanites who were converted. The fruits of his labor were abundant because of his love for the people and their love of him (see Alma 26:31). In fact, their love for their brethren was so great that they would not take up arms against them. The converted Lamanites refused to retaliate even when many of their numbers were slain. They would rather sacrifice their lives than to take the life of an enemy. They "buried their weapons of war deep in the earth, because of their love toward their brethren" (Alma 26:32). Because they had previously sinned so much in their battles against the Nephites, they wanted now to be free from the stain of killing again. Since their love for their brethren prevented them from killing even in self-defense, the Anti-Nephi-Lehies who were slain were thus able to return to God because of their love and because of their corresponding hatred of sin (see Alma 26:34).

With another concern in mind, Moroni tells us that when God's grace is sufficient for us, we may become perfect in Christ. We are promised that if we "love God with all [our] might, mind and strength, then is his grace sufficient" (Moroni 10:32).

Though the word "love" is not mentioned in connection with the events at the waters of Mormon, I believe that the words of Alma describe a loving people when he says, "Ye are desirous to come into the fold of God, and to be called his people, and are willing to bear one another's burdens, that they may be light, yea, and are willing to mourn with those that mourn; yea, and comfort those that stand in need of comfort, and to stand as witnesses of God at all times" (Mosiah 18:8-9). When we love others, we want to help, comfort, or share their grief.

The Book of Mormon is explicit in naming whom we should love, and even in identifying objects that are not worthy of our love. Let us consider first whom we should love. Alma reminds us "that *every* man should love *his neighbor as himself*, that there should be no contention among them" (Mosiah 23:15; emphasis added). The word "every" means that *all* of us should love all our neighbors, without exception. Sometimes those who are called to particular leadership positions have a gift for loving those over whom they hold a stewardship. For example, a bishop usually has a great love for all the members of his ward. But "every" person could have as great a love for all the members of the ward. One might not have the stewardship a bishop has, but there are no limitations to whom one can love.

In this connection, the Savior commands us to love our enemies. "But behold I say unto you, love *your enemies*" (3 Nephi 12:44; emphasis added). The Lord was certainly an example in this. Some of us have very difficult lives, but our plights do not often reach the magnitude of those which befell the early Saints, the Ammonites or Christ. Their love of God and others superseded their temporal agonies.

Reflecting love's matchless reach, King Benjamin told his people that it was possible for them to "be filled with love towards *God and all men*," thus reminding us to love God and *all* men (Mosiah 2:4; emphasis added). A little later he mentioned children and cautioned parents against allowing them to fight, quarrel, and serve the devil. Rather, they should be taught "to love one another, and to serve one another" (Mosiah 4:15).

On the other hand, Moroni noted that some loved their substance more than they loved the poor and needy, or the sick and afflicted (see Mormon 8:37). At times, we too may feel that we have neither the time nor the resources to love or care for such people. Those individuals who live in poverty and want, or who are ill or suffer afflictions could very well be in these circumstances as a result of lack of love either of or for others or themselves. Demonstrations of love, expressed or made visible, can sometimes make the difference between life and death. We must learn, somehow, not to be so concerned with our own problems that we fail to observe that those around us need love.

In summary, we have been admonished to love our neighbors, ourselves, our enemies, the poor, the needy, the sick and afflicted, God, and all men. This list appears to be all-inclusive, does it not?

By contrast, we are cautioned about placing our love on riches, vain things of the world, and glory. For instance, in the confrontation between Amulek and Zeezrom, Amulek accused Zeezrom of loving lucre more than God (see Alma 11:24). Further, we are often cautioned about the improper use of riches. It may be easier to be more humble and dependent on God if we do not possess great wealth. For example, those who followed Nehor loved the vain things of the world. "They went forth preaching false doctrines . . . for the sake of riches and honor" (Alma 1:16). In another instance, Moroni accused Pahoran of being iniquitous because of his love of glory and vain things (see Alma 60:32). Even though it turned out that Pahoran had not been iniquitous, Moroni's caution still stands. We simply cannot do right if we place love of glory or wealth ahead of being righteous. Christ warned the Nephites that the hypocrites loved to pray so as to be "seen of men" and observed that "they have their reward," that is, they were seen of others (3 Nephi 13:5).

All of these examples concern people during the Book of Mormon era. But the prophet Moroni summons us who live today to the forefront and addresses us directly on the matter. He begins: "Behold, I speak unto you as if ye were present and yet ye are not. But behold, Jesus Christ hath shown you unto me, and I know your doing. . . . Ye do love money, and your substance, and your fine apparel, and the adorning of your churches, more than ye love the poor and the needy, the sick and the afflicted" (Mormon 8:35, 37). He obviously perceived our generation and the temptations that exist. Several practical questions naturally arise. How many of us would willingly give our hard-earned possessions to those who need them more than we do? How many of us could get along without our surplus substance? When my husband was in graduate school, we could rather easily have given up any of our possessions because we didn't have very much of value. Now we find ourselves with surplus possessions. How easily can we give them up? Will our love be tested by whether or not we are willing to share them?

In looking for examples, we find love stories in the Book of Mormon. The scarcity of the mention of women eliminates the romantic love story. But we do not doubt the love Sariah had for Lehi and her family, as reflected in the loyalty she displayed in following her husband into the wilderness and to the promised land. Only one incident is recorded in which her troubles so weighed her down that she temporarily lost confidence in her husband and complained, calling him "a visionary man." She feared that her sons had been lost and that they had perished in the desert. Lehi admitted to being a visionary man, but not in a negative sense. Moreover, he assured her that the Lord would bring her sons back safely from Jerusalem. After her husband comforted her and her sons returned, she had the faith and courage to endure the coming difficult journey (see 1 Nephi 5:1-8).

Nephi earned the love of his people. "The people having loved Nephi exceedingly, he having been a great protector for them, having wielded the sword of Laban in their defence, and having labored in all his days for their welfare" (Jacob 1:10), they wanted his name to be remembered, and thus named successive rulers after him. Further, we do not doubt that Nephi loved God and his fellowmen. For instance, his love for his family was severely tested. He labored for and with his brothers throughout his life, and though they tormented and ridiculed him, he hoped for their salvation and tried to convince them of their errors. In a very personal glimpse into the soul of Nephi in 2 Nephi chapter 4, one cannot help but be filled with tender emotion for him as he revealed himself, in both his weaknesses and his strengths, his joys and his temptations. One senses that Nephi was trying to brace himself to face whatever was before him and to rededicate himself to the service of God. He says, "[My God] hath filled me with his love, even unto the consuming of my flesh" (2 Nephi 4: 21).

This statement may mean either that God abundantly granted his love to Nephi or that he gave Nephi the power to love as God himself loves. In either case Nephi experienced this gift as a consuming power. Those of us who have felt either of these kinds of love can begin to appreciate what a force or power love can be. When we have a consuming love, we want to be faithful to God. We desire to please him and to do his will. We want others to feel of his love. We are saddened by others' inability to recognize his love. We are strengthened and have power to do things we otherwise might think impossible. Likewise, when we feel consuming love for others, we are able to do all things for them that love requires. A consuming love for all men would be the zenith which Christ was able to attain.

Another example of love was that shown to Lamoni by Ammon. Perhaps the key to the change of heart experienced by King Lamoni's father, aside from the fact that his life was being threatened, was the great love Ammon had for his son: "And when he also saw the great love [Ammon] had for his son Lamoni, he was astonished exceedingly" (Alma 20:26). One recalls that Ammon had initially shown his love for Lamoni by offering to be his servant. By serving him well and saving his flocks, Ammon achieved a position of trust. Lamoni was then willing to listen to Ammon and thus began his conversion. When they later met Lamoni's father, Ammon saved Lamoni's life.

Christ showed great love to the Nephites. Compared to his time in Jerusalem, he spent very little time with the Nephites. But he felt great compassion for them and showed great love to them as he taught them things too sacred to be recorded, blessed their children, and healed their sick. All of these were acts of love. We can feel the emotion of the moment when we read: "And it came to pass that when Jesus had thus spoken he cast his eyes round about again on the multitude, and beheld they were in tears, and did look steadfastly upon him as if they would ask him to tarry a little longer with them. And he said unto them: Behold, my bowels are filled with compassion towards you" (3 Nephi 17:5-6). The Nephites knew that Christ would be with them only briefly. The one whom they loved would soon be gone. Yet how could they ask the Son of God to remain longer? He perceived this and a feeling of compassion welled up within him; and he was able to stay and minister to them a bit longer. He then asked that all the afflicted be brought to him, and he healed them. He also paid special attention to the children, blessing each one of them, one by one, and prayed to the Father for them. Any of us who have had to leave those whom we love, or have had loved ones leave us, can identify with this passage. As we spend time in one place or another, we grow to love those whom we meet. While we know that there will be others to love in other places, leaving remains difficult. Perhaps we are asked to speak in a sacrament meeting when we are about to move out of a ward and, as we look over the congregation, we are saddened by leaving and wish that we could tarry longer.

Jesus visited the Nephites as he had those in Jerusalem, and there were yet others to whom he must show himself after departing from the Nephites. "But now I go unto the Father, and also to show myself unto the lost tribes of Israel" (3 Nephi 17:4). Even so, because he loved the Nephites and because they reciprocated that love, he tarried.

Another example of one who loved was Mormon. He had become deeply discouraged by the wickedness of his people and consequently refused to lead the Nephite armies for a period. Yet he recorded, "Behold I had led them, notwithstanding their wickedness I had led them many times to battle, and had loved them, according to the love of God which was in me, with all my heart; and my soul had been poured out in prayer unto my God all the day long for them; nevertheless, it was without faith, because of the hardness of their hearts" (Mormon 3:12). Few of us are tried in our love for others as severely as was Mormon.

Whom does God love? "He loveth those who will have him to be their God" (1 Nephi 17:40). He has loved the world, even unto the laying down of [his] life for the world" (Ether 12:33). "He loveth his children" (1 Nephi 11:17). He also "loveth our souls" (Alma 24:14). Each of us, then, can be blessed by and with his love.

There are three scriptures that mention "redeeming love" in the Book of Mormon. "The chains of hell . . . were loosed, and [your fathers'] souls did expand, and they did sing redeeming love" (Alma 5:9). Moreover, "I say unto you, my brethren, if ye have experienced a change of heart, and if ye have felt to sing the song of redeeming love, I would ask, can ye feel so now?" (Alma 5:26). And finally, "[Our brethren the Lamanites] are brought to sing redeeming love, and this because of the power of his word which is in us, therefore have we not great reason to rejoice?" (Alma 26:13). It appears that the people were feeling the redemptive love of the Lord. However they expressed this, whether in song or praise or thanksgiving, they felt the love of their Redeemer.

There are several scriptures in which "the love of God" is mentioned. One can ponder whether this means "love *for* God" or "love *from* God" or the kind of love God possesses. The meaning of some scriptures can be enriched or enhanced by applying different senses to the words. Nephi, in interpreting Lehi's dream, described the tree as "the love of God, which sheddeth itself abroad in the hearts of the children of men; wherefore, it is the most desirable above all things" (1 Nephi 11:22). Love of God, then, is desirable above all things. Is this love God's love for us, or our love for God, or the state of being able to love as God does? In 4 Nephi we read that "there was no contention in the land, because of the love of God which did dwell in the hearts of the people" (4 Nephi 1:15). Again, did God's love dwell in their hearts, or did their love for God dwell in their hearts, or was it a general God-like love that dwelt in their hearts? Was there no contention because everyone felt God's love, or did everyone love God and therefore live peacefully?

Benjamin listed the ways in which we can become filled with the love of God. He taught that humbling oneself and remembering the greatness of God and one's own nothingness are part of the process (see Mosiah 4:11-12). Alma taught that we should have "the love of God always in [our] hearts, that [we] may be lifted up at the last day and enter into his rest" (Alma 13:29).

Though we have just mentioned the word *love* thus

far, the Book of Mormon makes it clear that *charity* is love and that all men should possess it (see, for example, 2 Nephi 26:30). Occasionally using the word *charity* in place of *love* gives the latter more depth. It is interesting to note that the word for *love* in Arabic (حب; hubb) is composed of the consonants " ح " (h) and " ب " (*b*). In order to make the word for *charity* (محبة), a " م " (*mem*) is added to the beginning of the word, which gives it a little more distinction. But in the Arabic Bible, "love" almost always appears to be the same word as "charity." They appear to be used in exactly the same way for all kinds of love. "محبة" (*mahaba*) is preferred because it sounds more elegant. *Cruden's Complete Concordance*, under the entry "love," has a note to the effect that all references to "charity" in the King James Bible should have been translated "love." Since the modern usage of the word "charity" no longer carries the meaning "love," "charity" can be misleading as it appears in the King James Bible.

In the Book of Mormon, charity is called "the pure love of Christ" (Moroni 7:47). It is "everlasting love" (Moroni 8:17). We are all familiar with the comprehensive description of charity which Moroni quotes from his father, Mormon:

> And charity suffereth long, and is kind, and envieth not, and is not puffed up, seeketh not her own, is not easily provoked, thinketh no evil, and rejoiceth not in iniquity but rejoiceth in the truth, beareth all things, believeth all things, hopeth all things, endureth all things. Wherefore, my beloved brethren, if ye have not charity, ye are nothing, for charity never faileth. Wherefore, cleave unto charity, which is the greatest of all, for all things must fail —but charity is the pure love of Christ, and it endureth forever; and whoso is found possessed of it at the last day, it shall be well with him (Moroni 7:45-47).

The fruits of charity are many. Some are mentioned here by Mormon. Alma taught that if one has charity he "will always abound in good works" (Alma 7:24). Moroni taught that charity brings the Gentiles to "the fountain of all righteousness" (Ether 12:28). Those who have charity "shall have talents more abundantly (Ether 12:35). The charitable will "not suffer the laborer in Zion to perish" (2 Nephi 26:30). And "love . . . for the children of men" is identified as charity in Ether 12:34.

If we lack charity, we "cannot inherit that place which [has been] prepared in the mansions of [the] Father" (Ether 12:34). Moroni makes it clear that without charity we "can in nowise be saved in the kingdom of God" (Moroni 10:21). And finally, "If [we] have not charity [we are] nothing; wherefore [we] must needs have charity" (Moroni 7:44). It is imperative that we come to possess this important gift.

Many examples of love and charity are found throughout the pages of the Book of Mormon. Perhaps love can be compared to the seed mentioned in Alma 32. Love is something that can be planted in our hearts; and if we nurture it and are diligent in our prayers concerning it, it will begin to enlarge our souls. It will even begin to be delicious to us, and our understanding concerning it will be enlightened. Alma encourages us to experiment upon the word of God. If we experiment with love and do as the Lord commands us, one day we shall hear the words, "Come unto me ye blessed, for behold, your works have been the works of righteousness upon the face of the earth" (Alma 5:16).

Before Columbus 10

George F. Carter

It is fitting here for me to take note of the work of The Church of Jesus Christ of Latter-day Saints in American archaeology. Their work in Mesoamerica is exemplary, an observation illustrated by the papers of the New World Archeological Foundation. I was alerted to this work early when cylinder seals from western Mexico were sent by this group[1] to W. F. Albright at the Johns Hopkins University, where we were both on the faculty at the time. Albright called me to his office to look at those items with him. He recognized a letter or two and concluded that these were degenerate cartouches of Mediterranean inspiration. He was roundly denounced for such a heresy, but, as usual, Albright was right.

Another pleasant memory grows out of my correspondence with then Dean George H. Hansen concerning the Utah Lake skull. It was found during the droughts in the 1930s, and Dean Hansen had the insight to see that it was quite an unusual skull. Neither of us has been able to get the anthropologists to give it the attention that it deserves. But I recall with pleasure his insight as well as his good-humored resignation to patiently enduring through the time that it takes to get new ideas accepted. His publication on this appeared in 1934,[2] just over fifty years ago!

George F. Carter, Department of Geography, Texas A&M.

Dr. Paul Cheesman and I not only share an interest in American prehistory, but both of us attended San Diego State College, though separated in time. And finally, this is not my first visit to Brigham Young University, for decades ago I was here to interview one of your biochemists, with the hidden hope that we could recruit him for the McCollum-Pratt Institute that we were then forming at the Johns Hopkins University. I have most pleasant memories of the hospitality extended to my family at that time. This is, then, a happy occasion for me, and one to which I am honored to have been invited.

The title "Before Columbus" gives me wide latitude in time, and suitably keynotes my interests. Did effective contact across the broad oceans begin with Columbus? Or was he a Johnny-come-lately? Was he preceded millennia before by many people who crossed both the Atlantic and the Pacific Oceans? Such is now my view, but it is one to which I have come reluctantly. It is not what I was taught.

It is hard for me not to begin with Columbus. Ever since his discovery, there have been persistent rumors about Columbus concerning both his person and his discovery. What might be called the Spanish version runs as follows. The so-called Columbus was actually Juan Colon from the island of Mallorca. He assumed the Christopher Columbus identity for religious reasons (he was part Jewish) and political reasons (he had fought against Spain). He married a Portuguese woman of good family, and her connections placed him in the Madeira Islands. There he met a ship captain who was returning from America. The captain died in the Madeiras, and Columbus inherited his papers. He also inherited two men who had been on the voyage, the Pinzon brothers, and they served as pilots on Columbus' voyage.

There is much more, and Morison,[3] the authority on Columbus, sweeps all of this under the academic rug. Having read the Spanish version and having considered several odd things related to Columbus' voyage, (such as his keeping two logs of the trip and his certainty of the length of the voyage), I suspect that the Spanish version may be correct. The importance of this lies less in what Columbus did or who he was than in how little one can trust history as it is usually presented. One should be critical of another's view of history, including mine.

The Carter Background

In listening to anyone on any topic you really need to know something about that person. Who is he? What ax does he have to grind? What school of thought does he represent? What tools does he employ to get at the particular problem under discussion? And a lot more. For these reasons, I shall be autobiographical in this presentation —not from ego, but to help the reader better understand what I was raised to think, and how my thinking became so radically different.

I was raised in archaeology. I started by collecting arrowheads and progressed to volunteer work in the San Diego Museum of Man. I went to the University of California at Berkeley and earned an A.B. degree in anthropology under such notable men as Kroeber and Lowie. I learned an immense amount about ethnology. I was immersed in cultural history, but it was a very particularized ethnohistory: a people-by-people study with little emphasis on the spread of ideas. That anyone at any time had sailed to America and influenced Amerindian cultural growth was unthinkable.

I was thereafter employed by the San Diego Museum of Man as an assistant curator, and worked happily at archaeology. When my thinking slipped too far out of line with that of the chief curator, who thought that the antiquity of man in America was about 4,000 years (my thinking was that it was more like 40,000), I left the museum job. By a happy accident I landed in geography—first at San Diego State College and very shortly at Berkeley, where I came under the influence of Carl Sauer, a giant in the field.

When it came time to start the research for a doctoral dissertation, I was given Southwestern Indian agriculture as my research topic. So I started by reading about the crop plants of the Southwest; and this set the line of research which I was to develop and which was destined to mark my scholarly life.

I discovered that there are several kinds of corn:

flint, flour, dent, and sweet. There are also several kinds of beans: *vulgaris*, *lunatus*, *acutifolius*. Pumpkins and squashes (*Cucurbitas*) are botanically *pepo*, *moschata*, and *maxima*; the common names do not match the botanical realities. These botanical designations represented initial perceptions which were to become keys to cultural history when illuminated by later work.

When I went into the Southwest, I collected the corn, beans, and squash that the Indians grew. I also ran into black-eyed peas, watermelons, wheat, and peaches—plants that the Spanish had brought. I collected names and usages; and at one pueblo I was given some strange squash seeds and told that the name of this squash was *mormonvatna*, Mormon squash. The names themselves were important in providing knowledge about the who, what, when, and where.

By the end of the summer I had a collection of corn, beans, and squash unlike any other that had been gathered. Most anthropologists study one tribe and are interested in things other than plants. They usually give only quite general descriptions of the crops. "They have corn, beans, and squash" would be a typical description. But what I had was corn and beans and squash from nearly every tribe from the Mexican border to the Mesa Verde, and from the Colorado to the Rio Grande. When attention was paid to the races of maize and the species of squash and beans, and their varieties, it immediately became apparent that there were two quite separate agricultures in the Southwest. Today it is obvious that the picture is even more complex. But my discovery of separate agricultural origins, with varied plants that had reached the area by different routes and at different times, was quite a radical finding for that time.

The Role of Plants

More important for the discussion here is what I had learned to do, and where it led me. I had learned to use plants as cultural tracers. The plants themselves were wonderful evidence. The dull-coated beans of Hohokam (modern Pima) came up the west coast of Mexico, as did the strange little tepary bean. The brilliantly colored and glossy-coated beans of the Pueblo region reached that area via the Mississippi valley and had their origin on the Caribbean coast of Mexico. The Pueblo corn was many-rowed and multicolored. By contrast, the Pima-Papago corn exhibited limited colors and few rows of kernels. Even the names for the plants told volumes: *mormonvatna*, for instance.

My dissertation was published, and this led to my being drawn into the transpacific controversy via *gossypium* (cotton).[4] The cottons of the world were a taxonomic mess. Hutchinson, Silow, and Stephens[5] set out to reorganize the genus by examining the chromosomes under a microscope. They then found that the picture was simple. All Old World cottons, wild or domestic, had one set of chromosomes; all American wild cottons had a different set. But American domesticate cottons had both sets. The explanation for this was that the differentiation was due to the cottons being separated, on a multimillion-year basis due to the drifting apart of the continents. This separation would automatically lead to such differences. The problem was that of reuniting these long-separated plants, leading to a hybridization so differentiated that a viable hybrid would have to carry both sets of genes. This, they suggested, must have happened relatively late, and must have been due to man's carrying Old World cotton to America. In the following decades the picture has become more complex, but the basic insight remains.

As a very properly trained anthropologist, I was scandalized. I knew with sophomoric certainty that no one at any time had reached America across the wide seas to influence our American Indians. But I had by now become something of a plant geographer, and I fully understood the significance of plants as evidence of contact. On the other hand, I was not a geneticist, and was not skilled in microscopic analysis of chromosomes. So I forwarded a manuscript that Stephens[6] had sent me in which he suggested transoceanic transport of Old World cotton to the Americas to the genetics department. They reported back that Stephens had proved his case about as definitely as one could in science. (And I always remark that this was a very sage observation. Science never proves things in absolute terms; it only arrives at very high degrees of probability.) The cotton picture has changed, and an African origin for the Old World cotton that was carried to America now seems more likely than an Asian type; it appears to be transatlantic rather than transpacific.

I felt compelled to look further. Hutchinson, Silow, and Stephens had pointed the way by noting that cotton was not the only plant in question. They noted the presence of *Cucurbita maxima* (the South American pumpkin) in Hawaii,[7] and the American sweet potato in Polynesia. Pumpkins and squash were familiar to me and I looked first into the pumpkin in Hawaii. That was a case of erroneous identification. The plant in question was *Lagenaria siceraria*, the dipper gourd, an Old World plant of African origin. Perhaps I should have stopped right there.

The Pacific: The Sweet Potato

Instead, I looked up the sweet potato. This had a long and controversial history which has since grown a bit longer. The first botanists into the Pacific noted that the sweet potato was deeply embedded in the culture of the Polynesians and noted with some surprise that the same plant was important in America and was known in one area by the same name that it had in Polynesia. The literature is extensive, but the upshot is interesting.[8] The sweet potato is certainly American. Botanically and linguistically it is clear that it has been carried out of America probably three times, and at least two of these are pre-Columbian. The sweet potato has been carbon-dated to before the time of its discovery on Easter Island and on Hawaii. This opens Pandora's box. You cannot let people carry plants out of America and simultaneously deny cultural contact.

The sweet potato alone indicates some kind of important contact. Consider the problem. Any domestic plant has a lot of knowledge associated with it; and without that knowledge, the plant is useless. For instance, one has to know how to plant it, how to tend it, when to harvest it, how to cook it, how to preserve it, and how to transport it. One even has to learn to like it. None of these steps is easy. We have good records of bitter resistance to new plants. The Peruvian potato (Irish potato) was first introduced in France when French royalty dined on potato soup, potato salad, and potato dessert. In Germany riots had to be put down when the potato was introduced there. So even the introduction of one agricultural plant indicates very considerable contact and extensive learning. These things never go one way. If someone in America was learning about sweet potatoes, one can be sure that the proprietors of the sweet potatoes were also learning of things from America.

Mountains of evidence that the people of America learned from transoceanic travelers have been put forward intermittently for over a century.[9] But such observations have always been knocked down by the argument that because anyone can invent anything, cultural parallels are simply classic cases of independent invention. That, of course, was my opinion until the plant evidence was thrust upon me. For the independent invention argument fails completely when one is dealing with biological items.

After I had become converted to the idea that contacts were made across the world's great oceans, I became what is known as a *diffusionist*—one who believes that ideas travel, and that parallel cultural items are more likely to be the result of the spreading of ideas than of independent invention. The opposite position is that of the *inventionists*. They view man as possessing unlimited inventive ability, and hence believe that the presence of similar things in widely separated regions is simply the result of independent invention.

To these people I say, "I invoke Kilmer's Law—'Hypotheses are made by fools like thee, but only God can make a sweet potato (peanut, maize, chicken, hibiscus).'" The list is now becoming very long.

I shall not try to write a definitive statement for the plants whose transpacific carriage well before A.D. 1500 is now in question to one degree or another. The sweet potato is hardly argued any longer, for it was carried out of America more than once, and well before 1500.

Other Plants

The peanut is very interesting. It appeared in China by at least 2500 B.C.[10] This gives us some idea of what kind of time we are dealing with. The case for the peanut was first seen by an economic botanist, Oakes Ames, at Harvard.[11] He noted that Chinatown had peanuts that were obviously not American commercial peanuts. The Chinese merchants were importing Chinese peanuts—a bit of nostalgia. Ames looked into peanuts in America and found that this kind of peanut was raised on the coast of Peru before A.D. 600, having disappeared long before the Spanish arrived. Decades later, peanuts turned up in Chinese archaeology, verifying Ames's insight.

There is a parallel case. Maize[12] of a type formerly grown on the coast of Peru, but having long disappeared from that region before 1500, is one of the kinds of maize found in the interior of China. The date of its introduction there is totally incompatible with a post-1492 introduction of maize into Spain and its diffusion down the Mediterranean, to India, over the Himalayas, and into China, where it would have become an established crop about fifty years after the discovery of America by Columbus. What begins to become obvious is that Columbus *was* a Johnny-come-lately.

Another plant that I read about intermittently over a long period is *Hibiscus rosa sinensis.* The plant in question is the hibiscus with the very showy, red, trumpet-shaped flower. The name is amusing. The plant is not a rose, and it is not native to China. You may find a taxonomist pugnaciously stating that this plant is an ancient endemic of Southeast Asia, but the facts are otherwise. A Dutch ornithologist interested in bird pollination of plants noted that this plant was seldom pollinated in Southeast Asia. And considering the shape of the flower, he concluded that the plant was dependent on a hovering, nectar-seeking bird. This describes the hummingbird, and hummingbirds are strictly American.

I picked this up and directed queries here and there. It quickly became a Catch-22 question. The plant was Asiatic until proven otherwise. If I proved that it was not

Asiatic, then I had to prove that it was in Asia before Magellan, but that it was not native there. Botanically, it is now conceded *Hibiscus rosa sinensis* would better have been named *rosamericanus*. It is an American plant that was taken early to China from Fu-sang (America). In Han dynasty accounts of the spread of the northern Chinese into south China, one finds ecstatic accounts of the wonderful flowers found in the south. Among these, the red-flowered hibiscus is described. The Chinese were exporting this flower to Persia in the second century B.C. That wraps up the *Hibiscus rosa sinensis* question.[13] It also throws an interesting light on what was carried by early travelers—an ornamental plant, forsooth! It had been argued that if anything was carried, it would be useful plants. But the evidence is all against that. What, for instance, went around the world as if jet-propelled? Maize? Not at all. It was that obnoxious weed called tobacco. Indeed, it went around the world so fast as to be quite suspicious in my view of things.

The Chicken

I turn now to another biological item, the chicken. Like the hibiscus, this was a long-term project. I accumulated notes and observations for a few decades and then, when asked for a paper, I put the whole thing together.[14]

The chicken is a pheasant and comes from Southeast Asia. It was domesticated somewhere east of India and south of China. A 15 April 1985 letter from William Plant in Australia tells me that he has a paper from Sally Rodwell in England that reports on the work of Professor Zhou Ben Xiong in northern China. This in itself is an interesting example of research: Texas, Australia, England, and China. The span of my interest in the question runs from 1940 to the present. From Cisham and other sites in northern China, quantities of chicken bones have been recovered and carbon-dated to 5,000 B.C. Since this is far from the homeland of the chicken, the original domestication must have taken place a good deal earlier. One has interesting biological checks on this. These Chinese chickens are very distinctive, indicating a long period of special breeding and selection. They are heavy-bodied, poor flyers, loose-feathered, low-combed, often feathered on their shanks. This race of chickens is distinctive to China.

Chickens can be viewed racially, and most usefully so. Mediterranean chickens lay white-shelled eggs. Most other chickens lay brown-shelled eggs. Mediterranean chickens are at the opposite spectrum from the Chinese chickens. They are great flyers, tight-feathered, spare-bodied, high-combed, and bare-legged. Malay chickens include another very marked race: naked-necked, nearly naked-breasted, very large, very erect, exceedingly strong, and very disease-resistant. And there are other equally marked races.

What first caught my attention with regard to chickens in America was the presence in Chile of chickens that laid eggs with blue shells. They are the only known examples in the world. The Spanish surely brought chickens to America, but they were Mediterranean chickens, for they were the only kind of chickens known to the Spanish. We have the good fortune to have a book written by an Italian scientist[15] describing all the kinds of chickens known to the Mediterranean world a hundred years after the discovery of America. He does not describe the chickens that the Indians had and, to a considerable degree, still have. From the scarce descriptions in the literature and from lengthy traveling in Mexico to view the chickens in the possession of the Indians, I can certify that even today, once one leaves the main roads, one will see mostly Asiatic races of chickens, and in the Indian markets one will see the brown-shelled eggs. Of course, this picture is being blurred now, for the egg and chicken factories are invading all areas, and with them go the Mediterranean white leghorns with their white-shelled eggs.

But among the Indians one finds brown-shelled eggs as well as naked-necked chickens of Malayan derivation and fluffy hens with feathered shanks, obviously of Chinese origin. Even melanotic silkies are found, the magical and religious chickens *par excellence* from India. Thus one has the odd picture that the Indians do not have the races of chickens that they would have if the Spanish alone had brought them. They have chickens that are appropriate for Asiatic introductions.

I made a survey of the names for chickens around the

whole world. This was an attempt to see whether we had any clues as obvious as *mormonvatna*. We do. The name for the chicken all over the Amazon basin is a variant of the Hindu name for the melanotic silky. *Karaknath* becomes in the Amazon basin, *karaka*, *kalaka*, and so on. These are very simple and obvious linguistic shifts. On the west coast of Mexico among the Tarahumara, the name for the chicken is *totori*, with variants thereof. This duplicates the Japanese word for domestic fowl. Curiously, this name seemingly was transferred to the domestic turkey in Mexico. *Cihuatotollin* obviously contains *totoli*. The modern Mexican word for the turkey is *guacalote*, but this is a Spanish introduction and its origin is unknown to me. The Aztec name for turkey at the time of the conquest, *totoli*, was preserved by Sahagun,[16] that marvelous compiler of Aztec history, economics, and religion. Someone should follow up this Tarahumara-Japanese link. By accident, I met a young anthropologist, Don Burgess, who had been in Japan and had married the daughter of missionaries among the Tarahumara. He had noted such parallels as the following:

Japanese		*Tarahumara*
kina sai	come here	kina simi
torikai	place of chickens	torichi
tori	chicken	otori

That there are no linguistic relationships between the Old and New World is dogma. That this dogma, like so many others, is "going to the dogs" is indicated by such studies as Mary Ritchie Key's "Polynesian and American Linguistic Connections" which appeared in 1984 in *The Edward Sapir Monograph Series in Language, Culture, and Cognition*, no. 12. Using modern linguistic methodology, she points to very extensive parallels between Polynesia and America. The work is introductory, but probably marks a turning point in our understanding of linguistic relationships between the Old World and the New.

Once interested in chickens I began to note such strange things as the fact that the American Indians who had chickens would not eat them or their eggs. This was not invariable but was very common. When one asks why they bother to keep chickens since they make no use of them, they expostulate, "But señor, you have to have chickens for sacrifice, divination, and prayer." This was something that the Indians would not have learned from the Spanish—at least not from the sixteenth-century Spanish; but it was still blandly assumed that the Spanish had brought the chicken to America. In Greco-Roman times one finds such sacrificial usages, but not a thousand years later. More interesting, when the particular religious usages are investigated and compared with the worldwide usages of chickens, one finds the whole set of American Indian usages in Southeast Asia.[17]

Notice now the compounding of the evidence. The races of the chickens point to Southeast Asia; the prohibitions and ceremonial usages point to Southeast Asia; and the names for chickens in America also point there. But let me illustrate how ideas influence scholars. When one reads in the handbooks about the economics of the tribes of South American Indians, chickens are often mentioned but seldom indexed. How odd! Not really odd, just an excellent example of the subtle (and sometimes not so subtle) working of ideas. If one sincerely believes that the chicken is a late introduction, then in attempting to describe the Indian culture one tends to slight the role of this latecomer, even to the extent of slighting it in the index.

When one goes back to Asia and inquires about origins and uses of the chicken, an interesting pattern emerges. Chickens were first domesticated for religious reasons: divination, sacrifice, and prayer. Later, cockfighting came along. Still later, eating of chickens and eggs. The American case fits into the early end of this spectrum of uses, for I know of no evidence for cockfighting among the Indians prior to the Spanish arrival with their fighting cocks. Chickens seemingly were introduced more than once, as the races and linguistic evidence indicate, and quite early, as the religious prohibitions and the absence of cockfighting suggest.

It would be possible to go on for many pages giving more biological evidence for transfers across the Pacific, both ways. This can even be extended into the human population. Blood groups especially indicate that sufficient racial contact occurred and, further, that the racial makeup of some parts of the Americas was strongly influenced by Asiatic arrivals. Similarly, one can present voluminous detailed evidence for art, architecture, and technological introductions across the Pacific, but one can consult Covarrubias, Heine-Geldern, Ekholm, and Shao for this.[18] What few seem able to grasp is the total complex picture, everything from alphabets and arts to zodiacs, literally A to Z. The literature will allow anyone to pursue this further. So I shall now turn to the Atlantic.

The Atlantic

The very early interest in the Pacific and the Asiatic influences in America led to a neglect of the Atlantic. Beginning about twenty-five years ago, I began to direct my students' attention to the Atlantic.

D. R. Beirne[19] made a study of axes. He found that in America there were only one or two axes of the Asiatic type, but that about 90% of the ax forms of the American Indian had parallels in Mediterranean and European, and one Peruvian ax shown has very specific Egyptian similarities, a fact also noted by Rowe, a vigorous anti-diffusionist. Even among the Old Copper culture, dating as far back as 3,000 B.C., one finds Mediterranean forms. Beirne's very detailed study indicates some early and important Old World influences affecting wide regions of America.

The Atlantic Ocean is small when compared to the Pacific. The winds and currents from the Strait of Gibraltar drive directly to America with great steadiness. Any mariner venturing out to sea beyond the ancient Pillars of Hercules and not having any mishap would arrive in America in a very short time. If he were making a deliberate voyage, then he would arrive even more quickly. We know that by the early Bronze Age, say about 3,000 B.C., there was a lively trade with Britain to obtain Cornish tin and Irish gold, among other things.[20] We also know that some of this shipping went by sea around Spain. It may have been about this time that the Madeiras and the Canaries were occupied, though perhaps earlier. But certainly by that time there was sufficient shipping exposed to the perils of the sea that contact with America was certain to occur, even if only by drift voyages.

The usual criticism of this view is that a drifter would have been unable to get back. But that is a mere assumption. Who can really say that after landing on a Caribbean island, mariners could not repair their ship and return? If they attempted a return and the Gulf Stream swept them northward and they caught the westerlies, they could return rather easily. But beyond such argumentation, of course, one would like to have some evidence.

Decades ago I began to notice what appeared to me to be quite clear examples of alphabetic writing in the archaeological reports from America. I often tried to interest my colleagues, especially those familiar with the ancient alphabets of the Mediterranean. They would, after casual inspection, state that my examples were neither Greek nor Roman nor Semitic.[21] But this did alert them to my interests, and one of the Latin scholars called my attention to a book on the centenary of the discovery of Pompeii. In it was a chapter by a botanist who identified the plants in the mural art at Pompeii. One of the things that he noted was the pineapple. He was fully aware that it is an American plant and, of course, that it cannot be grown in the vicinity of Naples. I noted this, and the usual furor erupted. When the smoke cleared, it was admitted that the pineapples were indeed portrayed at Pompeii,[22] a city which was buried at the end of the first century A.D.

One would like to have more such evidence. But it must be sought and developed, and little energy has been expended on the Atlantic question in comparison to the Pacific. But we do have some bits and pieces. The royal purple dye in the Mediterranean was made from a shellfish.[23] The dye was not only greatly valued by royalty, but it was commonly thought to be a fertility aid. In America the same color was derived from a closely related shellfish and, while one might think that this is just natural, what is striking is that some of the same ideas, such as fertility, are attached to this shellfish dye in America. When pressed, the independent inventionists suggested that the Spanish must have introduced it. However, textiles in Peru have been shown to have that dye as early as the second century B.C.

There is an interesting possible return flow. In America a brilliant red dye, cochineal, was made from an insect that grows on cactus. Cactus is strictly American, and the insect grows on nothing else. An American with a major dye business was in Mexico and admired the colors in the textiles of the Mexican Indians, and later he was in Palestine and was struck by the similarity of the colors in the clothing of the ancient Bar Kokhba people, some of whom had died in the desert and whose clothing had been preserved by the aridity in the caves of that region. He had his chemists investigate the dyes and they found that one of the chemicals was cochineal, the dye from the insect that lives on American cactus. The time of Bar Kokhba is the first half of the second century. But a difficulty exists with this bit of evidence. Chemists tell me that to make the identification certain, the analysis would have to be carried one side chain of molecules further.

Would dyestuffs be expectable? Most certainly. The economics of long-distance carriage of materials is such that high-value, low-bulk materials are those that can stand the transfer costs. In the sixteenth century it was dyestuffs that were avidly sought in America.

One would, of course, like to have further evidence. Ask and you shall receive. In an excavation in Mexico, under three intact layers of stone and cement, Professor Jose Garcia Payon found a small terra-cotta head that is easily identified as originating in Italy and dating to around A.D. 200. This is not often mentioned by the opponents of Old World influences in America, possibly because it was reported in German.[24] At the time, oddly, this find was viewed as more likely to have reached Mexico via the Pacific, though the Atlantic possibility was mentioned.

These finds cluster around the early centuries A.D. They are part of what, if gathered up, would be a strong case for Mediterranean, probably Roman, contact with America. Amphora-shaped vessels appeared at Teotihuacan near Mexico City at this time. Data on a classic amphora found in Mayan archaeology and dating from about A.D. 40 have been published by the National Geographic Society.[25] As part of this set of data one should, of course, include the finding of an inscribed tablet in Tennessee that refers to Bar Kokhba,[26] the finding of coins that date to that era,[27] and the preservation of the Jewish harvest festival of *sukkoth* by the Yuchi Indians of the same region.[28] All of this clusters around the time of Christ, usually a century or so after. I hasten to add that there is evidence that points to far earlier contacts as well as much later ones. For the earlier, there is the Old Copper culture of the Upper Michigan area, which dates to 3000 B.C., with its clearly European-style spear points and other implements.[29]

But to return to the Roman period, let us look at the maize situation. We have already touched on this in our discussion of the Pacific (see note 12 for the citations on maize), and I did not strain at the evidence there. There are two or more parts to this story. The Romans comment on the appearance of a new grain. It grows on a stalk like sugarcane but bears grain in an ear, and the individual grains are as large as peas.[30] I know of no plant other than maize that fits this description. What became of this introduction of whatever it was remains unknown.

Concerning later introductions we know more. Sauer and Jeffreys,[31] in papers that appeared almost simultaneously but totally independent of one another, using the same documentary materials, concluded that maize preceded Magellan in the Philippines. Anderson had a student, Finan, work on maize in the great herbals that were produced in Europe about A.D. 1600 (see note 12 for Sauer, Jeffreys, and Finan). The interesting fact emerged that maize was not mentioned as coming from the Caribbean for almost a hundred years. It was uniformly attributed to the Turks and called *frumentum turkicum*. Among the herbals, two kinds of maize are shown in fine botanical detail. One is a tropical flint corn typical of the Caribbean, clearly the grain that Europe had been getting recently from the land found by the Spanish. The other is quite clearly a mid-latitude type of maize. In the herbals, it is identified as maize and as originating in Turkey. Far too little attention has been paid to these data.

M. D. W. Jeffreys devoted great energy to this question. He was convinced that the Arabs had reached America and had carried maize back to Africa. He eventually proved that the Portuguese were getting maize well before Columbus' voyage.[32] Their source lay in West Africa, lands dominated by the Arabs. I am less certain of his claim that the Arabs spread maize into the Indian Ocean and on to the Philippines. It is quite possible that maize was carried across both the Pacific and the Atlantic before A.D. 1500, thus confusing the picture.

If I seem overly free in moving items across both oceans, let me cite another instance. This is the cylinder seal. Stamp seals are very ancient, and cylinder seals only a little less so.[33] They originated in the Near East and spread east and west. One set is found in Thailand. It has pure design, is deeply carved, and is often hollow. It is exactly this type of cylinder seal that appears in Central America. A distinctly different cylinder seal appears in Mexico. It is usually solid, the markings are engraved rather than deeply carved, and alphabetic letters of at least two separate alphabets flood the designs.[34]

As I noted in the introduction, my first brush with these seals occurred when the Mormon excavations produced two from early levels in Mexico. Casts were sent to W. F. Albright at the Johns Hopkins University, where I then was, and Albright called me over to review them. He called them degenerate cartouches, and pointed to individual letters that he could recognize. This was later discussed by David Kelley, who noted that some form of developed writing was present (see footnote 33). Still later, after I had worked with Barry Fell and had become familiar with western Mediterranean alphabets, I belatedly recognized that at least one of the alphabets present was Libyan.

I have strayed a bit from the biological evidence. I did so deliberately in order to indicate that the diffusionist evidence is not lopsided; it is not just biological. There is also bio-cultural evidence. I have in manuscript[35] a study of *Cyprea moneta*, the money cowry from the Indian Ocean. In West Africa it is used in medicine bundles in a manner similar to the use of this shell in medicine bundles among some Algonkin tribes. One would tend to think that this was some late introduction, improbable as that might seem. However, *Cyprea moneta* appears in an Adena (1000 B.C.-A.D. 500) mound in West Virginia. The presence of an Indian Ocean shell in an Adena mound is seldom mentioned, much less the cultural link it represents to the Old World.

Conclusion

The evidence of both Asiatic and European influences in Amerindian culture is exceedingly broad and deep. This refers both to time and to place. Currently, I would judge that contact with America across both the Atlantic and the Pacific began as early as 3,000 B.C. It is difficult to characterize the contact. I have come to call it intermittently continuous, and widely scattered as to place. When we come to understand it fully, we shall find it tied to the rise and fall of empires and dynasties of the Old World. We are very far from this understanding at present because of a certain fanatical resistance to the idea that there was any meaningful contact.

The issues here are large. We are dealing with the nature of man: either inventive or a very good learner. Clearly, I see man as relatively uninventive, but good at learning. We are also looking at the origins of civilization: one or many? Within my lifetime we have gone from assuming separate origins for the Egyptian, Mesopotamian, Indian, and Chinese civilizations to seeing them as stemming from a single beginning. In America we have also seen that the Mexican and Peruvian (really Andean) civilizations developed from shared roots. I see the probability that the Amerind civilizations stem from Old World contacts, and this seems to be leading to the notion of a single origin of civilization. This is not a small conclusion.

Finally, I offer a defense against the claim that the diffusionist is a racist, especially when he credits civilization in America to outside influences. Some claim that this amounts to saying that the American Indians were stupid louts incapable of developing civilization on their own. My reply is that no one developed civilization on his own. Civilizations grew up where there was an exchange of ideas, leading to new combinations and a multiplication of innovations. I know of no exceptions. Indeed, I enjoy running this in reverse. Consider the noble British, until recently rulers of the earth (almost). What did they invent? Not agriculture, domestication of animals, metallurgy, printing, alphabets, arches, wheels, zeros–and the list can be made almost infinitely long. Surely by this measure they are among the most backward people on earth. They are also Johnny-come-latelys to civilization. Read Caesar's description of them sometime.

The lesson is obvious. No people did it all by themselves, and a people's genius is measured by what they did with what they were able to borrow. By this measure, the aborigines of Australia were not stupid. Given their immense isolation, their rich ceremonial life and ingenious returning boomerang indicates considerable ability. Thus, to attribute the Amerind civilizations to outside stimuli is to categorize the Amerinds as normal humans–able learners, gifted innovators.

This discussion could be extended indefinitely, but I shall end by saying that the plant and the chicken evidence proves in absolute terms that the great oceans were crossed, very early, and seemingly fairly easily, for plants and animals were carried so easily that they did not have to be eaten. I consider that the biological data has proved the case for diffusion. This, then, changes the odds and makes more admissible all the cultural evidence. To be sure, this cannot become an excuse for careless use of cultural data. But it should free us to use that data with no apologies.

Notes

1. See Thomas S. Ferguson, *One Fold and One Shepherd* (San Francisco: Books of California, 1958), pp. 22-24 for the letter sent to Albright and Albright's reaction.

2. "Utah Lake Skull Cap," *American Anthropologist* 36 (1934): 431-33.

3. Samuel Eliot Morison, *Admiral of the Ocean Sea* (Boston: Little, Brown and Co., 1942); and *Christopher Columbus, Mariner*, (Boston: Little, Brown, 1955).

4. G. F. Carter, "Plant Evidence for Early Contacts with America," *Southwestern Journal of Anthropology* (now renamed *Journal of Anthropological Research*) 6 (1950): 161-82; "Plants Across the Pacific," *Memoirs of the Society for American Archeology* 9 (1953): 62-71; "Disharmony Between Asiatic Flower Birds and American Bird Flowers," *American Antiquity* 20 (1954): 176-77; "Pre-Columbian Chickens in America," in *Man Across the Sea*, Carroll L. Riley et al. (Austin, Tex.: University of Texas Press, 1971), pp. 178-218; "Hibiscus Rosa Sinensis," *Anthropological Journal of Canada* 15, no. 4 (1977): 26-27; "The Money Cowry and the Medeingwin Society," *The Epigraphic Society. Occasional Papers* 15 (1986): 160-69.

5. J. B. Hutchinson, R. A. Silow, and S. G. Stephens, *The Evolution of Gossypium and the Differentiation of the Cultivated Cottons* (London: Oxford University Press, 1947); they observe (p. 53) that "the outstanding feature of . . . [cotton] . . . is the way in which diversification has accompanied geographical distribution."

6. S. G. Stephens, "Cytogenetics of Gossypium and the Problem of the Origin of New World Cottons," *Advances in Genetics I*, ed. M. Demerec (New York: Academic Press, 1947), pp. 431-42. The cotton picture has advanced greatly and one must see later papers to keep up; see also Stephens' "Some Problems of Interpreting Transoceanic Dispersal of the New World Cottons," in *Man Across the Sea*, pp. 401-15.

7. *The Evolution of Gossypium*, p. 138, in which cucurbita and other plants are shown to have both Old and New World centers, which "supports the theory of a transPacific . . . link."

8. On the sweet potato see Donald D. Brand, "The Sweet Potato: An Exercise in Methodology," in *Man Across the Sea*, pp. 343-65; and Douglas Yen, "Sweet Potato Variation and Its Relation to Human Migration in the Pacific," in *Plants and the Migrations of Pacific Peoples*, ed. Jacques Barrau (Honolulu, Hawaii: Bishop Museum Press, 1963), pp. 93-117, as well as his "Construction of the Hypothesis for Distribution of the Sweet Potato," in *Man Across the Sea*, pp. 328-42.

9. Lists of traits shared by the Old World and the New World can be enormously long. See John L. Sorenson, "The Significance of an Apparent Relationship between the Ancient Near East and Mesoamerica," in *Man Across the Sea*, pp. 219-41, esp. 227-41 for lists. For a shorter and more specific list, see John Howland Rowe's "Diffusionism and Archaeology," *American Antiquity* 31 (1966): 334-37. Rowe views the comparisons as constituting "no proof of direct contact." For the opposite view see Stephen C. Jett and G. F. Carter, "A Comment on Rowe's 'Diffusionism and Archaeology,'" *American Antiquity* 31 (1966): 867-70.

10. Kwang-chih Chang, *The Archaeology of Ancient China* (New Haven, Conn.: Yale University Press, 1968), pp. 142, 157.

11. Oakes Ames, *Economic Annuals and Human Cultures* (Cambridge, Mass.: Botanical Museum of Harvard University, 1939), pp. 44-49.

12. Maize outside of America before A.D. 1500 has had some lengthy and controversial treatments. Some of the papers on the pre-Columbian evidence are: C. R. Stonor and Edgar Anderson, "Maize Among the Hill Peoples of Assam," *Annals of Missouri Botanical Garden* 36, no. 3 (1949): 355-405; Carl O. Sauer, "Maize into Europe," *Akten des 34. International Amerikanistenkongresses*, (1960), pp. 777-88; M. D. W. Jeffreys, "Milho zaburro = Milho de Guynee = Maize," *García de Orta* 2 (1963): 213-26; and M. D. W. Jeffreys, "Pre-Columbian Maize in Asia," in *Man Across the Sea*, pp. 376-400. Further bibliography on Jeffreys can be found in *Man Across the Sea*, p. 493. Also consult John J. Finan, *Maize in the Great Herbals* (Waltham, Mass.: Chronica Botanica, 1950).

13. G. F. Carter, "Hibiscus Rosa Sinensis," *Anthropological Journal of Canada* 15, no. 4 (1977): 26-27.

14. G. F. Carter, "Pre-Columbian Chickens in America," in *Man Across the Sea*, pp. 178-218.

15. Ulisse Aldrovandi, *Aldrovandi on Chickens. The Ornithology of Ulisse Aldrovandi (1600)*: vol. 2, book 14, trans. L. R. Lind (Norman, Okla.: University of Oklahoma Press, 1963).

16. Three Aztec names for the turkey were *totoli*, *quauhtotoli*, and *acoiotl*, as recorded by Fray Bernardino de Sahagun; see his *Florentine Codex: General History of the Things of New Spain*, Book 11 (Santa Fe, N. M.: School of American Research, University of Utah, and Museum of New Mexico, 1963), pp. 53, 29, 30, respectively.

17. Carl L. Johannessen, "Folk Medicine Uses of Melanotic Asiatic Chickens as Evidence of Early Diffusion to the New World," *Social Science and Medicine* 15D (1981): 427-34; and Carl L. Johannessen, "Melanotic Chicken Use and Chinese Traits in Guatemala," *Revista de Historia de America* 93 (1982): 73-89.

18. Of his many papers, see Gordon Ekholm's "Diffusion and Archaeological Evidence" in *Man Across the Sea*, pp. 54-65, and the bibliography therein, p. 478. Robert Heine-Geldern was associated with Ekholm and has written many important papers on diffusion. Consult the bibliography for Heine-Geldern in *Man Across the Sea*, pp. 487-88; for their joint works, see p. 488. Also see Miguel Covarrubias, *The Eagle, the Jaguar, and the Serpent* (New York: Alfred A. Knopf, 1954), esp. pp. 32-72; and Paul Shao, *Asiatic Influences in Pre-Columbian American Art* (Ames, Iowa: Iowa State University Press, 1976); and Shao's *The Origin of Ancient American Cultures* (Ames, Iowa: Iowa State University Press, 1983).

19. Daniel Randall Beirne, "Cultural Patterning as Revealed by a Study of Pre-Columbian Ax and Adz Hafting in the Old and New Worlds," in *Man Across the Sea*, pp. 139-77.

20. See, for example, Lionel Casson, *The Ancient Mariners* (New York: Macmillan, 1959), pp. 22, 71; at a later date, Herodotus mentions gold in northern Europe (Book III.116) and Caesar frequently speaks of European trade with Britain (e.g. IV.21). Compare Barry Fell, *Saga*

America (New York: Times Books, 1980), pp. 51-53, 60, in which he cites Arribas, who thinks Cornish tin mines were depleted by the fourth century B.C.

21. Much later I sent some of this material to Barry Fell, who was then centering his interest in the Pacific and forming the Polynesian Epigraphic Society. My tiny samples changed the emphasis; we now have the Epigraphic Society, and Fell's work is scandalizing the anthropologists who cling desperately to their anthropological Monroe Doctrine. See Fell's three books, *America, B.C.* (New York: Times Books, 1976), *Saga America* (New York: Times Books, 1980), *Bronze Age America* (Boston: Little, Brown and Co., 1982), and the volumes of the Epigraphic Society.

22. On the pineapple see G. F. Carter, "Plants Across the Pacific," *Memoirs of the Society for American Archeology* 9 (1953): 62-71, esp. p. 62; and Domenico Casella, "La frutta nelle pinture Pompeiane," *Pompeiane: Raccolta di studi per il secondo centenaria degli scavii di Pompei* (Napoli: Gaetano Marchiaroli, 1950), pp. 355-86. Also Elmer Drew Merrill, in his *The Botany of Cook's Voyages* (Waltham, Mass.: Chronica Botanica, 1954), p. 367, had to concede that the pineapple did appear to be known at Pompeii, p. 367, but see also pp. 216, 251, and 267 for opposite opinions. He still suggests a possible African origin for the sweet potato (p. 195), a point now thoroughly refuted.

23. Phoenician "Tyrian purple," for example, came from a shellfish called the murex. See for instance *Collier's Encyclopedia* under "Phoenicia," article by T. B. Jonis (New York: Macmillan, 1986), 18: 728. Compare Barry Fell, *Saga America*, p. 50.

24. An English translation can be found in Robert Heine-Geldern's "A Roman Find from Pre-Columbian Mexico," *Anthropological Journal of Canada* 5, no. 4 (1967): 20-22.

25. See Luis Marden, "Dzibilchaltun: Up from the Well of Time," *National Geographic* 115 (1959): 125 for a photo of a broken amphora retrieved from an underwater mine.

26. Cyrus Gordon, *Before Columbus* (New York: Crown Publishers, 1971), pp. 179-87.

27. Gershon Jacobson, "Mataba'ot von Bar Kochbas Zeiten Gufunden in Teil von Kentucky," *Day Jewish Journal* 53, no. 22, (April 17, 1967): 220; cf. Barry Fell, *Saga America* (New York: Times Books, 1980), p. 168.

28. Cyrus Gordon, *Before Columbus*, pp. 89-90.

29. Barry Fell, *Saga America*, pp. 35, 358-61.

30. Peter Martyr in Italy in 1493 described such a grain; ibid. Compare Frederick J. Pohl, *Atlantic Crossings Before Columbus* (New York: W. W. Norton, 1961), who argues that Leif Eriksson brought Indian corn to the Old World from North America (p. 220) and that the Welsh knew of this grain (pp. 172-73). Jeffreys, in "Pre-Columbian Maize in Asia," *Man Across the Sea*, p. 397, cites Leonardo da Vinci (in 1495-97) making a list of commodities including maize (melica/miglio).

31. M. D. W. Jeffreys, "Origin of the Portuguese word 'Zaburro,'" *Bulletin de l'Institut Francais d'Afrique Noire*, vol. 19 (1975).

32. For the Arab-African and Portuguese maize question see M. D. W. Jeffreys, "Pre-Columbian Maize in Asia," *Man Across the Sea*, pp. 380-81.

33. Cylinder and stamp seals are part of the growing body of evidence of alphabetic writing in pre-Columbian America. See G. F. Carter, "Mexican Sellos: Writing in America, or the Growth of an Idea," in *Diffusion and Migration: Their Roles in Cultural Development*, Proceedings of the Tenth Annual Conference, the Archaeological Association of the University of Calgary (Calgary, Alberta, Canada: University of Calgary, 1978), pp. 186-201; G. F. Carter and Sol Heinemann, "Pre-Columbian Sellos: Another Artifact Showing Possible Cultural Contact and Transpacific Diffusion," *Anthropological Journal of Canada* 15, no. 3 (1977): 2-6; and David H. Kelley, "A Cylinder Seal from Tlatilco," *American Antiquity* 31 (1966): 744-46. On the topic of writing in America, the volumes of the Epigraphic Society are by now essential reading.

34. G. F. Carter, "Mexican Sellos: Writing in America, or the Growth of an Idea," in *Diffusion and Migration*, esp. pp. 187-88, 190-91, 197.

35. The manuscript is now published under the title "The Money Cowry and the Mideiviwin Society," *The Epigraphic Society. Occasional Papers* 15, 1986, pp. 160-69. Meanwhile, Thor Heyerdahl has published on the Maldive Islands, pointing out that these islands, just west of the tip of India, were the major source for these shells. See Thor Heyerdahl *The Maldive Mystery* (Bethesda, Md.: Adler & Adler, 1986).

Categories of Evidence for Old World Contacts with Ancient America

11

Norman Totten

When Columbus refound America for Europe in 1492, he believed that the Bahamas, Haiti, and Cuba were parts of the East Indies in eastern Asia; so naturally he named the people whom he encountered on that initial voyage "Indians." His and subsequent Spanish trips caused the church this curious problem: were native Americans humans or not? In 1512 at the Fifth Lateran Council, Pope Julius II declared that Americans had descended from Adam and Eve, and thus are humans–as well as candidates for conversion to the Christian faith.

Julius left open another issue: from which son of Noah–Shem, Ham, or Japheth–had Americans descended? This question hardly bothered merchants, soldiers, soldiers of fortune, colonists, and slaves arriving in this hemisphere, eventually by the millions. But the question of American origins remained vivid for churchmen and scholars. Rephrased in today's terms, the question meant: had

Norman Totten is chairman of the History Department at Bentley College.

Americans migrated here primarily from Europe, Africa, or Asia?

It seemed obvious to most early European explorers that Americans varied widely in physical appearance, language, and life-style, and represented various amalgamations of people. East Coast tribes physically resembled European or Middle Eastern populations more than Far Eastern ones, while the reverse was usually true on the West Coast. Some American tongues had no known affinities with other languages; others could be grouped easily or with difficulty into language families. A few such as Canadian Takhelne,[1] have been grouped with Gaelic or some other Old World language family.

Pottery made its appearance in the Northeast about 1000 B.C. In its type, it was closer to then-contemporary northern European ware than to other American pottery.[2] The earliest pottery at Valdivia, Ecuador, arguably the first anywhere in America (c. 3100 B.C.), bore the same range of decorative patterns as Middle Jomon ware of western Japan.[3]

Such observations merely state facts. In no way do they denigrate the innate intelligence, creative potential or achievements of anyone. The biological bases for temperament and intelligence vary far more between individuals than between groups. In this connection, the label "racist" has been applied and continues to be misapplied by some members of academia to the more far-reaching diffusionist interpretations for which I would like to present a defense. The position of racism has very specific meanings when judging individuals by their ethnic group of origin without regard to individual worth. Some of us within the Epigraphic Society have actually risked our lives to combat racism, and some of us are part or entirely Indian. This particular charge made hypothetically in defense of isolationism is inappropriate and, at best, a misunderstanding. Any explanation of America's ancient cultural developments that does not take into account some combination of diffusion and indigenous achievements is not in keeping with the way civilizations have arisen everywhere on earth.

In referring to post-1492 European colonization of America, the poet Robert Frost noted, "The land was ours before we were the land's." The isolationism that characterizes most current archaeological theory is not just an alternative view; it is one, in my mind, that causes misunderstanding and considerable harm to our common cultural heritage. In just one example, reported by Warren Cook, a well-intentioned but incompetent archaeology judgment has resulted in the dispersal and loss of most of the Crespi collection.[4] Isolationism sometimes results in not reporting or even worse in hiding evidence which supports opposing views. No member of the Epigraphic Society has been allowed to view the Davenport Tablets, much less make detailed studies of them (among others, I telephoned the director's office and went to the museum in Iowa where the tablets are housed but was denied access). Collectors of ancient coins continue to be informed, incorrectly in my view, that all Greek, Roman, and Jewish coins found in American soil and on its beaches are hoaxes or modern losses.[5] Thus evidence that academia itself may someday come to realize to be of immense value continues to be destroyed through current misunderstanding and bias.

Oral traditions in various American tribes refer to ancestors who arrived by sea. Strangers were sometimes sacrificed, as depicted in the Toltec-Maya mural fragments found at Chichen Itza more than half a century ago and never reported by Mexican archaeologists. Those murals, as von Wuthenau and others have pointed out, depicted an Old World type dragon-boat, with shields attached, and the deaths of white and black strangers. The fact is that new ideas are not easy to come by indigenously; and whether better technology is developed in isolation or by introduction, it has often been attributed to culture-bringers who are honored: Quetzalcoatl, Kukulcan, Wiracocha.

Although diffusion from the Old World to the New World prior to 1492 occurred infrequently within long stretches of local time, its impact was often far out of proportion to its quantity because of the nature of human *conservatism* versus *creativity* (which occurs most frequently when ideas are in tension and conflict). One must understand why and how creation occurs in order to develop balanced accounts that incorporate both local developments and outside influences. The burden for fairness and accuracy lies not simply with those who challenge prevailing theory, but also with those who hold older, more established views.

In modern times, oceans have been navigated in various directions by hundreds of rigs with one- and two-man crews carrying only a few supplies such as paddles, sails, caulking, and something for catching fish and pressing out their juices. The Atlantic, for example, has been crossed intentionally during this century in kayaks, dugouts, inflatable rafts, reed-bundled boats[6] (Carter called the Ra II, in admiration, a "floating haystack"[7]), and a stitched animal skin curragh.[8] Once steered into a prevailing wind and current, only an accident will prevent craft, large or small, from eventually landing on a far-distant shore.

Charles Wolcott Brooks, who served as Japanese consul in San Francisco during the mid-nineteenth century, spent many hours researching the history of Japanese fishing boats ("junks") that had beached on American shores prior to 1850. He was able to document about a hundred such landings—accidental voyages to be sure—and found that in most cases crew members had survived the trip. The Japanese sailors seldom returned home, but rather blended into local Indian populations from Alaska to South America, adding some new words to local languages.[9]

Although a vessel's size has little to do with its seaworthiness, size does affect the movement of large numbers of peoples and goods. Among Barry Fell's important findings through the decipherment of ancient scripts are his identifications and translations that indicate the existence of pottery compass bowls in Liria, Spain, and in New Mexico, both long before Columbus, about a thousand years earlier than any form of compass was previously known to be in use in Europe.[10] Our knowledge of ancient navigation skills, exploits, and supportive techniques and technology is still so limited that, if the early navigators could read our reconstructions, in many cases they would probably have a good laugh—maybe not at Paul Chapman's work,[11] but at that of most of us.

Ptolemy IV (221-204 B.C.) had built in Alexandria, Egypt, a twin-hulled catamaran designed to carry marines; it was propelled by four thousand rowers—quite a ship![12] In 56 B.C. Julius Caesar recorded details of his battle with a fleet of the Celtic Veneti tribe, off the Atlantic coast of modern France. Caesar wrote that the 220 Celtic ships were considerably larger than his own and more seaworthy.[13] They were built of heavy oak beams with large iron fittings and employed supple leather sails and iron anchor chains. All in all, the Celtic fleet was much better constructed than Roman ships to withstand the violent Atlantic storms.

It is also worth noting that, in size, Roman merchant ships of the first century A.D. averaged 340 tons unladen. This compares to about 106 tons for Columbus' flagship and 180 tons for the Pilgrims' *Mayflower*. In A.D. 64, when the historian Flavius Josephus sailed across the often stormy Mediterranean Sea to Rome, he was just one of six hundred passengers in the ship—certainly a respectable size even by mid-twentieth-century standards. Grain freighters built to sail only with prevailing winds from Egypt to Rome reached the enormity of 1200 tons unladen, about twelve times the size of the ship that Columbus sailed.[14]

Looking westward from America across the Pacific to China, let us next consider another bit of pre-Columbian navigation. Zheng He departed China in A.D. 1430 commanding a fleet of sixty vessels manned by a crew of 27,000 men. His flagship measured 140 meters long (one-and-a-half times the length of a modern football field) and could sail against or with the wind.[15] Such massiveness was not reached again in the known history of navigation until we began to build aircraft carriers in this century. Following visits to Arabia and East Africa, Zheng He returned to China. On one trip his cargo included a live giraffe for the imperial zoo that was recorded in an extant contemporary painting.

Certain cultural parallels between ancient China and Peru suggest Chinese influence in the Cupisnique-Chavin, Moche, Nazca, and Chimu cultures that existed along Peru's coastal desert from about 500 B.C. to A.D. 1400. Numerous nineteenth- and twentieth-century scholars have observed linguistic, epigraphic, artistic, religious-cosmological, and technological parallels suggestive of such influence.[16]

Unfortunately, many once-great ancient libraries have been either deliberately or accidentally destroyed and their records lost—including those at Alexandria, Carthage, Merv, and cities of the Maya. Moreover, as is well known, cartographic information and knowledge of voyages were often well-guarded state secrets in the ancient world, for reasons of military and economic advantage and for the advantage of potential sites for refuge and colonization. What made possible the irregular voyages to and from America on ancient seas? Not compasses, nor ship dimensions and types, for experienced seamen devised many ways to make such crossings. To be sure, there were accidental drift crossings caused by storms–broken rudders and masts, or ships blown far off course. But there was also the daring skill of the navigators, an unending search for wealth in trade, curiosity, and the often desperate desire of passengers to improve their lives.

From my studies, the evidence for ancient, occasional, transoceanic contacts between America and the Old World, including Asia, Polynesia, Africa, and Europe, can be summarized in the following categories:

1. *Languages*. Some languages spoken in pre-Columbian America were as mutually unintelligible as modern Chinese and English. Other languages were related to one another in their structures and vocabularies. During the past decade, Barry Fell has attempted to show that some American and Old World languages were related to each other, especially in cases in which the quantities of shared vocabulary and structure are too great to have been independently invented, or to have developed independently in isolation following a postulated original diffusion thousands of years ago.[17]

2. *Epigraphy*. Some Old World scripts have been discovered in America and published prior to being recorded during modern times in the Old World itself, making forgery improbable. For instance, prior to Fell's decipherment of Basque inscriptions found in Pennsylvania, no one knew how to read similar examples preserved in museums in Spain and Portugal. Fell's achievement was confirmed and republished by the world's foremost authority on the etymology of the Basque language (Euskera),

the late Imanol Agire.[18] In addition, during thirty-seven years of exploration in Oklahoma and surrounding states, Gloria Farley has been able to record more than a hundred inscriptions on stone which appear in a variety of Old World scripts.[19]

3. *Place Names*. The linguistic roots and meanings of place names have sometimes survived millennia of changing inhabitants and their languages. While this has been pointed out by many scholars, perhaps the most provocative investigation is John Philip Cohane's *The Key*, which shows the phenomenon to be worldwide, including the Americas.[20] Cohane's studies indicate an ancient diffusion of word roots and meanings throughout large parts of the Old and New Worlds.

4. *Visual Symbols*. A variety of symbols has been employed, sometimes erratically, with common meanings throughout much of the ancient world, including America. Some symbols of the phosphene type—that is, caused to appear without light and induced by either pressure on the eyeballs, a blow to the head, drugs, or electricity—may be in our genetic makeup or irresistibly suggested by their universal appearance in nature, such as circles, concentrics, spirals. But what about symbols as complicated and specific as classical labyrinths? Labyrinths have not appeared universally in time or space, nor are they phosphene-elicited or found naturally. Yet they were used in areas of both ancient Europe and pre-Columbian America.[21]

5. *Artistic Styles*. Styles lacking universal application but traceable in geographical regions through certain parts of the Old and the New World may also suggest migration. Andreas Lommel focused on the "X-ray Style" in art and came to such conclusions.[22] Chinese characteristics, including what appear to be written script characters, have been found in Peru's ancient Nazca and Chimu cultures.[23] Further, some Moche pottery from Peru's

north coast depicts physical features, tattooing, and clothing typical of certain North African Berbers, and a few depict Negroid facial features. One Tiwanaku (Tiahuanaco) pot contains an inscription referring to North Africa in the early period of the common era.[24] Ivan Van Sertima's *They Came Before Columbus* discusses possible African presence in ancient America, based partly on artistic styles and features.[25]

6. *Technologies.* Serious questions arise concerning unusual, difficult techniques, as in smelting, soldering, and gold working, which involve steps not easy to discover and not universally employed. For instance, how can their developmental stages be discerned and where do they appear to have been fully developed? Paul Tolstoy detailed 121 traits in manufacturing bark cloth and bark paper in Southeast Asia and Mesoamerica and concluded that the technology must have diffused from the Celebes to America.[26]

7. *Religious Rituals.* Numerous authors have been struck by significant similarities between particular American and Old World ceremonies. Some similarities in ritual, belief, iconography, and rank symbols express universal human psychological factors. But when considered with other categories here enumerated, these comparisons may also support contact rather than isolated parallelism. For example, Joseph Mahan has provocatively traced seeming connections with Asia in the earth-sky symbolism of America's Yuchis.[27]

8. *Belief Systems.* Ancient mythologies shared generally an underlying basis in a common astronomy and cosmology. It is perhaps of importance that art historians and mythologists have tended to understand this better than archaeologists. Different in conception but interesting in their conclusions are de Santillana and von Dechend's *Hamlet's Mill* and Joseph Campbell's *The Way of Animal Powers.*[28] Although not concerned with bridging

hemispheres, Marija Gimbutas provides a rare bridging between archaeology and mythology.[29]

9. *Native American Traditions.* Most tribes once had traditions about both their own origins and peoples who appeared in their midst. At times the traditions were couched in mythology and sometimes they consisted of straight oral history. While occasionally such records have been maintained to the present, they were generally recorded by sixteenth- to eighteenth-century explorers and scholars, or even in the late nineteenth- and early twentieth-century volumes of the American Bureau of Ethnology of the Smithsonian Institution. Examples are numerous. I used an early Spanish account of Inca oral traditions about writing in the pre-Inca Andes to shed some light on this curious problem.[30]

10. *Old World Sagas and Histories Referring to Travel to America.* Apparent trips to America have been recorded in Viking sagas such as *Hauksbok* and *Eyrbyggja* (c. A.D. 1250), by the Greek historians Plutarch and Diodorus Siculus, in several Chinese documents, and in medieval European accounts of voyages by Ireland's Saint Brendan, the Welsh Prince Madoc, and the Scotsman Henry Sinclair. Artifacts have been found in America that accord with each of these accounts. Barry Fell also deciphered an engraving *in situ* on a large cliff face at Figuig, Morocco, that told of a fifth-century Moroccan emigration.[31]

11. *Explorer and Colonial Accounts of Americans When First Encountered.* Christopher Columbus wrote on the sixth day of his first arrival in America, referring to his crew: "They found a man who had in his nose a piece of gold, which might have been half the size of a castellano, on which they saw letters. I was angry with them because they had not bargained for it and given whatever might be asked in order that it might be examined and seen what money it was, and they replied to

me that they had not dared to bargain for it."[32] One well-known historian mistranslated this passage to make Columbus's note accord with the modern bias that the hundreds of ancient coins found in America, even those deeply embedded in the soil, are modern losses or hoaxes.[33]

12. *Comparative Anatomy*. Balboa and other early explorers in America referred to scattered groups of white Indians and black Indians and to traditions of pygmies, in fact, peoples of just about every type. Mexico's art historian Alexander von Wuthenau offers explicit photographic documentation, in the pottery and carvings of Mesoamerican and South American pre-Columbian artists, of all the races and virtually every known physical type.[34] While old charts of group gene frequencies in blood types are now known to be virtually useless when employed without caution about selectivity and changes through the influences of diseases, studies of earwax and other body chemistries are promising.

13. *Animal Dispersions*. George Carter has shown that ancient American chickens are the domesticated descendants of a Southeast Asian pheasant.[35] In both Asia and America, where pre-Columbian tradition has been maintained, chickens have been kept primarily for their feathers and to be used as sacrifices. The Greeks were the first to begin to raise them for eating and for their eggs. Significantly, Asian fowl types and names have been maintained in South America, and Japanese names are used among the Tarahumara of western Mexico. Another curiosity suggesting migration is that hairless dogs were eaten and castrated in both Mexico and China. The *alqo*,[36] an almost extinct, nearly hairless dog, is still raised on boiled sweet potatoes in coastal Peru.

14. *Plant Dispersions*. Let us ask several specific questions that will make the point about diffusion

of cultures. How and when did the Old World bottle gourd (*Lagenaria siceraria*), used for containers, become America's first domesticated plant without known wild ancestors in America?[37] Did coconut palms and plantains arrive in America without human assistance? Did American peanuts make it to China by 2000 B.C. by some means other than human craft? Under what circumstances did strains of cotton grown in Mexico (hybrid 26-chromosome *Gossypium hirsutum*) and Peru (hybrid 26-chromosome *Gossypium barbadense*) each develop from 13-chromosome wild cottons in Polynesia and America?[38] How is it that American pineapples are depicted in a Pompei fresco buried since A.D. 79.[39] Maize, an American plant, is reported to have been growing in West Africa and Asia (Assam, Philippines) when the first Europeans arrived.[40] Also, as Professor Carter has long pointed out, one does not independently invent sweet potatoes and chickens.[41]

15. *Disease and Immunology*. Questions of parasite transmittal, contagion, immunity, and even the presence of certain diseases in the Old and the New World need further study and should cast some light on the issue of human contacts. At present, we would not be able to detect through archaeology the known effects of devastating plagues without historical records about them. When have plagues occurred for which we lack historical records? What were they? Why did they occur? How long and under what circumstances does general resistance to disease last in a population? Two human hookworm species that supposedly could not survive a slow land migration through Arctic regions are found in certain American Indians and in China and Japan; one of them is not present in Polynesia.[42] How are we to explain this?

16. *Comparisons of Old and New World Artifacts*. When Old and New World artifacts are virtually identical, are complex in their nature, and have

been chosen from workable alternatives but not universally so, then diffusion is suggested and the burden of counterproof logically lies with those who would insist upon independent invention. South American and Solomon Island panpipes almost identical in tone, pitch, and shape are a case in point. Pachisi, a board game of India, and Aztec patolli are another such case.[43] The list could go on, including flat and cylinder stamps, trumpets, flutes, and so forth.

17. *Old World Artifacts Found in America.* I have four coins of the Roman emperor Hadrian (A.D. 117-138) acquired from workers who found them several feet below the ground's surface in Los Llanos, Dominican Republic, while excavating a building foundation. Hundreds of Old World coins have been and continue to be found in America, few reported, some modern losses or frauds, but many recovered under circumstances that indicate their presence in America before 1492 (as Columbus himself was the first to report, see above item no. 11). This is also true of Old World pottery, tools, and figurines, ranging in date from the Neolithic period to A.D. 1500.[44]

18. *American Materials in the Old World.* This category of potential evidence exists at present only minimally, for who is looking? A breakthrough may eventually occur with the analysis of the sources of raw materials, such as copper in bronze, and gold, when significant testing of Old World museum collections becomes possible. New findings of deep sea wrecks may be important. The archaic "lunate knife" may have been dispersed to Europe and to the Eskimos (as the ulu form) after its initial development in the Northeast.[45]

19. *Ancient Maps, Math, Astronomy.* Of course, the great libraries of Alexandria, Carthage, and Iberia, of Central and Southeast Asia, of the Mayas and Aztecs, were destroyed. But the spherical shape of the earth, its approximate diameter, and systems of

latitude and longitude were once known and used to some extent from Europe to China, before being lost and later rediscovered.[46] The Piri Reis map raises the possibility of the existence of ancient cartography.[47]

20. *Cultures at Times of Basic Changes.* This point constitutes a focusing of all categories. The archaeological record (as with the broader fossil record of species) indicates that isolated communities tend to be conservative and retentive. My unpublished study of the 5,000-year sequence of pottery lamps in the Holy Land was my own initial data bank for demonstrating this principle. Others who have studied long artifactual sequences have agreed independently with its validity. Even fossil languages and pronunciations tend to be preserved in isolated pockets after disappearance in mainline areas (e.g., Jukta in Surinam, Gullah in South Carolina, Elizabethan English on islands off Virginia and the Carolinas). Significant changes and creative developments are stimulated by environmental alterations and cultural interactions. Reasons for change require explanation; they do not just happen.

It is a social scientist's dream to have a whole geographical hemisphere where peoples developed for thousands of years in virtual isolation from the rest of the world. This hypothetical laboratory simply did not exist in America. The illusions of the hypothesis itself have been challenged by the evidence of many fields: epigraphy, art history, bibliographic archives, archaeology, comparative mythology and symbolism. The shame is that the response formulated thus far to these challenges has generally been less than scientific. Some have turned the isolationist hypothesis into an article of faith, a dogma defended through neglect of counter-evidence or with scorn, derision, and mischaracterization.[48]

When a scientific approach comes to prevail, the issue will not be between diffusion and isolation, nor will it be decided by the continued use of a model so restrictive as to exclude and misinterpret relevant data. The issue, rather, will be, What took place, when, and how much change resulted from which kinds of diffusion and indigenous creation? Regrettably, that day has not yet dawned; American archaeology remains committed to an isolationist model destructive of certain anomalous facts. The case for diffusion will continue to be made in a focused, lopsided way until the case itself is incorporated into a prevailing theory.

In the meantime, it might be helpful to define "Indians" as any peoples who lived in America or whose ancestors lived in America before 1492. That definition is broad enough to include immigrants before 1492 from any part of the world at any time, arriving by foot or by boat. And who are "Americans"? Simply those who are now here, no matter when they or their ancestors arrived. The injustices of the past—including the dispossession of native Americans from their lands and values, the importation of African slaves, and the combined genocides and oppressions that earlier institutions caused—can never be rectified, but they can be resolved.

The American petroglyphs, fading messages left by people here long ago, bring again to mind Frost's perception: "The land was ours before we were the land's." Perhaps it is the Choctaw part in me reaching out. If so, then who were the distant ancestors of the Choctaw? And why could they not get along better with those Greek-like Muskogees? Native Americans have long known what it means to be observed and misunderstood, then catalogued, by academics mostly concerned with advancing the cause of their own careers and reputations. Why not treat native Americans and their ancestors as something other than specimens? If and when that challenge is taken up seriously within academic halls, it will have to be acknowledged that the Indian peoples of America have never espoused the concept of isolationism, neither in their lives nor in their oral histories.

Frost spoke also to the English, Irish, and Scottish parts in me: "The land was ours before we were the land's." In the natural beauty of America's canyons, plains, forests, mountains, and rivers, the disinherited once viewed these features as sacred: the land keeps reaching out to claim us for its own. It is my hope that this discussion will help to reestablish some of the intrinsic unity between past and present upon which good futures are constructed.

Notes

1. Barry Fell, *Saga America* (New York: Times Books, 1980), p. 299.

2. Alice B. Kehoe, "A Hypothesis on the Origin of Northeastern American Pottery," *Southwest Journal of Anthropology* 18 (1962): 20-29; cf. her "Small Boats Upon the North Atlantic," in *Man Across the Sea*, ed. C. Riley et al. (Austin: University of Texas Press, 1971), pp. 287-88.

3. Betty Jane Meggers, Clifford Evans, and Emilio Estrada, *Early Formative Period of Coastal Ecuador* (Washington: Smithsonian Institution, 1965); see especially pp. 158-72.

4. Warren Cook, "The Crespi Collection of Cuenca, Ecuador," *Epigraphic Society Occasional Publications* (hereafter *ESOP*) 11, no. 272 (1983), pp. 216-30.

5. For this view on coins, see Jeremiah F. Epstein, "Pre-Columbian Old World Coins in America: An Examination of the Evidence," *Current Anthropology* 21, no. 1 (Feb. 1980), pp. 1-19.

6. Robert A. Kennedy, "A Transatlantic Stimulus Hypothesis for Mesoamerica and the Caribbean, circa 3500-2000 B.C." in *Man Across the Sea,* pp. 266-74; cf. Alice B. Kehoe, "Small Boats Upon the North Atlantic," in *Man Across the Sea*, pp. 275-92; also Clinton R. Edwards, "Commentary: Section II," in *Man Across the Sea*, pp. 293-305.

7. See George Carter, "Before Columbus," in this volume.

8. Timothy Severin, *The Brendan Voyage* (New York: Avon, 1979) and "The Voyage of the 'Brendan'," *National Geographic,* 152 December 1977, pp. 770-97.

9. Hubert Howe Bancroft, *The Native Races of the Pacific States of North America*, in *Bancroft's Works* in 39 vols, vol. 5 (San Francisco: Bancroft & Co., 1883), p. 52: "There have been a great many instances of Japanese junks drifting upon the American coast, many of them after having floated helplessly about for many months. Mr. Brooks gives forty-one particular instances of such wrecks, beginning in 1782, twenty-eight of which date since 1850. Only twelve of the whole number were deserted. . . . The author of the paper assures me that he has records of over one hundred such disasters." Bancroft referenced the *San Francisco Evening Bulletin* of March 2, 1875. Schuyler Camman, emeritus University of Pennsylvania art historian and authority on Asian mythology and symbols, supplied me with the following additional reference: Charles W. Brooks,

"Reports of Japanese Vessels Wrecked in the North Pacific," *Proceedings of the California Academy of Science* 6 (1875):50-66; see especially p. 62. Alex Patterson of the Epigraphic Society pursued the matter for me a bit further and discovered an 1876 reprint of the academy's proceedings with another paper Brooks read before it March 15, 1875, entitled "Early Maritime Intercourse of Ancient Western Nations Before the Christian Era."

10. Barry Fell, "Ancient Iberian Magnetic Compass Dials from Liria, Spain," *ESOP* 3, no. 57 (1976); "Additional Lirian Compass Dial Inscriptions from Spain and New Mexico," *ESOP* 7, no. 142 (1979).

11. Paul Chapman, *The Man Who Led Columbus to America* (Atlanta, Ga.: Judson Press, 1973) and *The Norse Discovery of America* (Atlanta, Ga.: One Candle Press, 1981). The latter is an up-to-date discussion of Viking sagas and other sources relating to the Viking discovery of America.

12. Vernard Foley and Werner Soedel, "Ancient Oared Warships," *Scientific American,* April 1981, pp. 148-63, especially 160-61.

13. Julius Caesar, *Commentaries* 3:13-16.

14. Discussed comparatively by Wake Forest University historian Cyclone Covey in *Calalus* (New York: Vantage Press, 1975), pp. 1-3. For more basic references see Lionel Casson's *The Ancient Mariners* (New York: Macmillan, 1959) and *The Ships and Seamanship in the Ancient Mariners' World* (Princeton, N.J.: Princeton University Press, 1971). Also Willard Bascom's *Deep Water, Ancient Ships* (New York: Doubleday, 1976).

15. The exhibition catalog *China: 7000 Years of Discovery* (Toronto, 1982), pp. 8-9, discusses Zheng He's seven voyages into the western oceans 1405-1433, and shows a photograph of a model of his flagship and a map of his routes. The exhibition itself, which I visited twice in the summer of 1985 at Boston's Museum of Science, was outstanding. Unfortunately, but characteristic of a line of modern thinking about ancient navigation, the catalog text ends its discussion of Zheng He's achievements with this unwarranted assumption (demonstrably erroneous for numerous ancient voyages): "None of these triumphs of navigation would have been possible without the compass which had been invented in China."

16. See George Carter's good summary, "Chinese Contacts with America," *Anthropological Journal of Canada* 14, no. 1 (1976), pp. 10-24; Joseph Needham, *Science and Civilization in China*, vol. 4 (Cambridge, Mass.: Cambridge University Press, 1971, Part III, esp. pp. 540-43; R. A. Jairazbhoy, *Ancient Egyptians and Chinese in America* (Totowa, N.J.: Rowman and Littlefield, 1974); Paul Shao, *Asiatic Influences in Pre-Columbian American Art* (Ames, Ia.: Iowa State University Press, 1976); and recently deceased Henriette Merz's more speculative *Pale Ink: Two Ancient Records of Chinese Exploration in America* (Chicago: Swallow Press, 1953; revised 1972).

17. Barry Fell, *America B.C.* (New York: Quadrangle/New York

Times Books, 1977); *Saga America* (New York: New York Times Books, 1980) see, for example, pp. 398-406; *Bronze Age America* (Boston: Little, Brown, 1982); see, for instance, pp. 85-66, 288-89.

18. Imanol Agire, "The Origin of Writing and Language," *ESOP* 9, no. 211 (1981), particularly p. 47.

19. See, for example, Gloria Farley, "Inscriptions from Mid-America," *ESOP* 3, no. 69 (1976), pp. 1-10.

20. John Philip Cohane, *The Key* (New York: Crown, 1969).

21. Clyde Keeler, "Tree of Life and Labyrinth," *ESOP* 5, no. 107 (1977); Norman Totten, "The Eye of God and the Agricultural Grid," *ESOP* 4, no. 86 (1977). Classic labyrinths, dating 1500 B.C. to A.D. 1500, have been preserved in stone, clay, and metal in Greece, Italy, North Africa, England, Ireland, Scandinavia, France, Arizona, and Peru—but were apparently never used in most places on earth.

22. Andreas Lommel, *Prehistoric and Primitive Man* (London and New York: Paul Hamlyn/McGraw Hill, 1966); see, for example, pp. 5-7, 30-32, 71.

23. See Carter's "Chinese Contacts" referred to in note 16, in which article he illustrates several characters.

24. My article dealing with some of this material, provisionally titled "King Juba Remembered," is to appear in the forthcoming volume 16 of *The Epigraphic Society Occasional Publications.*

25. Ivan Van Sertima, *They Came Before Columbus* (New York: Random House, 1976), pp. xiii, 188-89, 249-50.

26. Paul Tolstoy, "Cultural Parallels Between Southeast Asia and Mesoamerica in the Manufacture of Bark Cloth," *Transactions of the New York Academy of Science* 25, ser. 2 (1963), pp. 646-62.

27. Joseph B. Mahan, *The Secret* (Columbus, Ga.: published by the author, 1983).

28. Giorgio de Santillana and Hertha von Dechend, *Hamlet's Mill* (Boston: Godine, 1940, 1969; 1971 reprint); Joseph Campbell, *The Way of Animal Powers* (New York: A. van der Marck; San Francisco: Harper and Row, 1983).

29. Marija Gimbutas, *The Goddesses and Gods of Old Europe* (Berkeley: University of California Press, 1982), previously published by Berkeley as *The Gods and Goddesses of Old Europe 7000-3500 B.C.* (1974).

30. Norman Totten, "Documentary Evidence for Writing in the Pre-Inca Andes," *ESOP* 13 (1985): 63-66.

31. Barry Fell, "A Fifth Century Moroccan Emigration to North America," *ESOP* 3, no. 46 (1976). I began but have never completed a commentary on Greek sources for ancient voyages to America and artifacts that appear to corroborate them. Plutarch's account, for example, can be found in Greek and Latin texts as chapter 26 of *Plutarchi*

Chaeronesis Scripta Moralia, vol. 2 (Paris, 1841), pp. 1151-53. Most medieval accounts of voyages exist in a variety of manuscript versions summarized in part by Frederick J. Pohl, *Atlantic Crossings Before Columbus* (New York: W. W. Norton, 1961).

32. Christopher Columbus, *Journal,* Hakluyt Society Extra Series, no. 38 (London: Hakluyt Society, 1960), p. 36.

33. No metal coinage is known to have been made in America prior to the May 11, 1535, decree of Doña Juana de Castilla, la Loca ("the mad"), authorizing the minting of silver and copper coins in Mexico. The Spanish silver "real" was a medieval version of the gros denier (grosso, groschen, groat), the principal coin of Europe after its introduction in 1266. Small change was provided by the copper quarto (four maravedies, tariffed at 34 maravedies to one real). Quartos were minted in Mexico City 1536-42, when copper coins were discontinued until 1814, as the Aztecs considered them worthless. A second mint at Santo Domingo, Dominican Republic, had a much longer history of copper coinage beginning in 1544. Miguel Muñoz, "The Mexico Mint," *The Numismatist,* May 1985, pp. 882-92; Miguel Gómez, *Monedas Dominicanas* (Santo Domingo, 1979).

34. Alexander von Wuthenau, *Unexpected Faces in Ancient America* (New York: Crown, 1975); see, for example, pp. 131, 156, 162, 186, 196-97, 209-14.

35. George Carter, "Pre-Columbian Chickens in America," in *Man Across the Sea*, pp. 178-218.

36. I observed and photographed this rare breed at a place near Lima on two different trips to Peru. In an effort to prevent its extinction, the family has been divided now to two locations. Many pots from the Colima culture of western Mexico depict a pot-bellied, nearly hairless dog raised for food. In the Nahuatl language of the Aztecs it was called *techichi* ("stone dog") because of its appearance.

37. Thomas W. Whitaker, "Endemism and Pre-Columbian Migration of the Bottle Gourd, *Lagenaria siceraria,*" in *Man Across the Sea,* pp. 320-27. Indigenous to tropical Africa, the bottle gourd was found with beans in Spirit Cave, Thailand, perhaps 6000 B.C. Its presence in America is attested for certain at Huaca Prieta, Peru, by 3000 B.C., but possibly earlier in Mesoamerica.

38. J. B. Hutchinson, B. A. Silow, and S. G. Stephens, *The Evolution of Gossypium* (Oxford: Oxford University Press, 1947).

39. Domenico Casella, "La frutta nelle printure Pompeiana" *Pompeiane: Racolta di studi per il secondo centeraria degli scavii di Pompei*, (Napoli: Graetaur Marchiaroli, 1950), pp. 355-86.

40. C. R. Stonor and Edgar Anderson, "Maize Among the Hill Peoples of Assam," *Annals of the Missouri Botannical Garden* 36 no. 3 (1949): 355-405; W. R. Stanton and Frank Willett, "Archaeological Evidence for Changes in Maize Type in West Africa: an Experiment in Technique," paper 150, 63 (1963): 117-23. M. D. W. Jeffreys, "Pre-Columbian Maize in Southern Africa," *Nature* 215 (1967): 695-97.

41. George F. Carter, "Movement of People and Ideas Across the Pacific," in *Plants and the Migrations of Pacific Peoples*, ed. Jacques Barrau (Honolulu: Bishop Museum Press, 1963), pp. 7-22.

42. S. T. Darling, "Observations on the Geographical and Ethnological Distribution of Hookworms," *Parasitology* 12 (1920): 217-33.

43. Edward Burnett Tylor pointed out the patolli-pachisi correspondence in "On the Game of Patolli in Ancient Mexico and Its Probable Asiatic Origin," *Journal of the Anthropological Institute of Great Britain and Ireland* 8 (1878):116-31 (now the *Journal of the Royal Anthropological Institute of Great Britain and Ireland*; and again in "On American Lot-Games as Evidence of Asiatic Intercourse Before the Time of Columbus," *Internationales Archiv für Ethnographie,* Suppl. zu Bd. IX (Leiden: E. J. Brill, 1896), pp. 55-67 and plate 5.

44. I have not yet formally reported the Dominican coin find, but they are from North African mints and in too poor condition to be considered collectors' pieces. Of the many sources reporting Old World artifacts found in America, the most accessible would probably be Barry Fell's books *America B.C.*, *Saga America*, and *Bronze Age America* (see note 17).

45. I have listed this category because of its potential importance; in part, it can become meaningful as appropriate technologies are developed. In her article dealing primarily with European origins for the earliest pottery in the U.S. Northeast, Alice B. Kehoe noted in conclusion: "Conversely, the earlier use of ground slate knives in America implies a transoceanic origin for the slate implements appearing in Europe." See "Small Boats Upon the North Atlantic," in *Man Across the Sea,* p. 292. Perhaps a detailed, comparative study has since been published, but I am unaware of one. I have several ground slate tools of the early part of the Late Archaic period, about 3000-2000 B.C., from New England: a "Red Paint" culture spearpoint from Maine, a Laurentian-Brewerton tradition gouge from New Hampshire, and three ulus of the same phase from Connecticut. A flint spearpoint, ritually "killed" (broken at burial) from Danbury, Connecticut, dating perhaps 6500 B.C. (Early Archaic), is as fine as any I have ever seen anywhere on earth, indicating to me an extraordinary level of artistry from some culture in that area, as yet archaeologically unexplained. Much work remains to be done in comparing Old and New World artifacts and their chronologies.

46. Original documentation for this statement would be quite extensive, but perhaps more important are the reasons for discovery, loss, and rediscovery-plus. The most provocative essay I have read on this, focused on astronomy, was Arthur Koestler's *The Sleepwalkers* (New York: Macmillan, 1959).

47. Charles Hapgood, *Maps of the Ancient Sea Kings,* rev. ed. (New York: Dutton, 1979).

48. My defense of Barry Fell's research in North American epigraphy against abusive, incorrect, emotional critics (such as Daniel, Cole, Davies, and McKusick) is a point by point documented refutation: "Epigraphic Research in America: Reply to Archeologists' Denunciations," *ESOP* 9 (1981): 71-115.

Cultural Parallels Between the Old World and the New World 12

Paul R. Cheesman

The idea of ancient contact between the Old and the New World has been studied by so many scholars with so many varying solutions that there appears to be no consensus concerning the origin of the group whom we call the American Indians.

During the course of many years, investigators have adopted and refined the method of comparing one culture with another. In instances in which no written documents were available, artifacts formed the means by which scholars constructed a history. Naturally, the persuasive power of such comparisons of cultural parallels increased with the number of similarities successfully identified. To be sure, three or four cultural parallels could be due to chance. But as one reviews thoroughly the similarities, for instance, between the cultures of the Old World and the New World, one can now catalogue well over two hundred features common to both areas.

Paul R. Cheesman is director of Book of Mormon in the Religious Studies Center and professor of Ancient Scripture at BYU.

The emerging picture points to a multiplicity of contacts between the two worlds. As an example of the impact of recent study, most museums in the United States dealing with the origin of the American Indian used to display maps indicating that they had migrated only across one route—the Bering Strait. Today, however, many major museums freely indicate the possibility of ancient transoceanic migration across both the Atlantic Ocean and the Pacific Ocean.

In this connection, the Book of Mormon carefully records three such migrations—one about 2400 B.C. and two others near the year 600 B.C. It is my personal opinion that many other groups came to this continent anciently, among whom were the Vikings and the Orientals.

In an interesting prophecy recorded in the Book of Mormon, Nephi quotes Lehi:

> But, said he, notwithstanding our afflictions, we have obtained a land of promise, a land which is choice above all other lands; a land which the Lord God hath covenanted with me should be a land for the inheritance of my seed. Yea, the Lord hath covenanted this land unto me, and to my children forever, and *also all those who should be led out of other countries by the hand of the Lord* (2 Nephi 1:5; emphasis added).

In the world of scholarship, one notes two opposing viewpoints—that of the diffusionists and that of the independent inventionists. Advocates of the diffusionist view attribute similarities between the civilizations of the Old and the New World to transoceanic migrations between the Eastern and Western hemispheres. Independent inventionists maintain that the many similarities are accidental, exhibiting no contact, and are thus to be ascribed to parallel and independent developments in both worlds.

As research has continued, however, it has become increasingly clear in scholarly circles that the civilization of the New World resembles that of the Old in significant ways. The earlier question has now become more crucial: could all of these cultural similarities really be due to independent development or should they be attributed to contacts and trade between these major continents? In response, let us review several telling pieces of evidence, beginning with the issue of transoceanic travel.

According to modern research, a fairly small craft, if well constructed, is more likely to survive a long sea voyage than is a large vessel. Surprisingly, seaworthiness has little to do with size.[1] Perhaps this is a reason that Lehi and his small group included only one other family in their sea voyage. Although the earlier migrating Jaredites consisted of a few more families, that group came in eight vessels.

Concerning transoceanic contacts, Eric Reed supports the idea of such communication. From the multi-authored publication *Man Across the Sea* he quotes J. D. Baldwin, who said, "Certainly there is nothing unreasonable or improbable in the supposition that the countries on the Western Mediterranean . . . communicated with America in very remote antiquity; nor is it improbable that there was communication across the Pacific."[2] J. Hornell agrees in his conclusion that "the rafts of Ecuador and of coastal Asia probably are connected genetically."[3] It is now believed that of sixty known drifts of Japanese junks into the Pacific, at least a dozen reached the American coast.[4] In light of this, Edwin Doran, Jr., concludes: "There appears to be no question that rafts could have crossed the Pacific, repeatedly [and] in appreciable numbers."[5] Moreover, while it is difficult to gauge the end result, Joseph Needham observed that "a fleet of 3000 young men and women, in 219 B.C., . . . sailed from China into the ocean, never to return."[6]

It is significant that the idea of transoceanic contacts is also supported by modern trans-Pacific and trans-Atlantic journeys made by explorers who have duplicated primitive conditions. For instance, one notes Thor Heyerdahl's excursion from Peru to Tuamotu in the Pacific, as well as his expedition in the *Ra II*, which sailed across the Atlantic. Further, in six months Eric de Bisschop sailed from Tahiti to the Juan Fernandez Islands, a distance of five thousand miles. He also made a trip of similar duration from Chile, via Callao in Peru, to Manihiki, a trip of seven thousand miles. Such cumulative observations argue persuasively for a theory of cultural diffusion between the Old and New World.

In this vein, Clinton R. Edwards supports the idea of

diffusion as follows: "From the standpoint of available nautical capabilities, ancient crossings of the Atlantic were entirely possible."[7] Surely there cannot now be any question that before 1492 there were visitors between the New and the Old World in historic and even prehistoric times. The important question, however, is whether these visits brought a significant cultural import to the Americas.[8]

Not only has transoceanic contact from the Old World to the New gained the support of Dr. Gordon F. Ekholm and Dr. Robert Heine-Geldern of the staff of the American Museum of Natural History in New York City, but they also agree, for example, that the columns and balustrades of Chichen Itza in Yucatan, as well as its decorative serpent motifs, are almost identical with those found in Java. Furthermore, they note similarities in the thrones and the artistic lotus motifs between India and Mayan countries.[9]

With regard to agricultural connections, the bottle gourd provides another interesting piece of the puzzle when one studies the mystery of the early inhabitants of America. Botanists observe that the gourd is very likely native to tropical Africa, or possibly southern Asia. Moreover, they suggest that the importing came by way of the Atlantic and insist that the seed must have been brought by man since it could not have survived lengthy soaking.[10]

Regarding the variety of racial characteristics found in pre-Columbian America, Constance Irwin writes:

> How [are we] to account for such a conglomeration [in America]: an Egyptian sphinx, the Egyptian god Ra, and Assyrian style, and Negroid types—and in addition, as we have just seen, a bearded face of Semitic aspect? Where else on the face of the earth were these once blended?
>
> Where else? In the ancient Orient, a term employed in scholarly convention to indicate the ancient Near East or the "Mediterranean East." More specifically, in the Syro-Palestinian region, including Phoenicia, which linked together the great river valleys of Egypt and Mesopotamia and freely partook of the cultures nurtured by both.[11]

Concerning contacts with the Far East, it was archaeologist James A. Ford who suggested that the oldest type of pottery known in the Americas may have been introduced on the coast of Ecuador about five thousand years ago by voyagers from Japan.[12] And the historian Alvin M. Joseph, Jr., noted: "Certainly, by at least 1500 B.C., Asians were capable of making long sea trips. Much later, perhaps as late as A.D. 500-1000 when the islands of Polynesia were first populated, other long-distance oceanic voyages may have been made in one or both directions between America and the Pacific Islands."[13] In this connection, botanists have concluded that cotton seeds were carried to America from Asia in the second millennium B.C. Because the wind and birds have been eliminated as possible carriers, Constance Irwin suggests that a man in a vessel was the only alternative: "This much is certain: he came; civilized man from the Old World sailed across an ocean and landed somewhere in that general area where the higher American culture flourished in pre-Columbian times."[14]

In a related vein, some researchers conclude that burial practices as well as the mummies themselves indicate that white men must have come to the Peruvian plain in very early times. But Pierre Honore is even more emphatic, asserting that "there is stronger evidence still, amounting to positive proof, from plant life, particularly cotton and the sweet potato, and possibly maize as well."[15]

Many believe that America has been "discovered" several times. Some are of the opinion, for instance, that Leif Eriksson and his Nordic adventurers landed on the coast of Massachusetts some years before Columbus left Spain.[16] Further, phallic symbols found in Central America have caused some speculation as to whether the people of India had made contact in the Americas. In addition, many Hebrew and Semitic resemblances appearing in the American Indian have led to the theory that there may be a connection here.[17] While it is possible that many Old and New World similarities could be coincidental, there are so many similarities being found almost daily it would be better to remain open-minded. We should receive such observations as those noted above as lines in an emerging picture whose faint and bold strokes tend distinctly to portray cultural contacts rather than accidental traits that constitute mere curiosities.

Immediately following Columbus' discovery of America, Spain was the only country among all the European powers that was in a position to enter upon conquests in the New World on a large scale. This, of course, was partly due to prior European wars which had already drained the resources of the other powers. From Adair's *History of the American Indians* we learn that the first Spanish priests who followed the conquistadors to this country were so amazed by the similarities between the Old and the New World that they believed the American Indians to be Hebrews.[18]

Similarly, the theory that the American Indians were the lost ten tribes of Israel was also a very popular notion at one time in colonial America. For example, William Penn wrote of the Indians of Pennsylvania as follows:

> I found them with like countenance with the Hebrew race; and their children of so lively a resemblance to them that a man would think himself in Duke's Place or Barry Street in London, when he sees them. . . . Their worship consists in two parts, sacrifice and cantice [songs]. . . . They reckon by moons; they offer their first ripe fruits; they have a kind of feast of tabernacles; they are said to lay their altars with twelve stones.[19]

In a similar vein, Hyatt and Ruth Verrill wrote:

> Unquestionably the real truth is that man came to America from the Old World via all of these various routes. Some came from Europe by way of Greenland, others across the Atlantic to South America, some via the Bering Straits, and others across the Pacific.[20]

Elsewhere in their work, the Verrills pinpoint an exact people—the Sumerians—as being more like the people of Peru than any other Near Eastern people of whom we have record.

> The results of Mrs. Verrill's work in conjunction with the author's wide first-hand knowledge of the ancient civilizations of Peru, would seem to prove conclusively that the pre-Incan civilization was brought to Peru ready made and fully developed by Sumerian (Phoenician) explorers and colonists 2000 to 2500 B.C.[21]

Indeed, for ancient peoples to find their way to America is well within the range of possibility. For example, a Buddhist monk in A.D. 400 was reported to have sailed from China to America and back in a Chinese junk.[22]

Plenty of evidence, both valid and erroneous, has been advanced in numerous books and articles by professionals and amateurs alike. What was needed now in order to give the diffusionists a firm foundation for their views was the discovery of an eastern Mediterranean inscription, professionally excavated in an intact American archaeological context. Dr. Joseph Mahan ransacked the scientific literature from beginning to end in the late 1960s in an effort to find such an inscription in the annals of American archaeology. After years of painstaking investigation, Dr. Mahan came across an inscription found in 1885-86 by Cyrus Thomas at Bat Creek, Tennessee, under the auspices of the Smithsonian Institution. Digging to the bottom of an "Indian" mound, Thomas had discovered nine undisturbed skeletons with an inscription partly under the skull of the main personage of the group. The sketch of the nine skeletons in the tomb and a photograph of the inscription, along with the report of the excavation, were published in Thomas's *Report on the Mound Explorations of the Bureau of Ethnology*.[23] Unfortunately he published the inscription upside-down and presumed it to be Cherokee, although the writing bears no resemblance to the Cherokee syllabary. After the inscription had been turned right side-up by Henriette Mertz, she recognized it as a Phoenician script. In August 1970 Dr. Mahan sent Dr. Cyrus H. Gordon a photograph of the inscription made from the stone itself, now deposited in the museum of the Smithsonian Institution in Washington, D.C. He requested Dr. Gordon's opinion as a Semitist; Gordon subsequently confirmed the distinctively Jewish nature of the text.[24]

The archaeological circumstances of this discovery rule out any chance of fraud or forgery, and the inscription confirms a migration of Jews from the Near East, possibly to escape the long hand of Rome after the disastrous Jewish defeats in A.D. 70 and 135. Thus the diffusionist view has been bolstered by this archaeological find, called the Bat Creek Stone, which was unearthed under the direction of professional archaeologists working for the Smithsonian Institution.[25]

Let us also mention ancient coins in the New World. Dr. Norman Totten from Bentley College in Waltham, Massachusetts, has pursued research on ancient Old World coins found in America. And although he has yet to publish the results of his work (see his contribution to this volume), other material has come to light from the southeastern United States through an accidental discovery. In the 1820s, John Haywood, Chief Justice of the Tennessee Supreme Court, gathered material for his book entitled *Natural and Aboriginal History of Tennessee*, which was republished in 1959.[26] In this publication, Haywood described Roman coins found in Tennessee and adjacent states. Moreover, on 17 April 1967, the New York Yiddish newspaper *The Day-Jewish Journal* ran an article on Hebrew coins of the Bar Kokhba Rebellion (the second Jewish rebellion against Rome in A.D. 132-35) found by farmers near Louisville, Hopkinsville, and Clay City, Kentucky.[27]

If some will persist in claiming that the civilization of the Americas developed independently from the Old World, they must adduce as much impressive evidence as have those who favor the theory of diffusion between the Old and the New World. From the information reviewed in this study, it would seem that ancient multiple contacts from the Old World are highly likely. At the same time, to be sure, it can also be agreed that one may hold a diffusionist view and still acknowledge that some cultural traits developed independently.

Although this chapter constitutes only a preliminary study, it is designed to emphasize the increasing number of cultural parallels to be found in both hemispheres. And while it is true that some cultural features could have developed independently, other examples noted above rather compellingly support a diffusionist view.

In the summer of 1985 I conducted a research study on this subject, visiting major museums and historical sites of the world in order to view, photograph, and catalogue the most prominent cultural similarities between the Old and the New World. The results of this research, along with the contributions of Thomas Ferguson and John Sorenson, provide us with an important aggregate of cultural parallels between these two global regions. It is summarized in the following list, arranged alphabetically, in order to give to the reader a brief overview.

Some Cultural Similarities Between the Old and the New World

A
Adobe brick manufacturing
Altar (horned)
Altars (other)
Anointing
Aqueducts
Arch (true/corbelled)
Architecture of 1000 pillars of S. India
Arrowheads of metal
Artificial tears on masks
Avocado

B
Balance scales
Ball courts
Banners
Baptism font
Bark cloth
Beard (false)
Bearded men
Beaten sheets of metal
Bells
Bird-man deities
Blood sacrifice
Bloodletting
Blow gun
Bone ornaments
Bottle gourd
Bottle-shaped underground cistern
Bow and arrow
Bread (sacred)
Breastplates
Bucket (ritual)
Burial techniques
Burials
Burnt offerings

C
Calendars
Cannibalism
Caps
Carved steles
Casting by lost wax
Cement
Ceramics
Chickens
Chisels
Color representing
Colors (tribal)
Confession
Cotton
Creation story
Cross
Cylinder seals

D
Drain Pipes
Double S sign
Double walls with mud for insulation

E
Eagle and serpent motif of India
Earplugs
Embalming with oil
Embossed designs on pots

F
Fasting
Feline
Fertility figurines
Festivals
Figures holding up tables
Fishhooks
Flint blades of obsidian
Flutes

G
Gold plates (writing on)

H
Hair types
Half-pillars as door frames
Hand with eye
Headdresses
Helmet of Olmec
Hierarchic society
Hieroglyphs
Highways
Holy water
Horses
Human sacrifice (adult and child)

I
Idolatry
Incense burners
Intentional deformation of skull
Irrigation

J
Jade carving
Jewelry

K
Knitting

L
Life symbol
Lima beans

Lime plaster
Loom
Lotus or water
lily

M
Maces
Maize
Masks (gold on
corpse)
Masks
Mathematics
Metal disc in
roof of mouth
of corpse
Metallurgy
Mirrors
Mosaic masonry
Mummification
Mural painting
Musical instruments
Musical scale

N
Needles
Net fishing
Nose rings

O
Obelisks
Observatories
Obsidian blades
Oil lamps
Overflowing vase
motifs

P
Paintings on
pottery
Panpipes
Paper or writing
surface
Parasol
Parcheesi
Parchment
Petroglyphs
Phallic symbols
Plants (amaranths;
bottle gourd;
coconut; cotton;
maize; peanut;
pineapple; plantain; sweet potato)
Plastic floors
Plating
Potter's wheel
Pottery
Pregnant women
holding breasts
Priesthood
Purple dyes
Pyramid burial
Pyramid building

Q
Quipu

R
Red dye
Reed boats
Roads
Rope
Rudder-oar on
boats

S
Sacrifice of
doves and quail
Sandals
Sarcophagus of
stone
Scales
Seer stones
Self-mutilation
Serpent with 7
heads
Seven-day time
cycle
Shields
Short skirts for
warriors
Silk
Slavery
Slings
Sphinx
Spindle whorl
Spoon, plate, comb
Stamp seals
Stamps (flat)
Star of David
Stela
Stone boxes
Stucco
Sun worship
Sun dials
Swastika
Sweat rooms
Sweet potato

T
Tattoo
Temple atop
Temples and platform
Terrace agriculture
Textiles
Tree of life symbol
Trephination
Tribes and chiefs
Tweezers of
metal

U
Umbrella (as a
symbol)

W
Weaving techniques
Wheel toys

Z
Zero concept

Notes

1. C. A. Borden, *Sea Quest* (Philadelphia: MacRae Smith, 1967), pp. 25, 164.

2. Eric K. Reed, "Commentary: Section I," citing J. D. Baldwin's *Prehistoric Nations* (1869), in *Man Across the Sea*, ed. Carrol L. Riley et al. (Austin: The University of Texas Press, 1971), p. 111.

3. J. Hornell, "South American Balsas: The Problem of Their Origin," *Mariners Mirror* 17 (1931): 355.

4. C. W. Brooks, "Report of Japanese Vessels Wrecked in the North Pacific from the Earliest Records to the Present Time," *Proceeding of the California Academy of Science,* 6 (1875): 50-66, especially p. 64 and the map following p. 50.

5. Edwin Doran, Jr., in *Man Across the Sea,* p. 135.

6. Joseph Needham, *Science and Civilization in China*, vol. 4, pt. 3 (Cambridge, England: Cambridge University Press, 1971), p. 553.

7. Clinton R. Edwards, in *Man Across the Sea,* p. 299.

8. Herbert Baker, in *Man Across the Sea,* p. 438.

9. See, for example, Gordon F. Ekholm, "Diffusion and Archaeological Evidence," in *Man Across the Sea*, pp. 54-65, and the bibliography cited there for studies by both Ekholm and Heine-Geldern.

10. For a useful summary, consult Thomas W. Whitaker, "Endemism and Pre-Columbian Migration of the Bottle Gourd, *Lagenaria siceraria,*" in *Man Across the Sea,* pp. 320-27.

11. Constance Irwin, *Fair Gods and Stone Faces* (New York: St. Martin's Press, 1963), p. 71.

12. Alvin M. Joseph, Jr., *The Indian Heritage of America* (New York: Alfred A. Knopf, 1968), p. 101.

13. Ibid., p. 40.

14. Irwin, p. 281.

15. Pierre Honore, *In Quest of the White God* (London: Hutchinson and Co., 1961), p. 143.

16. A number of medieval accounts of various crossings exist; see the partial summary in Frederick J. Pohl, *Atlantic Crossings before Columbus* (New York: W. W. Norton, 1961).

17. An example of this sort of study is that by Alexander von Wuthenau, *Unexpected Faces in Ancient America* (New York: Crown, 1975).

18. James Adair, *The History of the American Indians* (London: E. & C. Dilly, 1775), pp. 17-18, 37-38, 80-107; see also Samuel Cole Williams, *Adair's History of the American Indians* (Johnson City, Tenn.: Watauga Press, 1930), pp. 83-108.

19. Quoted in Ethan Smith, *View of the Hebrews*, 2d ed. (Poultney, Vt.: Smith and Shute, 1825), pp. 107, 108.

20. A. Hyatt Verrill and Ruth Verrill, *America's Ancient Civilizations* (New York: G. P. Putnam's Sons, 1953), p. 11.

21. Ibid., p. 293.

22. Charles G. Leland, *Fusang* (London: Curzon Press, New York: Barnes and Noble, 1973), pp. 25-26.

23. In the twelfth annual report of the Bureau of Ethnology to the Secretary of the Smithsonian Institution (1890-91), pp. 393-94.

24. See Cyrus H. Gordon, *Before Columbus* (New York: Crown Publishers, 1971), pp. 179-82.

25. Further information can be obtained in *Science*, 2:5 (May 1971); Smithsonian Institution, Washington, D.C., Manuscripts vol. XXI.

26. *Natural and Aboriginal History of Tennessee* (Nashville: George Wilson, 1823), see pp. 178-84.

27. Gershon Jacobson, "Mataba'ot von Bar Kockbas Zeiten Gefunden in Teil von Kentucky," *Day-Jewish Journal*, 53:22, p. 220.

The Bering Strait and American Indian Origins 13

James R. Christianson

The purpose of this chapter is to examine, contrast, and question the widely held and generally accepted beliefs concerning America's aboriginal inhabitants and the manner of their arrival in the Western Hemisphere.

Among the sources cited are those which assert, either directly or by implication, that the Bering Strait formed a land, ice, or water bridge for countless numbers of Old World immigrants entering the vast, unoccupied expanses of the Americas. Although the literature has been virtually unanimous on this point, the hypothesis that the Bering Strait was the only or even the primary route of access used by the ancestors of the American Indian is inescapably open to question.

The virtual absence of artifacts necessary to establish cultural parallels between habitation sites located on opposite sides of the strait should have encouraged doubt and fostered debate. In addition, the ancestral origins of the Paleo-Indian and the time of their arrival in the Americas are subjects that have not been conclusively established. An uneasiness in this regard is expressed in the writings of

James R. Christianson is associate professor of Church History and Doctrine at BYU.

some thoughtful scholars who are bothered by wildly inflated dating and questionable artifact claims. One of these scholars, H. Marie Wormington,[1] though herself an advocate of man's early presence throughout the Americas, cautions against unwarranted speculations at excavations such as the Texas Street and Calico Hills sites in California, where experts have dated artifacts at more than 80,000 years B.P. (before present). Even though the latter dig is a project headed by Richard Leakey, son of the famed African pre-historian Louis Leakey, Wormington suggests that the dates are open to question and the artifacts found may be natural rather than man-made.

Declaring that all research in the area of American Indian antiquity must meet reasonable standards, such as a clearly defined stratigraphy, reliable and consistent radiometric dates, and contextually acceptable human artifacts, Dennis Stanford rules that "none of the currently known archeological sites found south of the ice sheets, and for which great age is claimed, meets these criteria at this time."[2] Stanford criticizes interpretations given of all such sites, concluding that "we cannot decisively push back the time of human occupation beyond 12,000 B.P."[3]

Roy L. Carlson points out that truly early dates, 70,000 B.P. and older, are acknowledged primarily by the excavators alone.[4] The scientific community as a whole rejects them, believing that the overlap between naturally flaked objects and those of possible human origin, plus the absence of an acceptable cultural context, compromises the finds as credible evidence of man's presence. Carlson admits that the period from 63,000 to 23,000 B.P. was best suited for man's arrival from Asia, but declares that the evidence of this arrival is rare.[5] Stone tools said to have come from the period are clearly questionable, and human bones located at Delmar and Sunnyvale, California, previously dated at 48,000 and 70,000 B.P., have more recently had their ages set at 11,000 and 8,300. Also, remains of the Tabor Child from southern Alberta, originally said to have lived 40,000 years ago, is currently assigned an age of 3680 ± 4800 B.P.

Although not all of these assertions are sympathetic with the findings of this chapter, they do hint at divisions that persist concerning the issues of Indian antiquity and Indian origins. While neither the conclusions drawn nor much of the evidence presented in the following pages will be greeted with enthusiasm by some students of the subject, the sources utilized typify the large body of materials consulted which further substantiate these conclusions.

The Earliest Americans

Kenneth MacGowan and Joseph A. Hester, Jr., describe the earliest human residents of the Americas as being archaic in appearance, having long heads with straight sides and heavy brow ridges.[6] In their opinion, these early finds do not demonstrate Mongoloid characteristics and are not typical of the present American Indian. George Woodbury draws a similar conclusion, declaring that the fossilized bones exhibit "no affinity" with those of historic American Aborigines.[7]

Earnest Hooton states that the long-headed, heavy-featured crania are the remains of peoples who were closely akin to the Europeans of the same period. He describes them as being primarily white with "Nigritic elements and with whatever else was kicking around Asia before they crossed the Bering Strait."[8]

Harold Gladwin measured the skull of a pygmy-eating Australoid called Talgai and found a distinct resemblance between it and the several early American finds.[9] He concludes that the earliest American was an Australoid, not a great deal different from the present Australian Bushman. Since it would have been rather difficult for this ancient personage to have journeyed successfully from Australia to the Bering Strait and from there into North and South America, Gladwin suggests he originated either in Africa or Central Asia. From there, two factions of the original group parted company and eventually made their way to two widely separated locations, the Americas and Australia.[10] Richard Schutler supports this common-origin theory, suggesting a pre-Mongoloid ancestor in southern China some 70,000 to 100,000 B.P.[11]

Others who have pursued the non-Mongoloid theme are James B. Griffin, Paul S. Martin and Alex Hrdlicka.

Griffin stated that these earliest skeletal finds were of Europoid physical type,[12] while Martin wrote that both round heads and long heads came early to America, but that the long heads were definitely here first.[13] Hrdlicka, who toured Siberia early in this century, saw among the Siberians clear traces of an older, pre-Mongolian, especially pre-Chinese, population whose vestiges were identifiable in the American Indian.[14] Harold Driver likewise concludes that the Indian physical type is closer to that of marginal Mongoloids, who represent an earlier, less specialized racial type than the Mongoloids of China, Mongolia, and Japan.[15] At one time living in most of Asia north and east of India, they shared more characteristics with Europeans than with traditional Mongoloids. Some scholars believe that the peoples of Indonesia, west central Asia, and Tibet descended from them.

Following the Australoids from 17,000 B.P. to 4,500 B.P. Harold Gladwin writes of a migration of Negroids or Folsom men who made their way up the east Asian coast and crossed successfully into the New World.[16] From the close of this migration until 2500 B.P., his third group arrived. This aggregate of individuals, being a combination of Mediterraneans and whatever else may have been picked up en route, made its way from Africa through Spain, France, Bavaria, and Silesia to Siberia, and on to North America, settling across the continent from Oregon to New England.[17] Presently called Algonquin, these people were supposedly carriers of cord-marked pottery, which ceramic not only identified them but also marked their route of travel. Gladwin's fourth migration consisted of the Aluets and Eskimos, who arrived sometime prior to the first century B.C.[18] Hooton, who drew his conclusions following a careful examination of available skulls and skull fragments, like Gladwin, thinks in terms of multiple migrations, the last being the Mongoloids. Of this group he writes:

> At a somewhat later period there began to arrive in the New World groups of Mongoloids coming by the same route as their predecessors. Many groups of these were probably purely Mongoloid in race, but others were mixed with some other racial element notable because of its high-bridged and often convex nose. This

> may have been either Armenoid or Proto-Nordic (or neither one). These later invaders were capable of higher cultural development than the early pioneers and were responsible for the development of agriculture and for the notable achievements of the New World civilization. In some places they may have driven out and supplanted the early long-heads, but often they seem to have interbred with them, producing the multiple and varied types of the present American Indians–types which are Mongoloid to a varying extent, but never purely Mongoloid. Last of all came the Eskimo, a culturally primitive Mongoloid group, already mixed with some non-Mongoloid strain before their arrival in North America.[19]

An opposing view is that of Clark Wissler, who states that the first Americans not only came from Asia via the Bering Strait, but were closely related to the historic Chinese Mongoloids.[20] His examination of their remains led him to declare that they were Indian in type. He arrived at this decision, in part, by assuming that the Mongoloids controlled Asia during the earliest migrations and were masters of the area. No foreign migrations, Negroid, Australoid, or otherwise, could have made it through to the northeast Asian outlet adjoining Alaska.[21] Wissler is supported in his conclusion by almost all other authorities. Robert Clairborne has even written that "no scientist today doubts that American Indians are genetically most akin to the present peoples of East Asia."[22]

In addition to assuming that thc earliest immigrants to the Western Hemisphere had to be Mongoloid due to their geographic proximity and because they formed an insurmountable barrier which discouraged other migrations, scholars generally point to an obvious likeness of hair and facial features as well as less known but equally profound dental comparisons. Among those examining dental similarities is Christy Turner, who has demonstrated the possible common ancestral roots of these New and Old World peoples.[23] Using all suitable Paleo-Indian remains, including Minnesota Lady and Midland, Texpexpan, Lagoa Santa, Cerra Sota, and Palli Aike Man, as well as archaic finds from California, Saskatchewan, Quebec, Alabama, Tehuacan and Cuicuilco, and later prehistoric Aleut-Eskimos and Indians–in all more than 4,000 individuals–Turner demonstrates that all apparently possessed crown and root trait frequencies similar to those of northeastern Asiatics.

Among the seventeen traits analyzed, incisor shoveling, double shoveling, single-rooted upper first premolars and three-rooted lower first molars are relatively common. For example, 91.2% of American Indians have shovel incisors and 71.3% have double shoveling. Such trait intensification and addition is called *sinodonty* and occurs only in northeastern Asia and the Americas.

Turner's findings led to the conclusion that American Indians are of Mongoloid stock, that multiple-origin hypotheses have no validity, and that, except for some Aleut-Eskimo and other related peoples, all North and South American Indians are descendants of an original Paleo-Indian population.[24] Turner also found that, given the small, almost immeasurable amount of evolutionary change or divergence among Indians living from the Arctic south to Tierra del Fuego, the time of Paleo-Indian entry into the New World was as recent as 15,000 years ago. Their point of origin, Turner noted, was the Lena Basin in Siberia, a site far enough west to have been subject to some European influences. This explains a slight European condition in Indian dental conformation.[25]

Issues That Muddy the Waters

These conclusions drawn by Turner, Wissler, Clairborne, and others are clearly at odds with some of the previously mentioned data. For example, as Wissler points out, there are Indians who resemble in some respects the remains of what are thought to have been their earliest American ancestors. These ancestors, however, are not representative of the Mongoloid physical type, past or present. This was further demonstrated by Edgar B. Howard, who described them as being a composite of Mediterranean, Negroid, and archaic white elements with Mongoloid blending of a later date.[26] James B. Griffin claimed that "the Indian did not belong to a single physical type," as evidenced by the "great many linguistic groups in America." [27]

This statement by Griffin introduces a further significant point. If, as indicated, the Indian is truly Mongoloid, either recent or prehistoric, there should be some language similarities between the two groups. It appears, however, that, with the exception of the Aleut-Eskimos, there are virtually none. Further, as Griffin, Kroeber, and others have noted, there is greater language variation among and within the many North and South American Indian tribes than among any other related peoples on earth. The number and variety is such that some agent other than time must provide an explanation. This is especially true if the time frame is as recent as that set forth by Turner. Whereas the validity of her data on dental comparisons necessitates a postglacial entry of early man into the New World, the language differentiation within North and South America and the lack of affinity between these languages and northeast Asian tongues[28] requires either a beginning far back in antiquity or a multi-origin tradition of considerable breadth.

The situation is further complicated by the question of blood types, a condition which the passing of millennia alone cannot resolve. From birth, every individual belongs to blood group A, B, AB, or O. Each segment of the world's population has one or more of these in various proportions. In Spain, for example, the breakdown is 46.5% A, 9.2% B, 2.2% AB, and 41.5% O. A typical Mongoloid runs 25.1% A, 34.2% B, 10.0% AB and 30.7% O. The high incidence of B is typical of East Asian subgroups, but of no other people on earth.[29] Given their assumed Asiatic origin, onc would naturally expect a similar incidence of B among New World aborigines, but such is not the case. Except for the Aleut-Eskimos of the far north, B is not present within relatively uncontaminated societies. Ratios as high as 80% to near 100% O are common, along with a slight incidence of A. Present evidence suggests a near-total absence of A, B, and AB in prehistoric times among early inhabitants of the New World.[30]

As can readily be seen, the questions raised by such matters as skeletal characteristics, dental peculiarities, language differentiation, and blood types translate into a complex level of inquiry into the origins of American Indians and raise doubts concerning such commonly held beliefs as those expressed by Alex Hrdlicka[31] and others, who assert that the differences between Indians and Indian groups are more imagined than real and that time, isolation, and inbreeding, along with unquestioned Mongoloid ancestry, are responsible for America's aboriginal inhabitants.[32]

Despite what appears to be a veritable "can of worms" in terms of unresolved issues and an absence of concrete answers, there is one issue and one answer with which almost everyone nevertheless declares himself to be in agreement: that the Bering Strait was the route of entry for virtually all the ancestors of the Americas' aboriginal inhabitants. With this matter supposedly settled, all related problems are treated as easily resolved or yet-to-be-explained minor differences. Thus the question for most is not whether they emigrated via Siberia and Alaska, but rather when and how.

The Bering Strait

Any discussion of the Bering Strait, a 56-mile-wide, 180-foot-deep body of water separating the Asian and North American continents, as a prehistoric port of entry for early Americans must reckon with the Late or Upper Pleistocene glacial period, labeled the Wisconsin. It was during the middle, late, and postglacial periods of this most recent of several great ice epochs that man presumably crossed into and firmly established himself in the Americas. As Knut R. Fladmark has noted, and most other authorities agree, "Any specific discussion of Early Wisconsinan [pre-60,000 B.P.] environmental parameters significant to human occupation would be so speculative as to be essentially meaningless."[33]

The post-60,000 B.P. middle period of the Wisconsin was significant in human history. It was then that Homo sapiens neanderthalensis was replaced by Homo sapiens or modern man. It was during this interval that man, equipped with Upper Paleolithic technology, may have arrived in eastern Siberia. During much of this era, 60,000 to 25,000 B.P., most of the land mass on either side of the Bering Strait was ice-free, and the strait itself was a broad, unencumbered land bridge for a 6,000-year span from 32,000 to 38,000 B.P.[34] (Since there is no way of knowing the exact years associated with the various phases of the Wisconsin or any other ice age, those used are the ones thought best suited to the available evidence.)

This was a time when both flora and abundant mega-fauna such as the mammoth, mastodon, musk ox, horse, bison, elk, moose, and camel, all of which presumably originated in the Old World, may have crossed into Alaska and eventually southward into other parts of North America. Most of the plant and animal exchange that biologists affirm occurred between the two hemispheres, however, supposedly took place thousands of years earlier when the shallow plain that is today's Bering Strait was a 1,300-mile-wide, elevated land mass that tied the two continents together.[35]

There appears to be little doubt that mega-fauna in large numbers were present in both eastern Siberia and western Alaska throughout this phase of the Wisconsin. The long years between stadials or ice advances are described as relatively mild. Animal life would have flourished and, for indefinite periods, likely moved southward along an unglaciated coastline or down an ice-free interior valley.

During this rather pleasant era, according to many authors, man made his initial entry into North America. Taking advantage of the Cherry Tree Stadial between 32,000 and 42,000 B.P., he crossed the then water-free Bering Strait in pursuit of large game animals upon which he depended for sustenance. As the Wisconsin glacier or glaciers reached maximum limits 40,000 years ago, the Bering bridge remained ice-free, as did some parts of coastal and interior Alaska, making possible a relatively uninhibited southward journey for both men and animals. This condition persisted to 29,000 B.P., when the climate began to deteriorate rapidly. By 18,000 B.P., all of Canada from east to west was sealed off by the last Wisconsin ice mass.[36] It was not until 13,000 to 12,000 B.P. that conditions ameliorated, permitting both man and animals once again to move safely and credibly into and southward through North America.

The scenario given here is a fair reflection of what most authorities believe actually transpired. The query, however, is not whether early man could have traveled eastward and southward as suggested, but whether there is, in fact, evidence to suggest that he did.

Looking at the Evidence

The area between north China and the Bering Strait was for many decades a virtual blank as a source of factual information for early human occupation. In recent years, the discovery of chopper and flake tools at a number of sites has altered previous perceptions, and a smattering of carbon 14 dates have established tentative time parameters.

Two sites, Mal'ta and Buret, located on the Angara River, are characterized by unusual bone art, stone tools with bone and antler handles and stone flakes. Dates established for the two are 18,000 to 15,000 B.P.[37] The Yenisei Basin farther west contains bifacial chopping tools, scrapers, bone tools, and knives and is dated by carbon 14 at 20,000 to 13,000 B.P.[38] Farther east on the lower Aldan River, the Diuktai tradition contains leaf-shaped bifacial points, triangular bifacial knives, and wedge-shaped cores. The carbon 14 dates recorded by Y. A. Mochanov[39] are 35,400 ± 600 to 30,000 ± 500 B.P. These dates are derived from Ust'Mill II, which contained wedge-shaped cores, pebble cores, and flakes. The Hokkaido assemblages located in the far north of Japan contain micro-blades, bifacially prepared core preforms, burins, and scrapers, all thought to postdate 14,800 ± 350 and 15,800 ± B.P. Berelekh, located farther north than any other Paleolithic site in the works, is dated 11,000 B.P.[40]

All of these northeast Asian locations, except those reported by the Russian scientist Y. A. Mochanov, fall within the 20,000 B.P. or younger ranger and are typical of other Paleolithic sites in the same general area. Given the consistency of all other dates and the level of artifact sophistication at Mochanov's Diuktai sites, there may be reason to doubt the accuracy of his data. Aside from this, each of the sites contained an identifiable lithic technology that was essential to its inhabitants' way of life and would have accompanied them in all their wanderings. Positioned as they were on the doorstep of the New World, better acclimatized, and in every way the best suited of all potential immigrants, it presumably must have been they who first entered Beringia and became the earliest Americans.

If any of these or if other Old World wanderers entered Alaska at any time between 35,000 and 13,000 B.P., there should be some concrete evidence verifying their presence. W. N. Irving, who approached his work at Old Crow Basin (located in the north central Yukon valley) convinced that man's presence there went beyond these dates, found no stone artifacts to identify its early occupants and lamely concluded, "Stone implements at present simply do not figure in the definition of a Pleistocene industry or tradition of Old Crow Basin." The material evidence of man's early presence, he concluded, "though compelling was far from eloquent."[41]

Richard E. Morlan, who also studied the Old Crow as well as other sites, was convinced that those who crossed Beringia were well adapted to prevailing environmental conditions and had an adequate technology to assure their success.[42] Still, he was unable to explain the near total absence of lithic artifacts, claiming only that their marks left on pieces of bone and antler were sufficient evidence of their existence.[43] Man's early presence as far back as 80,000 years ago was attested by mammoth and other bones that appeared to have been artificially worked or splintered. But the tools for such were not present, neither were any human remains located, nor have they been confirmed in any pre-postglacial sites.

The problems faced by Morlan, Irving, and other advocates of man's mid-Wisconsin presence in Alaska are not only the absence of available Asiatics and their artifacts at that time, but also the acknowledged possibility that 80,000-year-old bones could have been broken, chipped, polished, and flaked in numerous ways, and the probability that they were redeposited on any number of occasions. There is, in fact, "no way to know which pieces belong together historically, or even which animals may have formed living communities."[44] The latter problem is so extreme that a thorough mixing of middle and late Wisconsin fauna has occurred, resulting in a misreading of the prehistoric record. Fladmark noted that scholars have pictured the mammalian community of the late Wisconsin as equivalent to that of West Africa, along with a similarly rich environment.[45] While this may have been true of the mid-Wisconsin, carbon 14 dates from central Alaska reveal no animals commonly listed between 18,000 and 21,000 B.P. and only the musk ox, bison, and perhaps mammoth between 12,000 and 15,000 B.P. At Old Crow, no faunal remains date from 22,000 to 14,000 B.P. At other sites, the musk ox alone was recorded from 26,000 to 15,000 B.P. All data combined indicate that no "hunter's paradise throughout Beringia" existed during the period from 26,000 to 15,000 B.P.

J. D. Richie and Les C. Cwynar deal a further blow to the widely held concept that the Arctic of that period was conducive to the immigration of central Eurasian big-game hunters into North America.[46] Based on a study of pollen cores taken near the front of what was once the Laurentide ice pack, they conclude that polar desert or fall tundra conditions existed in that part of Beringia during a period from 14,000 to 30,000 B.P. Such an environment would be as harsh as that of the modern-day high Arctic.

It is this era, 20,000 to 14,000 B.P., that some scholars point to as the time of man's arrival in the New World. Sites such as the Blue Fish Caves near Old Crow Basin have yielded dates of 15,500 ± 130 B.P. and 12,900 ± 100 B.P.[47] Scientists located bone and stone artifacts, but none demonstrated any affinity with known Asian discoveries. Since the dates were established from bones described as being from a "large ungulate population during full glacial times," a population which included the horse, mammoth, bison, sheep, wapiti and caribou, they were obviously redeposits from an earlier or later period, and the dates can be discounted.

Except for microchips or microblades located under hard-to-verify circumstances, and distantly similar bifaced, disk-like scrapers found at the lower or pre-6500 B.P. level of Onion Portage site in northwest Alaska,[48] researchers have found nothing of substance to clearly relate North American artifacts to those of northeast Asia. Even the fluted point which stands as the best evidence of a historical connection between continental and northwestern North America, though abundant at both locations, is strangely absent in northeast Asia or Siberia. It was circumstances such as this that led A. L. Kroeber to make a statement thirty years ago that is as pertinent today as it was then: "It remains one of the great enigmas that, at the top of the continent, where presumably the ancestors of all American natives crossed from Asia, no real connection links have been recognized between glacial times [or before] and shortly before the time of Christ."[49] Clearly, the question is not when but *if* early man, except in incidental and accidental instances, ever made the assumed journey.

Conclusions

If Asiatic tribesmen journeyed into North America anytime between 13,000 and 20,000 B.P. (there is no real evidence to show they were on site prior to this time), the environmental conditions they faced would have been unlike anything known to man in historic times. We cannot postulate concerning preparations or travel requirements, since nothing so severe has ever faced modern man. A glacial epoch is unknown to us. Not even conditions in Antarctica compare with an event so awful that it entombed one-third of the earth's surface with an ice mass one or more miles thick. An ice front converged on central Alaska, from both east and west, at a rate of 1000 meters or more a year. What kind of climatic extremes produced it, and what was the nature of those resulting from it? If the centuries during its buildup were beyond comparison, what were the millennia like which encompassed its demise?

If man ventured into North America during the period when a land bridge was available to him, following the animals that drew him after them, he would have entered an ice-free but cold, sterile, hostile environment. Once there, sometime after 20,000 and before 14,000 B.P., he would have been forced to wait out the ice age for an indefinite period prior to the opening of an ice-free corridor running down the east side of the rockies into North America sometime between 12,000 and 13,000 B.P. Though free of ice, the corridor was not without unimaginable difficulties. Fladmark[50] describes it as a veritable wind tunnel, pouring arctic temperatures off the ice mass into the Great Plains. En route, massive rivers, steep and treacherous terrain, and enormous ice-water lakes—Lake Agassiz was larger than all the Great Lakes combined—would have cluttered the course of travel. A journey along the west coast of Alaska and Canada was no less improbable. A fjord-like mainland, encumbered with great ice lobes reaching out into the sea and either extreme cold or enormous amounts of water discharge from the melting glaciers all spelled defeat for even the most determined travelers.

Even with the limited knowledge available of actual conditions in Beringia, Alaska, and Canada, given the assumed extremes of the Wisconsin glacial period for a decade of millennia from 24,000 to 14,000 B.P., we can rightfully suppose that our wildest speculation concerning probable conditions fall short of reality. How, then, in the absence of concrete evidence other than looking at a man and saying there was no other way available, can we begin to assume that early man out of Asia chose this time to discover a new world? With the wide-open, more-inviting expanses of Siberia to the west, it defies logic to suppose he would continue living in a geographically, climatically, economically inhospitable Alaska for perhaps thousands of years with no way of knowing but that conditions east and south were far worse than those he was experiencing. Viewed in this manner, one might correctly wonder why scholars have concluded that the Bering Strait was the primary route of access to the Americas with so little evidence to substantiate their findings.

A Peopling Hypothesis

If not via the Bering Strait, then how? For many, the answer to this query either lies hidden beneath the garbage and other remnants of successive civilizations or has been distorted, if not destroyed, by the altering, burying, crushing forces of nature. Either way, it can at best be only guessed at, and so approached, actual truth will always be beyond man's grasp.

For the few who know and for others who care to listen, there is an answer to the above question. Latter-day Saint doctrine avers that Adam and his early posterity were native to what is currently North America.[51] Whatever the degree of their expansion into inhabitable parts of the world, it came to an end with the biblical flood which encompassed all the landmass and, except for Noah and his family, extinguished the human species. From this we understand that the original peopling of the Americas, however long ago, was by Adam and his posterity—a race truly distinct from and not the immediate ancestors of the American Indian.

The next known inhabitants of the "New World" were the followers of a man named Jared and his prophet brother. Their arrival may have been as early as 2000 to 2200 B.C. following the dispersion of mankind at the time of the Tower of Babel. For an indeterminate period of time, an undisclosed number of individuals made their way over land and water until they came to a great sea. Their course of travel may have taken them across Asia to the Pacific and from there, in specially constructed vessels, to the uninhabited Americas (Ether 6:1-12).

Based on figures given sometime after their arrival, these 150 to 200 pilgrims multiplied and spread throughout the land (Ether 6:13-21). Whatever their ancestral composition, these Jaredites were the true Paleo-Indians and must have carried with them the inheritable characteristics that came to typify modern American aborigines. The widespread O blood type, the dental peculiarities, the hair, and facial features were common within the group and became standardized as they intermarried and moved unrestricted, often compelled by war and insurrection, to all points of the compass. In time, language and customs changed, but these basic traits remained dominant.

The next known group to arrive, in 589 B.C., was small (1 Nephi 18:1-25). It too experienced divisions and strife and soon migrated into the wilderness (2 Nephi 5:1-25). There, the followers of Laman, called Lamanites, and some of those who allied themselves with Laman's brother Nephi, called Nephites, met and intermarried with the remnants of the original Jaredite population, thereby becoming part of the established and more ancient gene pool. Within one or two generations, basic physical and cultural characteristics were greatly altered. As they received, however, they also gave, and in time the language, the culture, and the physical makeup of the Paleo-Indian or Jaredite population was indelibly influenced.

Soon after the arrival of the Nephites and Lamanites came a third group, the followers of Mulek, a son of the Jewish King Zedekiah. The Mulekites crossed the ocean and located some distance north of the central Nephite settlements (Helaman 6:10; Mosiah 25:2). In time the remnants of these two societies merged, but retained the Nephite designation. Again their languages and cultures "blended," and within a few generations a new, more complex society emerged. Centuries passed and peripheral mixing of all the inhabitants occurred. A new and distinctly American gene pool was forming, radiating outward from several major areas of influence.

The process heightened following A.D. 33, stimulated by a general combining of the principal Nephite and Lamanite factions. Major divisions followed a two-hundred-year period of integration, resulting in a total breakdown of Nephite society (4 Nephi 1:1-45; Mormon 6:1-20). The ensuing assimilation was final. The foundation population was in place, scattered throughout the Americas. Composed of remnants from prior Jaredite, Lamanite, Nephite, and Mulekite societies, it was further impacted over a 2,500-year period by countless other transoceanic and Bering Strait arrivals. Depending on individual numbers and the extent of their subsequent assimilation, such ingraftings may have profoundly enhanced cultural—especially language—variations among peripheral elements of the population. Thus viewed, the Americanization of the Indian was complete.

The substantial number of Mongoloids who undoubtedly made a water crossing into the New World also comprise a late post-flood entry. Their impact southward, confined as they were to the far northern habitation of historic Aleuts and Eskimos, which people they became, was far less significant than scholars have supposed. In actual fact, the predominant exchange of both culture and genes may have been south to north from cultural climax centers deep within the Western Hemisphere.

Notes

1. H. M. Wormington, "Early Man in the New World: 1970-1980," by Richard Schutler, Jr., ed., *Early Man in the New World* (Beverly Hills, Calif.: Sage Publications, 1983), pp. 192-94.

2. Dennis Stanford, "Pre-Clovis Occupation South of the Ice Sheets," in Schutler, *Early Man in the New World*, p. 65.

3. Ibid., p. 72.

4. Roy L. Carlson, "The Far West," in Schutler, *Early Man in the New World*, p. 73.

5. Ibid., p. 74.

6. Kenneth MacGowan and J. A. Hester, Jr., *Early Man in the New World* (New York: Doubleday-Anchor, 1962), pp. 134-35.

7. Ibid., p. 135.

8. Earnest Hooten, *Up from the Ape* (New York: Macmillan Co., 1940), p. 134.

9. Harold Gladwin, *Men Out of Asia* (New York: McGraw-Hill Book Co., 1947), p. xl.

10. Ibid., pp. 60-64.

11. Richard Schutler Jr., "The Australian Parallel to the Peopling of the New World," in Schutler, *Early Man in the New World*, pp. 43-45.

12. James B. Griffin, "Some Prehistoric Connections Between Siberia and America," *Science* 131 (1960): 801-12.

13. Paul S. Martin, G. I. Quimby, and D. Collier, *Indians Before Columbus* (Chicago: University of Chicago Press, 1947), p. 6.

14. Alex Hrdlicka, "A Search in Eastern Asia for the Race That Peopled America," in *Smithsonian Miscellaneous Collections* 60 (1913): 10-13.

15. Harold Driver, *Indians of North America* (Chicago: University of Chicago Press, 1969), p. 5.

16. Gladwin, pp. 92-94.

17. Ibid., pp. 137-46.

18. Ibid., pp. 167-71.

19. Hooton, pp. 361-62.

20. Clark Wissler, "The Origin of the American Indian," *Natural History Magazine*, September 1944, p. 313.

21. Ibid., p. 318.

22. Robert Clairborne, *The First Americans* (New York: Time-Life Books, 1973), p. 11.

23. Christy G. Turner, "Dental Evidence for the Peopling of the Americas," in Schutler, *Early Man in the New World*, pp. 147-58.

24. Ibid., p. 153.

25. Ibid., p. 156.

26. Edgar B. Howard, "An Outline of the Problem of Man's Antiquity in North America," *American Anthropologist* 38 (1936): 396.

27. Griffin, p. 801.

28. Driver, p. 6.

29. T. D. Stewart, *The People of America* (New York: Charles Scribner's Sons, 1973), p. 52.

30. Ibid., p. 54.

31. Alex Hrdlicka, *The Coming of Man from Asia in the Light of Recent Discoveries*, Smithsonian Institution Annual Report, 1935, p. 484.

32. T. D. Stewart, "A Physical Anthropologist's View of the Peopling of the New World," *Southwest Journal of Anthropology* 16 (1960): 263-64.

33. Knut R. Fladmark, "Times and Places: Environmental Correlates of Mid-to-Late Wisconsinan Human Population Expansion in North America," in Schutler, *Early Man in the New World*, p. 13.

34. Ibid., p. 14.

35. William G. Haag, "The Bering Strait Land Bridge," in *Pre-Columbian Archaeology: Readings from Scientific American* (San Francisco: W. H. Freeman and Co., 1979), pp. 17-18.

36. Fladmark, p. 16.

37. C. S. Chard, *Northeast Asia in Prehistory* (Madison, Wis.: University of Wisconsin Press, 1974), p. 27.

38. Ibid., p. 30.

39. Yuri A. Mochanov, "Stratigraphy and Absolute Chronology of the Paleolithic in Northeast Asia," in Alan L. Bryan, ed., *Early Man in America* (Edmonton: Alberta Printing Services, 1978), pp. 54-66.

40. Ikawa-Smith, "The Early Pre-History of the Americas as Seen From Northeast Asia," in Jonathon E. Erickson et al., eds., *Peopling of the New World*, (Los Altos, Calif.: Ballena Press, 1982), p. 26.

41. Irving, "Pleistocene Cultures in Old Crow Basin," in Erickson et al., *Peopling of the New World*, p. 79.

42. Richard E. Morlan, "Pre-Clovis Occupation North of the Ice Sheets," in Schutler, *Early Man in the New World*, p. 47.

43. Ibid., p. 56.

44. Ibid., p. 60.

45. Fladmark, p. 23.

46. Ibid., p. 22.

47. Morlan, p. 58.

48. Douglas D. Anderson, "A Stone Age Campsite at the Gateway to America," in *Pre-Columbian Archaeology: Readings from Scientific American*, pp. 27, 29.

49. A. L. Kroeber, *Anthropology Today: An Encyclopedia Inventory* (Chicago: University of Chicago Press, 1953), p. 246.

50. Fladmark, p. 28.

51. Zerah Pulsipher, "Zerah Pulsipher's History" (Special Collections, Harold B. Lee Library, Brigham Young University), p. 12. (Also Doctrine and Covenants 107:53; 116:1.)

Book of Mormon—Transmission from Translator to Printed Text 14

George A. Horton, Jr.

Translator to Scribes

After completing the translation of the sacred Nephite history, the Prophet Joseph Smith said, "Through the medium of the Urim and Thummim I translated the record by the gift and power of God."[1] He gave no other explanation of the process.

During the translation, as many as eight people may have served as scribes.[2] Some of them, and others then and now, have tried to explain how the translation took place, but the question remains unresolved. In an interview with one of her sons, Emma Smith, who acted as scribe for brief periods,[3] said: "When [I was] acting as his scribe, your father would dictate to me hour after hour; and when returning after meals, or after interruptions, he would at once begin where he left off, without either seeing the manuscript or having any portion of it read to him. This was a usual thing for him to do."[4]

George A. Horton, Jr., is department chairman of Ancient Scripture and associate professor of Ancient Scripture at BYU.

Regarding the translation, Oliver Cowdery wrote:

> Near the time of the setting of the Sun, Sabbath evening, April 5th, 1829, my natural eyes, for the first time beheld this brother. . . . On Monday the 6th, I assisted him in arranging some business of a temporal nature, and on Tuesday the 7th, commenced to write the book of Mormon. These were days never to be forgotten—to sit under the sound of a voice dictated by the inspiration of heaven, awakened the utmost gratitude of this bosom! Day after day I continued, uninterrupted, to write from his mouth, as he translated with the Urim and Thummim . . . the history, or record, called "The Book of Mormon."[5]

Oliver was the scribe for most of the Book of Mormon as we now have it, except for a few pages.[6] To view the pages of the remaining original manuscript is to be convinced that it has been transcribed from dictation.

Typesetting

Upon completion of the translation, precautions were taken to protect the manuscript, and a "printer's" second copy was made by Oliver Cowdery.[7] The typesetting started in August 1829, and the book was published in March 1830.

John H. Gilbert, the non-Mormon typesetter who worked for E. B. Grandin (a Palmyra, New York, printer), said:

> When the printer was ready to commence work, Harris was notified, and Hyrum Smith brought the first installment of manuscript, of 24 pages, closely written on common foolscap paper—he had it under his vest, and vest and coat closely buttoned over it. At night Smith came and got the manuscript, and with the same precaution carried it away. The next morning with the same watchfulness, he brought it again, and at night took it away. This was kept up for several days. . . . On the second day—Harris and Smith being in the office—I called their attention to a grammatical error, and asked whether I should correct it? Harris consulted with Smith a short time, and turned to me and said: "The Old Testament is ungrammatical, set it as it is written."
>
> After working a few days, I said to Smith on his handing me the manuscript in the morning: "Mr. Smith, if you would leave this manuscript with me, I would take it home with me at night and read and punctuate it." His reply was, "We are commanded not to leave it." A few mornings after this, when Smith handed me the manuscript, he said to me: "If you will give your word that this manuscript shall be returned to us when you get through with

it, I will leave it with you." I assured Smith that it should be returned all right when I got through with it. For two or three nights I took it home with me and read it, and punctuated it with a lead pencil. . . . Every Chapter, if I remember correctly, was one solid paragraph, without a punctuation mark, from beginning to end.

Names of persons and places were generally capitalized, but sentences had no end. The character or short & was used almost invariably where the word *and* occurred, except at the end of a chapter. I punctuated it to make it read as I supposed the Author intended, and but very little punctuation was altered in proofreading.[8]

In review:

1. The text had been dictated by Joseph to eight different scribes–Oliver Cowdery being the main one.
2. The scribes seem to have written just what they heard, no more and no less.
3. There does not appear to have been any explanatory conversation between the translator and his scribes.
4. Capitalization, spelling, and punctuation were apparently not specified during the dictation process.
5. Whatever the process of translation, it allowed for human errors to appear in the grammar of the scribal copy.
6. Joseph had little to do with the supervision of the typesetting, proofreading, or printing of the first edition.[9]

Printed Editions

A quick review of some of the more important recent editions of the Book of Mormon[10] gives some insights as to why new editions were deemed necessary of what Joseph had called the "most correct of any book on earth."[11] For example, as soon as the first edition was out, the readers could not avoid noticing many typographical, spelling, and grammatical errors.

On 25 June 1833, Joseph wrote to W. W. Phelps (a printer), "As soon as we get time, we will review the manuscripts of the Book of Mormon, after which they will be forwarded to you."[12] However, due to the pressure of other matters, the second edition did not appear until 1837, having been prepared by the Prophet with the assistance of Oliver Cowdery. Over one thousand corrections were made, and some minor clarifications were added, the majority having to do with grammar. By 1837 the Prophet, who had had limited formal schooling, was reading Greek, learning Hebrew, and studying grammar.[13] This edition was followed in 1840 by a third edition.[14] Appearing on the title page of the third edition (1840) are the words "Carefully Revised by the Translator." It appears that improving the printed copy continued because on 15 January 1842, Joseph recorded in his journal, "I commenced reading the Book of Mormon, at page 54, American stereotype edition [the third] (the previous pages having been corrected), for the purpose of correcting the stereotype plates of some errors which [had] escaped notice. . . ."[15]

The first European edition in English (1841) followed the 1837 edition and consequently did not contain the changes Joseph had made in 1840. Later American editions (beginning in 1871) were taken from the first European edition and consequently they continued the lack of corrections.

In 1879, President John Taylor assigned Orson Pratt to prepare a new edition which would include a redivision of chapters (increasing the number from 114 to 239), reversification, and scriptural cross-references. He was followed after the turn of the century by a committee, serving under the chairmanship of James E. Talmage, which prepared the 1920 edition with double-column pages, revised references, a pronunciation guide, an index, and many grammatical improvements.[16] This latter edition was the most commonly used edition in the Church for over half a century. As work was under way for the new LDS edition of the King James Version of the Bible, it was felt that additional work should be done on the Book of Mormon. Consequently, with further corrections growing out of research over the last twenty-five years,[17] the 1981 edition of the Book of Mormon was prepared under the supervision of the Scriptures Publication Committee by direction of the First Presidency.

Transmission Problems

In examining the process of transmission from the original translator to the printed text of later editions, let us briefly consider problems so common that the publishing world has identified most of them with technical names. They include orthography, haplography, dittography, homoeoteleuton, homoeoarchton, and other simple problems. Only one or two brief examples will be considered in each category.

1. Orthography (spelling):

One of the first things a modern reader notices about the first edition of the Book of Mormon is some of its "unusual" spellings. The common assumption is that Oliver Cowdery was poorly educated even though he was a schoolteacher. However, an examination of this supposition raises questions about the historical development of the English in our English Bible and also the status of American English in 1829.

a. Spelling in the King James Version. We have long been aware that the spelling of words in our English Bible has undergone many changes through the centuries. For example, the word "sins" was "synnes" in the 1611 King James Version and later became "sinnes" before the present spelling was adopted. Moreover, the word "majesty" was spelled "maiestie" then "majestie" before being spelled as it is now.[18] Further, a selection of words from the first nine verses of Hebrews 1 in the 1611 edition includes such spellings as "diuers," "sonne," "heire," "brightnesse," and "oyle."[19]

b. Status of American English in 1829. Many changes were taking place in the English language used in the United States during the early 1800s. Many people were pressing for a variety of English that would be uniquely American. At the forefront of this movement was Noah Webster, publisher of the *Compendious Dictionary of the English Language* in 1806 and his famous *American Dictionary of the English Language* in 1828. The introduction to the latter indicated that there were five different English dictionaries on the market at the time. Some examples of spellings found in those dictionaries are as follows:[20]

SHERIDAN (1784)	WALKER (1794)	JONES (1798)	PERRY (1805)	JAMESON (1827)
claushur	clauzhure	clauzhure	clauzhure	clauzhur
courtshus	courtsheous	courteous	curtcheous	courteous
creatshur	cretshure	creatshure	creature	creture
scriptshur	scriptshur	scriptshure	scripture	scriptyur
stattshur	stattshure	stattshure	stature	statyur

When Webster's dictionary was published in 1828, that made six dictionaries[21] that were in use at the time though we don't know whether Oliver Cowdery had access to any of them during the translation of the Book of Mormon. We might well ask, "Did he use a dictionary?" And if he did, "Which one (or ones) did he use?"

Seven of Webster's proposed new American spellings were later adopted. For example, he changed the following in some contexts: "our" to "or," "l" to "ll," "x" to "ct," "re" to "er," "c" to "s," "dge" to "dg," and "ck" to "c." But Webster used and recommended many other spellings that were not adopted such as ake, beleeve, breth, hed, iland, iz, korus, lauf, mashine, munth, rong, thum, tung, wimmen, and yeer. These last recommendations reveal a common tendency of the time: of relying heavily on phonetic or sound spellings. Some of this tendency can be detected in Oliver's spelling.

c. *Spelling of Important Contemporaries.* Since the 1830 edition of the Book of Mormon had so many "unusual" spellings, it could appropriately be asked whether Oliver's contemporaries were spelling words in the same manner—approximating sounds. Consider the following: Nathaniel Hawthorne (1804-81) wrote *ancles*, *cieling*, *sithe*, *choaked*, *chrystal*, *musquito*, and *canvass*, etc. Washington Irving (1773-1859) used all of the following variations: *smoak*, *smocke*, *schmoke*, and *smoke.* He used *received* and *recieved* in the same sentence. He also used such short forms as *tho*, *brot*, and *thro.* President Andrew

Johnson (1808-75) used *whent*, *som*, *allways*, *determin*, *yealding*, *desid*, *decission*, *rediculous*, *anxus*, *immaganable*, *propper*, among others.[22]

One author has said: "One immutable fact about a living, spoken language is that it inevitably changes. The written language changes more slowly than the spoken language, but even that changes. Therefore, no one can make an absolutely authoritative statement about the correctness of spelling, punctuation, or even, in some cases, grammar and idiom."[23]

d. Oliver Cowdery's Spelling. Considering Oliver's situation, we should remember that he had to write what he heard. Let us put ourselves in his place for a minute and imagine that we have just heard Joseph use the word *straight*. How would we spell it? There are two possibilities even with today's standardized spellings. From fragmentary evidence, it appears that Oliver spelled that spoken word *s-t-r-a-i-t* nineteen out of twenty-two times. But for some reason most of these were changed, perhaps by John H. Gilbert, who offered to improve the manuscript and "correct it." So it was that *straight* dominates the 1830 through the 1879 editions, all following the 1837 edition. In 1920, six instances were changed to *strait*, and four additional places were corrected back to *strait* in the 1981 edition, which makes its usage in those instances harmonious with the King James Version and its underlying Greek.

There were other words that Oliver may have been hearing for the first time, and in some of those instances it appears that Joseph Smith corrected them in later editions.

Many of the words that we thought Oliver had misspelled are actually legitimate English variants and can be found in the *Oxford English Dictionary*. This means that they were used by other writers of the time of the translation of the Book of Mormon. For example, the spellings *adhear, adultry, ancles, babtized, befal, burthensome, condescention, devlish, fraid, journied, moulten, nought, phrensied,* and *writen*—all indicate that Oliver was not really an unlearned schoolteacher as some have thought.

e. Middle English Inflections. Another area of spelling that has received attention in later editions of the Book of Mormon is the use of Middle English inflections and related forms. These reflect the influence of the King James Version and Elizabethan English, both of which were popularized by early English versions of the scriptures. The endings have been dropped from many words such as the following: *answereth, ascendeth, avengeth, beareth, becometh, causeth, dieth*. Changes have also been made in the following: *art, hath, shew, thee, thine, thou, ye,* and so forth.[24] Other spelling changes will be considered in the next category.

2. Typography (setting of the type):

There were numerous misspellings in the first edition from inaccuracies which are common to typesetting. Examples that seem to fall in this category might include the following: *aaswer, acccording, amog, armss, bacause, beold, bgan, daghter, destoy, expdient, govereor, hia, irsael, khown, mekness, mnltitude, opon, plaees, prohesy, rufused, seeen, sould, theit, and utttered.*

Oliver's handwriting also presented a challenge. His *r* (which looks like a "Palmer r") and his *n* are difficult to distinguish from each other, as are his *b* and *l*. For example, in the 1830 edition Gadianton was once called "the nobler" rather than "the robber." In a similar way, the typesetter apparently elsewhere mistook Oliver's *rm* for *un*. In 1 Nephi 13 there are several instances in which the original manuscript read *formation*, but the typesetter apparently thought the printer's copy said *founation* and supplied what seemed to be a "missing" *d* to make it read *foundation*. This was finally corrected in the 1981 edition.

3. Simple Omissions (e.g., of letters, syllables, words, or lines):

Simple omissions of short words and accidental skipping of single letters are the most frequent unintentional errors made by scribes or typesetters such as John Gilbert.[25] An example of this was the accidental omission of a single letter leaving three letters that just happen to form another word. This came at Alma 48:21, where the last *r* had been left off the word *year*, found in the original manuscript.[26]

A rather vital letter was dropped from the word

immortality (1830) so that it read *immorality* (1837). It was fortunately corrected in the 1840 edition.

4. Homoeoteleuton (accidental omission due to similar endings):

An example of sentences being dropped due to similar endings is found in Alma 32:30. Note how much was in the original and printer's manuscripts[27] and the commonalities in the first and last parts of the verse by comparing the original verse with that found in most other editions not including the 1981, where the omission is restored:[28]

Original MS & 1981 Edition	*Most Other Editions*
But behold, as the seed swelleth, and sprouteth, and beginneth to grow, then you must needs say that the seed is good; for behold it swelleth, and sprouteth, and beginneth to grow. And now, behold, will not this strengthen your faith? Yea, it will strengthen your faith: for ye will say I know that this is a good seed; for behold it sprouteth and beginneth to grow.	But behold, as the seed swelleth, and sprouteth, and beginneth to grow, then you must needs say that the seed is good; for behold it swelleth, and sprouteth, and beginneth to grow.

A second example is found at 3 Nephi 10:4 in the 1837 edition, where the printer skips from one occurrence of the phrase "of Israel" to a second occurrence, thereby unintentionally eliminating eight words.[29]

1830	*1837*
O ye people of these great cities which have fallen, which are a descendant of Jacob; yea which are of the house of Israel; O ye people of the house of Israel, how oft have I gathered you as a hen gathereth her chickens under her wings, and have nourished you.	O ye people of these great cities which have fallen, which are a descendant of Jacob; yea who are of the house of Israel, [ ] how oft have I gathered you as a hen gathereth her chickens under her wings, and have nourished you.

5. Homoeoarchton (accidental omission due to similar beginnings):

In the first edition, the printers skipped from one "f" to another in the the same word, which shortened "genealogy of his forefathers" to read "genealogy of his fathers" in 1 Nephi 19:2. The longer word is supported by the original manuscript, the printer's copy, and the 1840 edition.[30]

6. Haplography (omission of adjacent letters, syllables, words, or lines):

This is a case of accidentally dropping one of two adjacent *t*'s at Alma 51:10, which changed "that *t*his promise" in the original manuscript to "that his promise" in the printer's manuscript. All the printed editions have followed the error.

7. Dittography (accidental addition of letters or words):

An instance of accidental repetition occurs at 3 Nephi 22:4 (the italicized words were those accidentally repeated): "for thou shalt forget the shame of thy youth, and shalt not remember the reproach of thy *youth, and shalt not remember the reproach of thy* widowhood any more." This is a quotation from Isaiah 54:4, and it has been pointed out that not only does the KJV Isaiah not have these added words, but those words appeared first in the 1837 edition, and that they were not in the corrected printer's copy. Also, the added words do violence to the poetic parallelism found in Hebrew poetry.[31]

8. Contextual Assimilation (mistakenly influenced by the context):

At 2 Nephi 4:26 in Nephi's Psalm, the 1830 printer's alteration of "me" (which is the reading in the printer's manuscript) to "men" may have been unconsciously influenced by the earlier occurrence of "men" on the same line. However, Larson has said that "It should be pointed out that the presence of a printer's line under 'me' may indicate that he paused and pondered concerning the very closely written words 'me in' and then consciously decided that 'me in' was Oliver Cowdery's scribal error for 'men in.' Whatever the reason for the change, the correct text is 'me,' with Nephi marveling at the Lord's love for him."[32]

9. Mishearing of a Homophone (similar sound but different spelling):

Malachi 4:2 is quoted in 3 Nephi 25:2; however, in the latter case "Sun of righteousness" has been changed to read "*Son* of Righteousness" (emphasis added). A question naturally arises as to whether this is a calculated change on the part of Joseph or Oliver. Whatever the case, if the extant Hebrew text for Malachi is correct, "the Hebrew word used is *shemesh*, meaning 'sun,' and not the quite different *ben*, which is the word for 'son.' Also, the Hebrew text says literally 'the sun of righteousness shall arise with healing in her wings,' so that the feminine pronoun 'her' agrees with the feminine gender of shemesh in this passage."[33] Unless we find an explanation that it was a calculated change, it appears that the variation constitutes a simple problem of homophones.

Two other examples are interesting. Oliver wrote *wrecked* instead of *racked*, as it now appears (Mosiah 27:29), and *arrest* instead of *wrest* (Alma 13:20).

10. Misreading of a Word (mistaking of similarly shaped letters):

Instances of this were already discussed in the section dealing with the typesetter's reading of Oliver Cowdery's handwriting. Consider another case in which Oliver apparently misread the original manuscript wording "he drove out the man" and copied it as "he drew out the man" (Alma 42:2). The latter rendering has remained in all the printed texts. Again, the typesetter apparently misread

Oliver's final *r* of the word *mediator* in the printer's copy and set it as *mediation* (2 Nephi 2:27),[34] which was corrected in 1981.

Now let's consider the changes that have been made to correct and improve the text in the various editions.

Textual Revision

As early as the second edition there were over a thousand changes made personally by the Prophet Joseph to improve the grammar.[35] The most frequent change, occurring 707 times, was a shift from *which* to *who.* Later editors, especially the committee chaired by James E. Talmage, also made similar improvements.

When all of the *grammar changes* found in each edition from the first edition to that of 1981 are totaled, the most frequent are the following:[36]

891	*which* to *who*	45	*were* to *was*
177	*exceeding* to *exceedingly*[37]	19	*that* to *who*
		11	*mights* to *might*
162	*was* to *were*	11	*them* to *those*
74	*is* to *are*	10	*straight* to *strait*
66	*which* to *whom*	10	*done* to *did*
54	*they* to *those*		

Similar changes have occurred in the King James Version of the Bible.[38] Turning to *deletions*, it is interesting that some readers have been critical of the repetitive use of the expression "and it came to pass," an authentic expression carried over from the Semitic. In Hebrew, the expression is a conjunction plus a form of the verb *to be*.[39] Nevertheless, the entire expression except the "and" was eliminated in forty-six places for the 1837 edition, probably by Joseph Smith himself. Other deletions include the following:

188	*that*	14	*he*
48	*the*	13	*of*
40	*a/and*	11	*to/thereof*
29	*had*	10	*&c*[40]
16	*for*		

Some of the changes were *additions* which might be considered in three categories:

(1) Addition of words to improve grammar:

12	*of*	4	*had/he/in/to*
7	*and/is/the*	3	*all/be/letter l*
6	*that*		*with*
5	*not*		

(2) Replacing (adding back) words dropped through transmission errors: An example already mentioned consisted of the restoration of the sentences that were omitted from Alma 32:30 of the original manuscript.

(3) Intentional additions to improve clarity: The most dramatic instance of clarifying a text is found at 1 Nephi 11:18, 21, 32 and 13:40, where the words "the son of" have been added before the names *God* and "the Eternal Father." Joseph Smith personally made these corrections in the 1837 edition. Given the fact that these texts are clearly talking about Jesus, the Son of God, the addition of "the son of" was appropriate to give additional clarity for the reader.

Other intriguing clarifications can be found in 1 Nephi 8:4 (1837), where "in my dream" is added, and in 1 Nephi 20:1 (1840), with the addition of "or out of the waters of baptism."

One of the more interesting *textual changes* relates to the changing of "white" (1830, 1837) to "pure" (1840) in 2 Nephi 30:6. Although this correction was made by Joseph Smith, it was not picked up in subsequent American editions, which followed the earlier Liverpool printings based on the 1837 edition. This was corrected again in the 1981 edition.

Perhaps the most difficult change to understand occurs at both Mosiah 21:28 and Ether 4:1. The first edition had "Benjamin" where "Mosiah" now appears. Since King Benjamin would not likely have still been living at the time of the text, the Prophet changed the 1837 edition reading of Mosiah 21:28. The change in Ether was made in the 1849 edition. We can only speculate about who made the original "error." Dr. Sidney B. Sperry asked, "Was it an inadvertent slip of the tongue on the part of Joseph Smith as he dictated his translation to Oliver Cowdery, or did he translate correctly enough an original error on the part of Mormon, the abridger of the Book of Mormon? The last of these suggestions is probably the correct one."[41]

Some Conclusions

1. The Book of Mormon has been subject to problems in its printing, as have other books.
2. The English language in America was not standardized in 1829.
3. The original grammar was Joseph's; the spelling was Oliver's; the punctuation was John H. Gilbert's.
4. The Prophet-Translator initiated the majority of changes in the first few editions.
5. There is a difference between word changes and idea changes—the basic meaning of the text has not been changed.

Based on his letter to W. W. Phelps in 1833, his 1837 and 1840 editions, his statement in 1842, and his 1842 edition (all previously referred to), it is clear that had Joseph lived longer, he would likely have continued to correct the text of the Book of Mormon to produce a book without human errors. It has been in this same spirit that corrections have been made in succeeding editions.

Some of the sharpest detractors of the Book of Mormon translation have confessed that "as we stated earlier, most of the 3,913 changes which we found were related to the correction of grammatical and spelling errors and do not really change the basic meaning of the text."[42] This reminds us of a statement the Prophet Joseph made when he was criticized in 1834 for "glaring errors" in a published revelation. He replied that shades of meaning or literary mechanics were not as important as the general message: "We did not think so much of orthography [spelling], or the manner, as we did the subject matter, as the word of God means what it says."[43]

"The Most Correct Book"

Even before the 1981 edition was published, a careful student of the original manuscript and printer's copy said, "A great value of these early manuscripts is that for the most part they substantiate the correctness of the present Book of Mormon text—fully 99.9% of the text is published correctly."[44]

Notwithstanding the fact that this sacred Nephite witness of Jesus Christ already towers far above many of the other scriptures in the integrity of its text, still the Church has endeavored to make it even more correct, as is shown by the following statement about the 1981 edition: "Some minor errors in the text have been perpetuated in past editions of the Book of Mormon. This edition contains corrections that seem appropriate to bring the material into conformity with prepublication manuscripts and early editions edited by the Prophet Joseph Smith."[45] The changes and corrections are not only correct but appropriate.[46]

When Joseph Smith said "the Book of Mormon was the most correct of any book on earth," it seems evident that he was not talking about grammar,[47] punctuation, or spelling. He was referring to the clarity and depth of doctrine, to the mission and message of the book, to the spirit of inspiration that it fosters, to the divine desire that it sparks in the soul to make the "mighty change," and to the abiding love of the Lord that it brings into our hearts. All of these correct things help make the Book of Mormon just exactly what the Prophet said it was: "The most correct of any book on earth, and the keystone of our religion, and a man would get nearer to God by abiding by its precepts, than by any other book."[48]

The Lord himself has similarly testified with a solemn oath—"And he [Joseph] has translated the book, even that part which I have commanded him, and as your Lord and your God liveth it is true" (D&C 17:6).

Notes

1. Wentworth Letter, *Times and Seasons* 3 (1 March 1842): 707.

2. Paul R. Cheesman, *The Keystone of Mormonism* (Salt Lake City: Deseret Book Co., 1973), pp. 55-56, lists Martin Harris, Emma Smith, Samuel Smith, Reuben Hale, Oliver Cowdery, David Whitmer, John Whitmer, and Christian Whitmer as one time or another scribes.

3. By 14 June 1828, at least 116 manuscript pages had been completed with the help of Martin Harris, Emma Smith, and Reuben Hale as scribes. These pages were subsequently lost and never recovered. See Joseph Smith, *History of the Church of Jesus Christ of Latter-day Saints*, ed. B. H. Roberts, 2d ed., 7 vols. (Salt Lake City: Deseret Book Co., 1948-51), 4:461, 537; cited hereafter as *HC*.

4. Joseph Smith III, "Last Testimony of Sister Emma," *The Saints' Herald* 26 (1 October 1879): 290.

5. *Messenger and Advocate* 1 (1834): 14.

6. There are a total of 144 pages of original manuscript extant, plus eight readable sheets and about 50 fragments of pages; Oliver Cowdery's handwriting has been identified on 124 pages (Cheesman, p. 64).

7. It was decided "First, that Oliver Cowdery should transcribe the whole manuscript. Second, that he should take but one copy at a time to the office, so that if one copy should get destroyed, there would still be a copy remaining. Third, that in going to and from the office, he should always have a guard to attend him, for the purpose of protecting the manuscript. Fourth, that a guard should be kept constantly on the watch, both night and day, about the house, to protect the manuscript from malicious persons." (Preston Nibley, *Joseph Smith, the Prophet* [Salt Lake City: Deseret News Press, 1946], p. 93).

8. Quoted in Wilford C. Wood, *Joseph Smith Begins His Work* (Salt Lake City: Wilford C. Wood, 1958), introductory pages.

9. Ibid. According to Gilbert, Joseph was in Grandin's shop on only one occasion for fifteen to twenty minutes.

10. Compare the following: Stanley R. Larson, "A Study of Some Textual Variations in the Book of Mormon Comparing the Original and the Printer's Manuscripts and the 1830, the 1837 and the 1840 Editions" (Master's thesis, Brigham Young University, 1974); Jeffrey R. Holland, "An Analysis of Selected Changes in Major Editions of the Book of Mormon—1830-1920" (Master's thesis, Brigham Young University, 1966); *The Book of Mormon Critical Text: A Tool for Scholarly Reference*, vols. 1 and 2 [1 Nephi-Alma] (Provo, Utah: Foundation for Ancient Research and Mormon Studies, 1984, 1986).

11. *HC* 4:461, 28 November 1941.

12. *HC* 1:363.

13. *HC* 2:390, 474, 3:26.

14. By now, Oliver Cowdery had been excommunicated and had taken the printer's manuscript with him.

15. *HC* 4:494.

16. "Dr. Talmage was a stickler for good English. . . . He knew as well as anyone the imperfections of the literary dress of the First Edition of the Nephite record and took a prominent part in correcting many of them in a later edition of the work." Sidney B. Sperry, *Problems of the Book of Mormon* (Salt Lake City: Bookcraft, 1964), p. 190.

17. Research before 1981 includes the following: Master's theses by Jeffrey R. Holland and Stanley R. Larson (see note 10); Richard P. Howard, *Restoration Scriptures: A Study of Their Textual Development* (Independence, Mo.: Herald Publishing House, 1969); Hugh G. Stocks, "The Book of Mormon, 1830-1879: A Publishing History" (Master's thesis, Graduate School of Library and Information Science, UCLA, 1979). Other studies and articles before and after the 1981 edition include: James Wardle, *Selected Changes in the Book of Mormon* (Salt Lake City: Modern Microfilms, 1963); Sperry, *Problems of the Book of Mormon*; Janet Jenson, "Variations between Copies of the First Edition of the Book of Mormon," *BYU Studies* 13 (Winter 1973): 214-22; Stan Larson, "Changes in Early Texts of the Book of Mormon," *Ensign*, September 1976, pp. 77-82; "Early Book of Mormon Text: Textual Changes to the Book of Mormon in 1837 and 1840," *Sunstone* 1 (Fall 1976): 44-55; "Textual Variants in Book of Mormon Manuscripts," *Dialogue: A Journal of Mormon Thought*, 10 (Autumn 1977): 8-30; "Conjectural Emendation and the Text of the Book of Mormon," *BYU Studies* 18 (Summer 1978): 563-69; George A. Horton, Jr., "Changes in the Book of Mormon and How to Handle Them," *A Symposium on the Book of Mormon* (Salt Lake City: The Church of Jesus Christ of Latter-day Saints, 1982), pp. 36-39; "Understanding Textual Changes in the Book of Mormon," *Ensign,* December 1983, 24-28; Hugh G. Stocks, "The Book of Mormon in English, 1870-1920: A Publishing History and Analytical Bibliography," (Ph.D. diss., University of California at Los Angeles, 1986); F.A.R.M.S. staff, *The Book of Mormon Critical Text: A Tool for Scholarly Reference*, 3 vols. (Provo, Utah: Foundation for Ancient Research and Mormon Studies, 1984-87); Lamoni Call, *2000 Changes in the Book of Mormon* (Salt Lake City: Modern Microfilm Co., n.d.); Jerald and Sandra Tanner, *3,913 Changes in the Book of Mormon* (Salt Lake City: Modern Microfilm Co., n.d.).

18. Sir Frederic Kenyon, *Our Bible and the Ancient Manuscripts* (New York: Harper & Brothers, 1958), Appendix II.

19. Ibid.

20. Noah Webster, *An American Dictionary of the English Language*, 2 vols. (New York: S. Converse, 1828), vol. 1, introduction.

21. There was at least one more available, with variant spellings: H. J. Todd's *[Samuel] Johnson's and [John] Walker's English Dictionaries, Combined*, ed. J. E. Worchester [Cambridge, 1927].

22. Elinore Hughes Partridge, "Nineteenth-Century Spelling: The Rules and the Writers," *Ensign*, August 1975, pp. 79-80.

23. Ibid., p. 76.

24. Middle English has apparently been retained in the Book of Mormon in passages in which Deity or a heavenly messenger is speaking, or for the sake of euphony.

25. Stanley R. Larson, "Scribal Scars on the Sacred Scriptures," A Symposium on the Gospels, Brigham Young University, 22 February 1985, p. 5; F.A.R.M.S. staff, *The Book of Mormon Critical Text: A Tool for Scholarly Reference*, 3 vols.

26. The word *yea* instead of *year* appeared in the printer's copy and all editions until 1841. A "secondary conflation" of "year, yea" has continued from 1849 to the present, though this is clearly an error.

27. Both of the manuscripts for this verse are extant. Larson, "A Study of Some Textual Variations," p. 155.

28. An exception was the RLDS edition which followed the 1840 third edition; but since the missing words were not in that edition, it was evident that the RLDS made use of the printer's manuscript also. See "Modern Pedigree of the Book of Mormon" in *The Book of Mormon Critical Text*, p. viii.

29. There were over two thousand revisions marked in the printer's copy in preparation for the 1837 edition, but this was not one of them. Howard, *Restoration Scriptures*, p. 41.

30. The 1981 edition did not restore the original word.

31. Larson, Master's thesis, p. 276.

32. Ibid., p. 82.

33. Ibid., pp. 229-30. However, there is always the remote possibility that the existing Malachi text could have been changed by biblical scribes in an attempt to make the genders agree.

34. "Proposed Changes in the Book of Mormon," no author given, unpublished manuscript, 1980, p. 25. [Used by the Scriptures Publication Committee of the Church.]

35. Howard, *Restoration Scriptures*, pp. 41-42.

36. Counting was done without a calculator and is subject to error.

37. Of the 225 acknowledged changes in the 1981 edition, 132 add *ly* to the word *exceeding.*

38. A comparison of the current text of the King James Version with the 1828 text (e.g., the H. & E. Phinney edition, which the Prophet used in the work of the Joseph Smith Translation) reveals such word changes as *of* to *from, which* to *where, am* to *is, be* to *are, to* to *unto,* and *aught* to *ought* (the last, for example, is in Matthew 5:23 and Mark 11:25).

39. *Gesenius' Hebrew and Chaldee Lexicon*, trans. Samuel Prideaux Tregelles (Grand Rapids, Mich.: Wm. B. Eerdmans Publishing Company, 1980), pp. 221-22.

40. Refer to the last paragraph of John H. Gilbert's statement as in note 9.

41. Sperry, *Problems of the Book of Mormon,* p. 203. See, however, Hugh Nibley, *Since Cumorah: The Book of Mormon in the Modern World* (Salt Lake City: Deseret Book Co., 1967), p. 7.

42. Jerald and Sandra Tanner, *The Changing World of Mormonism* (Chicago: Moody Press, 1980), p. 131.

43. Letter to William Edward, et al., 30 March 1834, from Oliver Cowdery's letter book, pp. 30-36, quoted in Dean Jessee, *Journal of Mormon History* 3 (1976): 28-29.

44. Stanley R. Larson, "Textual Variants in Book of Mormon Manuscripts," *Dialogue*, 10 (August 1977): 8.

45. *The Book of Mormon* (Salt Lake City: The Church of Jesus Christ of Latter-day Saints, 1981), introductory pages.

46. Horton, "Changes in the Book of Mormon and How to Handle Them," pp. 36-39.

47. Part of the definition for the word *correct* from Webster's *American Dictionary of the English Language* is as follows: "Literally, set right; conformable to truth, rectitude or propriety, or conformable to a just standard; not faulty; free from error. . . . Correct manners correspond with the rules of morality and received notions of decorum. Correct principles coincide with the truth."

48. *HC* 4:461.

“‘Lest Ye Become As the Nephites of Old’” 15

Susan Black

In 1831 the Lord assured his Saints that it was the will of the Father to give unto those who seek the “riches of eternity.” In addition, he confirmed that “the riches of the earth are mine to give; but beware of pride, lest ye become as the Nephites of old” (D&C 38:39).

The abundance of the earth has been promised to the obedient followers of Christ since the time of Abraham (Genesis 26:3-5), and this promise has continued on down to Lehi (2 Nephi 1:9), Joseph Smith,[1] and even to the obedient of our present day.[2]

In our day “the Lord has blessed us as a people with a prosperity unequaled in times past.”[3] Today, many members of The Church of Jesus Christ of Latter-day Saints are prospering temporally. Necessities and even luxuries in some cases abound with respect to good food, fine clothing, precious jewelry, comfortable homes, and much more. Today’s members have been called the “modern Nephites”[4] because they, like the Nephites of old, are constantly challenged with the temptation of a damning pride which arises so readily from abundant temporal prosperity.

Let us heed the ancient and modern prophets and

Susan Black is assistant professor of Church History and Doctrine at BYU.

search the Nephite records to discover what they teach about the relationship between temporal prosperity and spiritual life or death.

God Would Give Prosperity to All

From the beginning, the Lord taught the Nephites that he generously bestows temporal prosperity on the just and even the unjust (Jarom 1:8; Mosiah 11:8; 2 Nephi 1:9). He also taught the Nephites that when they began to be obedient to his commandments, they would begin to prosper both spiritually and temporally (Alma 1:29). Thus this strong relationship between obedience and temporal and spiritual prosperity was taught to the Nephites from the beginning. The promise was spiritual and temporal prosperity for obedience; however, if disobedience occurred there was a threat of destruction (2 Nephi 1:9-13; Jarom 1: 9; Ether 2:10).[5]

This blessing and its companion curse are recorded and demonstrated repeatedly during the centuries of Nephite history. The Nephites would repent and become more spiritual; then within a short time they would begin to increase in riches as had been promised (Jarom 1:9). The curse was also repeatedly witnessed as the Nephites became more wicked, refused to keep the commandments, and ultimately were destroyed (Mormon 3:9 through chapter 6).

The ancient Nephite experience can solve several puzzling questions about the dilemma of prosperity. They will guide our study of prosperity in the Book of Mormon.

Is there a promise of temporal prosperity as well as spiritual prosperity for obedience? If so, is it granted to the entire church or only to individuals within the church? Is this promise peculiar to the Nephites, or does it extend to all in our day?

From the time of Adam, God has invited man to "subdue" the earth and to "have dominion" over its creatures (Genesis 1:28). He has assured us that he has "made the earth rich" (D&C 38:17) for the "benefit and the use of man . . . and it pleaseth God that he hath given all these things unto man" (D&C 59:18, 20). Moreover, he desires to extend the material blessings of the earth to both poor and rich, for "all flesh is mine, and I am no respecter of persons" (D&C 38:16). For "he maketh his sun to rise on the evil and on the good, and sendeth rain on the just and on the unjust" (Matthew 5:45).

The temporal blessings of the earth are extended by God to all his children. We see throughout the Book of Mormon that even those who rebelled against him generally enjoyed possessions of gold and other material luxuries (3 Nephi 8). Despite their prolonged wickedness, God continued to extend his hand to them by sending both physical and spiritual nourishment in the form of love and hope (Helaman 7:4-5). These gifts are still extended by a loving Father, regardless of our righteousness.

In addition, there have always been promises of temporal blessing extended in extra measure to the righteous, the obedient, the repentant. Abraham and his descendants were given a "land of promise" (see Genesis 12:7). Similarly Lehi (1 Nephi 2:20), the brother of Jared (Ether 2:8), and the latter-day Church (D&C 38:18) were given choice lands.

The promised lands were abounding in milk and honey (D&C 18:8) and other temporal riches (1 Nephi 18:25). These lands were bestowed initially because of the bounty of God and the worthiness of one or a few great souls. The descendants of these few could continue to enjoy the "promised land" unless they reached a "fulness of iniquity" (Ether 2:9-10).[6]

The first set of temporal riches promised to Adam's posterity were given without regard to individual righteousness. The second set of temporal riches, illustrated by the patriarchal inheritances of Abraham and Lehi, were given because of the worthiness of a forebear. In both the Adamic and the patriarchal promises there existed a basis for humility because those who received the temporal gifts had not personally earned them but received them because of the worthiness and love of another (e.g., Christ, Abraham, Lehi).

The third set of temporal gifts consisted of the blessings of prosperity that came in accordance with the Lord's specific decree, "Inasmuch as ye shall keep my commandments, ye shall prosper" (1 Nephi 2:20).[7] This promise of spiritual and temporal wealth, extended to both Lehi and his seed (1 Nephi 4:14), was fulfilled many times among Lehi's posterity. For example, when Nephi and his family first separated themselves from the threatening Lamanites, they were obedient to the law of Moses and did "prosper exceedingly." This prosperity included reaping in abundance, working with precious ores, and building shelters, including a temple of "exceedingly fine" workmanship (2 Nephi 5:10-16).

Was the promise restricted to only the constantly righteous among the Nephites? No. Throughout the years, the Nephites increasingly hardened their hearts to the commandments and were inclined to prideful, selfish, and adulterous behavior (Jacob 2). However, the promise of prosperity continued with them. Were they being rewarded for unrighteousness? Not at all. Over these difficult years their kings and leaders (Jacob, Enos, and Jarom) were men of faith who preached with increasing harshness and ruled with strictness such that the law of Moses was generally observed. For many generations these increasingly reluctant but still ultimately obedient Nephites continued to prosper as promised by the prophets. They "became exceedingly rich in gold, and in silver, and in precious things" and were not overcome in battle (Jarom 1:3-8).

However, after approximately three hundred years, even the leaders began to falter. One leader described himself as "a wicked man" (Omni 1:2). At this time many people willfully rejected the prophets and were eventually destroyed as had been promised (Omni). However, the righteous residue was preserved, a result which also accorded with a promise (Omni 1:7; Mosiah 2:22; Mosiah 2:4).

The blessings of prosperity were not limited to the constantly obedient like those who first joined with Nephi, but also included those who struggled with righteousness —those stiff-necked Saints who readily fell into divers sins but were eventually repentant. However, these wavering Saints seemed to need unusually harsh and plain words from their righteous leaders. They required "mighty men in the faith" (Jarom 1:7) who taught diligently, "continually stirring them up unto repentance" (Jarom 1:12). By listening, the repentant were spared speedy destruction (Enos 1:23). Once again they "multiplied exceedingly . . . and became exceedingly rich in gold, and in silver, and in precious things, . . . in buildings . . . and all preparations for war" (Jarom 1:8).

But there were a few who would not obey, no matter how powerful the warnings or how strict the laws. And yet the hardness of their hearts, the deafness of their ears, the blindness of their minds, and the stiffness of their necks were not automatic signals to God to destroy them instantly. Rather, these circumstances became occasion for greater diligence by prophets, priests, and teachers (Jarom 1:3). These servants showed them patience and long-suffering beyond ordinary understanding. Yet even they stood amazed at the Lord's patience with the most resolutely wicked. In awe they wrote, "God is exceedingly merciful unto them" (Jarom 1:3).

However, when all ministrations in extended long-suffering yielded only continued rejection, then the few who totally refused to repent finally lost the promise of being preserved from destruction. According to the second promise, they were destroyed (Omni 1:5). In contrast, the righteous residue prospered (Omni 1:7; Mosiah 2:22; Mosiah 2:41).

It is clear that the consequences of disobedience were restricted to those who knowingly rejected the word of God and refused to obey it.[8] Is this a message for our day? Does the Nephite promise of prosperity to the obedient apply to the members of the Church today? President Spencer W. Kimball has answered this query by reminding us that the Lord has promised us "the fulness of the earth . . . upon condition that we unreservedly obey his commands."[9]

Why would the Lord make temporal prosperity a result of obedience if it can be so destructive? Is not spiritual prosperity sufficient as a reward for righteousness?

Whenever the prophets and teachers of the Book of Mormon received a gift, temporal or spiritual, their immediate, driving impulse was to share it with others (Mosiah 14-21; 4 Nephi 1:7). For example, after receiving revelations from the Lord, Lehi left his wealth to share the riches of eternity with his posterity.[10] Alma, a priest in the court of a wealthy king, after being converted, risked his life to lead and direct his fellowmen (Mosiah 17:2-3; 18:3). The wealth of Nephi, Alma, Benjamin, Mosiah and other righteous leaders was devoted to the welfare of their people.

Why were they so willing to share? It was because they were stewards and not owners of wealth and had learned, as President Kimball expressed it, to "hold all their possessions in trust, subject to the call of the Lord."[11]

The first step to righteous prosperity is obedience. The second step is consecration or true charity with a hope to be as the Lord himself is (3 Nephi 27:27). Prosperity can become a means of achieving this. Speaking of our unequaled prosperity, President Kimball wrote, "Forgotten is the fact that our assignment is to use these many resources in our families and quorums to build up the kingdom of God—to further the missionary effort and the genealogical and temple work; to bless others in every way, that they may also be fruitful."[12]

Just as obedience to the Word of Wisdom leads to increased physical strength (D&C 89:20), so obedience to gospel commandments leads to an increased desire to share with and to love our neighbors.[13] As we begin to master obedience, we become prosperous and are given increased strength and challenges to master the law of consecration—the law of charity. The lesson of charity is always present the moment that we are obedient enough to be called a Saint "through the atonement of Christ the Lord, and [become] as a child, submissive, meek, humble, patient, full of love" (Mosiah 3:19). As we learn to be full of love, we do "not send away any who [are] naked, or . . . hungry, or . . . athirst, . . . having no respect to persons as to those who [stand] in need" (Alma 1:30).

Why is the blessing of prosperity so significant to the obedient Saint? It is significant because it provides an opportunity to learn the more challenging law of consecration, the law of true charity, the role of steward in the Lord's vineyard (Moroni 7:46-47). Temporal prosperity provides us with a source of great joy as we use it to further the Lord's purpose while serving as his trusted stewards.

The question remains, why give the Saints prosperity if it causes so many to fail? President Kimball prayed, "Bless all people, our Father, that they may prosper, but not more than their faith can stand . . . that they may not be surfeited with . . . wealth which would bring them to worship false gods."[14]

> And after ye have obtained a hope in Christ ye shall obtain riches, if ye seek them; and ye will seek them for the intent to do good—to clothe the naked, and to feed the hungry, and to liberate the captive, and administer relief to the sick and the afflicted (Jacob 2:19).

The risk of pride, envy, lying, stealing, and idleness is great for the prosperous and appears to increase with the level of riches. However, we must learn to give by giving, to consecrate by consecrating, and to succor by succoring. However little the riches may be that follow obedience, our first challenge is to admit that we are rich enough to share, to practice charity. If we cannot admit that, we are in the negative sense rich enough to become blind to our spiritual and moral obligations.[15]

Given our unsurpassed modern prosperity, how can we avoid the destructive "Curse of the Nephites" and their fatal pride?

The key to avoiding dangerous pride in prosperity is to "seek . . . the kingdom of God; and all these things shall be added unto you" (Luke 12:31; Jacob 2:18).

First, we are to learn the lesson of King Benjamin, who served "with all the might, mind and strength which the Lord [had] granted unto [him]" (Mosiah 2:11), recognizing that "when ye are in the service of your fellow beings ye are only in the service of your God" (Mosiah 2:17).

Second, we are to learn President Kimball's lesson of the idolatry that lurks in every object—every temporal excuse for not having families, for not giving generously to the church and kingdom of God in means, time, and talents. We can be quick to see the false gods of power, wealth and influence in each of our lives. Moreover, when we see the idolatry we can confess it, repent of it, and most important, replace it with true consecration.

Third, we are to learn the lesson of stewardship. We

must learn that all we have is the Lord's. A portion may be assigned to us to care for, to nurture, or to further the Lord's purposes. But it is not ours to "own."

Why do the righteous often fail to receive the promised result of obedience–temporal prosperity? Why do the wicked often receive great temporal prosperity?

Many struggling Saints who feel that they have not received the promised prosperity err in this assumption. They are slow to concede their own wealth because their wants are so limitless.[16] Alma's followers recognized great prosperity when they escaped from slavery with few material goods (Mosiah 24:23-25; 25:24). Nephi's followers felt that they prospered when they could earn a basic living, live in some degree of safety, and have means to build a temple (2 Nephi 5:11-16). By these standards it appears that every community of modern Saints prospers.

Recognition that even the most meager of temporal possessions, the widow's mite, makes us rich enough to render gifts to God, to our families, and to our neighbors is what righteous Nephites knew. When this gift of having "eyes to see" is absent, no amount of earthly wealth is enough to exercise true charity, to consecrate all to the service of the Lord. Righteous Nephites recognized the temporal gifts which surrounded them, and seemed to delight in laboring to accumulate great riches for service in God's kingdom. As an example, the righteous recognized the land as the means to construct supplies of food, clothing, and shelter. They recognized the presence of ore and lumber as the means to build monuments to their God (2 Nephi 5:17; see the preceding six verses).

These perceptions were in direct contrast with the views of the wicked. With few exceptions, the wicked were idle and had inclinations to exploit the labors of others. Theft, murder for gain, subtle tactics of flattery, deceit, and unlawful taxation were the means most often employed by the wicked. However, the wicked sometimes used methods that were also used by the Saints to gain riches, such as cooperative efforts, increase of skilled laborers, and industry (Alma 30:17).[17]

It appears that the courses pursued by the wicked were not beneficial over the years and generations recorded in the Book of Mormon. The sacrifice-oriented community of Nephites grew stronger while the exploitive-parasitic community became fragmented (4 Nephi). Why was this the result? When the wicked work in secret societies (e.g., the Gadianton robbers), they multiply riches faster than those who work alone. However, they work together not for love of God or man but from a fear precipitated by secret oaths (Helaman 6:26, 29). These societies, organized to get gain at any cost, can be powerful and even transgenerational. But like carnivorous beasts, the secret societies can survive only when those who labor to accumulate wealth prey on those who permit predations.

Perhaps one of the most intriguing predations of the wicked was the successful adaptation of the prosperity principle of commerce (Mosiah 24:6). The wicked saw commerce as a means of having the benefits of plunder without costly warfare. For instance, the apostate Nephites taught the Lamanites to be literate and keep records in order to enhance their skills and strategies of trade, to be cunning and wise as to the wisdom of the world, and to plunder those outside their group through commerce while being friendly within their group (Mosiah 24:5-7). Elsewhere, apostate mentors avoided teaching of God, prophets, or the laws, thus assuring a belief that "whatsoever a man did was no crime" (Alma 30:17). Apparently, the only ethic they learned was the lesson of honor among thieves. Similarly, the robbers of Gadianton found that they could rob effectively without physical assault, and thus they became skilled in trafficking "in all manner of traffic," laying up "in abundance" gold and silver (4 Nephi 1:46). However, the end results of this sort of rapacious trade were increased exploitations that fed the fires of pride, hatred, and strife, resulting in extinction of families, communities, and nations (Mormon 1-8).

Is the prosperity challenge of greater urgency in our generation than among the Nephite generations?

Since the time of Joseph Smith, latter-day prophets have warned us of pride.[18] President Kimball taught that the willingness of many today to give all for things, power, prestige, and lustful sensation is unequalled in history and constitutes the modern manifestation of idolatry. "We fear that never in the history of the world have there ever been so many more people bowing to the god of lust than there were bowing to golden calves. . . . This idolatry, so closely associated with the destruction of mind and body, could inundate the world."[19]

When the prophet Mormon compiled records of the Nephites, he wrote, "Behold, the pride of this nation, or the people of the Nephites, hath proven their destruction except they should repent" (Moroni 8:27).

Moroni speaks further to us:

> Behold, I speak unto you as if ye were present, and yet ye are not. But behold, Jesus Christ hath shown you unto me, and I know your doing.
>
> And I know that ye do walk in the pride of your hearts; and there are none save a few only who do not lift themselves up in the pride of their hearts, unto the wearing of fine apparel, unto envying, and strifes, and malice, and persecutions, and all manner of iniquities; and your churches, yea, even every one, have become polluted because of the pride of your hearts.
>
> For behold, ye do love money, and your substance, and your fine apparel, and the adorning of your churches, more than ye love the poor and the needy, the sick and the afflicted.
>
> Yea, why do ye build up your secret abominations to get gain, and cause that widows should mourn. . . ? (Mormon 8:35-37, 40).

Moroni is talking to us! Let each of us consider whether we have adopted idol worship and have allowed the love of money, substance, fine apparel, lust, and vain ambition to become our false gods. Today is a day of unequalled prosperity, deadly pride, flagrant idolatry, and widespread lack of charity. Is it not time to examine the Nephite struggle with prosperity?

Should righteous Church members seek to obtain temporal riches? How essential is it to our salvation to seek and accrue riches?

The heart acts as a barometer registering the effect of temporal riches on each Saint. For in the heart, "Ye cannot serve God and Mammon" (3 Nephi 13:24). "For where your treasure is, there will your heart be also" (3 Nephi 13:21). The commandment is to "seek ye first the kingdom of God and his righteousness, and all these things shall be added unto you" (3 Nephi 13:33).

If we love God with all our heart, mind, might, and strength, then we have no room to serve mammon. As a consequence of total consecration we experience prosperity, both spiritual and temporal. For example, giving tithing opens "the windows of heaven" (Malachi 3:10) to a whole panoply of temporal blessings.[20] The Word of Wisdom "[shows] forth the order and will of God in the temporal salvation of all saints in the last days" (D&C 89:2). In essence, it could be said that all commandments include a promise of prosperity.

Therefore, "after ye have obtained a hope in Christ ye shall obtain riches, if ye seek them; and ye will seek them for the intent to do good" (Jacob 2:19).

Why would the Saints seek prosperity through obedience to commandments? One clear answer is to serve, to enrich, and to succor the lives of others.

What should the righteous "prosperous" member do with his riches?

Righteous Saints are to be charitable, for "a man being evil cannot do that which is good" (Moroni 7:10). They are to use their wealth to advance the kingdom of God on earth. They are to remember that they are stewards and not prideful owners. They seek direction from the owner of their riches and his leaders, and make their possessions "subject to the call of the Lord through his authorized servants."[21] They should give gladly from their hearts, for "except [a man] shall do it with real intent it profiteth him nothing" (Moroni 7:6).

Conclusion

The Book of Mormon teaches, from the vantage point of a thousand years' experience, that the Lord willingly extends the riches of the earth to his obedient servants. These temporal and spiritual riches are a fulfillment of the oft-repeated theme, "Keep the commandments and prosper." The prosperous Saint directs his stewardship by avoiding the dangers of pride and embezzled ownership, thus escaping destruction. He charitably gives of his stewardship in consecrated joy. Therefore, the true Saint will not "become as the [rich] Nephites of old" (D&C 38:39).

Notes

1. "I prophesied that the Saints would continue to suffer much affliction and would be driven to the Rocky Mountains. . . . [They will make] settlements and build cities and . . . become a mighty people in the midst of the Rocky Mountains." Joseph Smith, *History of The Church of Jesus Christ of Latter-day Saints,* ed. B. H. Roberts, 2d ed. rev., 7 vols. (Salt Lake City: Deseret Book Co., 1973), 5:85.

2. In a speech given 8 March 1975, President Spencer W. Kimball said, at the Buenos Aires Area Conference, "I often pray that the Lord will bless the people with prosperity. . . ." Edward L. Kimball, ed., *The Teachings of Spencer W. Kimball* (Salt Lake City: Bookcraft, 1982), p. 354. Hereafter cited as *Kimball.*

3. Spencer W. Kimball, "The False Gods We Worship," *Ensign,* June 1976, p. 4.

4. Hugh Nibley, *Since Cumorah: The Book of Mormon in the Modern World* (Salt Lake City: Deseret Book Company, 1967), p. 390.

5. Of the twenty-one verses that link keeping the commandments with prosperity, eight verses include, verbatim, the Jaredite curse: "Wherefore he that doth possess [this land] shall serve God or shall be swept off" (Ether 2:10).

6. The Book of Mormon describes at least four methods used to pass knowledge from one generation to another in order to keep the promise we have been considering foremost in the minds of Lehi's posterity:

> 1. The Lord declared this promise directly to the prophets of each generation who in turn wrote it down as scripture (e.g., Lehi [2 Nephi 1] and Nephi [1 Nephi 2]).
>
> 2. Fathers passed information on to their sons (e.g. Alma to Helaman [Alma 37:13] and Alma to Shiblon [Alma 38:17]).
>
> 3. The prophets disseminated this knowledge universally (e.g., King Benjamin reiterated the Lord's promises to his people who consisted of Lehi's descendants as well as the descendants of Mulek [Mosiah 1:7]).
>
> 4. The promises were reviewed intermittently by the population as they were found written on the metal plates (Jarom 1:9; Omni 1:6; Alma 9:13).

7. The word "prosperity" is mentioned nine times in the Book of Mormon. Four of these references are associated with growth in the Church, meaning that men and women had given heed to the word of God and had joined themselves to the Church (Helaman 3:25), with no direct or indirect inference to secular prosperity. Five times "prosperity" refers to both land and riches in combination. When we include the word "prosper," fifty-four verses may be added to the list. Of these verses, thirty-eight link "prosper" with the land, while eight link "prosperity" to

riches. Of the sixty-seven verses that mention either "prosper" or "prosperity" in the Book of Mormon, fifty-one refer to land and connect land with riches.

8. The Lamanites who in ignorance did not obey the law of Moses were spared final destruction (2 Nephi 4:3-7). Only those Lamanites who were taught and fully understood the gospel message received the full consequences of their obedience or disobedience (2 Nephi 4:6; see also Helaman 13-15 regarding Samuel the Lamanite).

9. Spencer W. Kimball, "When Is One Rich?" *Salt Lake Tribune-Telegram*, 28 May 1949; quoted in *Kimball*, p. 358.

10. "Lehi was very rich, and he was a trader, for his wealth was in the form of 'all manner of precious things' such as had to be brought from many places." Hugh Nibley, *Lehi in the Desert and The World of the Jaredites* (Salt Lake City: Bookcraft, 1952), p. 36. See also 1 Nephi 2:4.

11. "When Is One Rich?" *Kimball*, p. 358.

12. See also Spencer W. Kimball, "The False Gods We Worship," *Ensign*, June 1976, p. 4; also in *Kimball*, p. 357.

13. Samson's increased physical strength stemmed from obedience. His strength was not in itself righteous or evil but gave its possessor means to be more evil or more righteous. Also, Mormon was blessed with a large physical stature just as Samson was (Judges 13:24-16:30; Mormon 2:1). One chose to use his strength to magnify his service to God. The other chose to use his to advance selfish motives.

14. Dedicatory prayer for the Washington, D.C., Temple, 19 November 1974; *Kimball*, p. 354.

15. *Kimball*, p. 356.

16. "When Is One Rich?" *Kimball*, p. 356.

17. The righteous were very adept in finding mutual benefit from taking the fruits of their industry to "buy and sell and traffic one with another, that they might get gain" (Ether 10:22). Indeed, it was said of the righteous Jaredites under King Lib that "never could be a people more blessed than were they, and more prospered by the hand of the Lord" (Ether 10:28).

18. *Teachings of the Prophet Joseph Smith,* comp. Joseph Fielding Smith, (Salt Lake City: Deseret Book Company, 1938), p. 137.

19. "'Why Call Me Lord, Lord, and Do Not the Things Which I Say?'" *Ensign*, May 1975, p. 7; also in *Kimball*, p. 280.

20. James E. Faust, "The Responsibility for Welfare Rests with Me and My Family," *Ensign*, May 1986, p. 21.

21. "When Is One Rich?" *Kimball*, p. 358.

Subject Index

— A —

Aaronic Priesthood, 92
Abinadi, 53, 105–6, 123, 155
  prophecies concerning Christ, 29, 59–60, 62
Abinadom, 103
Abraham, 24, 65, 86, 256, 258
Accountability, 3, 20
Adair, James, *The History of the American Indians,* 211
Adam, 24, 53, 55, 57, 60, 61, 100, 187, 257, 258
  fall of, 34, 38–39, 42, 46, 57, 77–78, 78–80, 82, 88
  native to North America, 231–32
Adena Indians, 181
Africa, 188, 209, 220
  East, 191
  North, 194
  West, 180, 197, 228
Agire, Imanol, 193
Agriculture, 166–72
Ahab (king), 130, 132
Alabama, 222
Alaska, 224, 225–31
Alberta, Canada, 219
Albright, W. F., 164, 180
Aldan River, 227
Aleut-Eskimos, 222–24
Aleuts, 221, 233
Alexandria, library at, 192, 198
Algonkin Indians, 180
Algonquin Indians, 221
Allegory of Zenos, 121
Alma the Elder, 59, 130, 261, 263
  authority of, 123
  Church established by, 105–6, 112, 117, 124
  Melchizedek Priesthood held by, 106
  on love, 155, 156
  people persecuted, 41
Alma the Younger, 106–7
  confrontation with Zeezrom, 148
  conversion of, 42, 59, 130, 145, 147
  desire to preach gospel, 22–23, 26
  high priesthood exercised by, 123
  mission to Zoramites, 51–52
  on change of heart, 148–49
  on charity, 162
  on Christ, 74, 77
  on faith, 12–13, 88, 137, 139, 140–41, 144, 163
  on fall of Adam, 35–36
  on justification, 83
  on love, 153–54, 161
  on resurrection, 81
  on revelation through righteousness, 92
  on spirit world, 81–82
  on spiritual rebirth, 59, 88
Amaleki, 104
Amaron, 103
Amazon basin, 174
America, land of inheritance, 65
  land of promise, 85
  See also Jesus Christ, Nephite ministry
American archaeology, 164, 199–200
American Bureau of Ethnology, 195
American Indians, Hebrew and Semitic resemblances in, 210–13
  origins of, 164–236
American Museum of Natural History, 209
Ames, Oakes, 171
Ammon, 52
Ammon (son of Mosiah), 155, 159
  on faith, 138
  people of, 138
Ammonites, 156
Amphoras, 178–79
Amulek, confrontation with Zeezrom, 50–51, 56, 157
  on atonement, 36
  on faith, 139
  on resurrection, 81
Anatomy, comparative, 196
Angara River, 227
Angel, 14
  Alma visited by, 42, 59, 81
  King Benjamin visited by, 50, 55, 56, 122, 150
  Jacob visited by, 54, 95
  Joseph Smith visited by, 9
  three witnesses visited by, 10
Angels, 11, 87, 97, 139, 140
  Jacob visited by, 3

ministering of, 108
writers of Book of Mormon visited by, 3
Animals, 226, 228–29
Anointing, 133, 136
Anthropology, 164, 167, 168
Anti-Christs, 40, 51
Anti-Nephi-Lehies, 107, 155
Apathy, 103
Apostasy, 107, 108–9, 115, 117, 119
Apostles, 34, 96, 111, 124
Arabia, 191
Arabic language, 162
Arabs, 180
Archaeology, 189
American, 164, 199–200
Architecture, 176
Art, 176, 193–94
Art history, 199
Artifacts, 197–98, 206, 218, 227–29
Ashes, 133, 134, 135
Asia, 188, 208, 209, 220, 229, 232
Astronomy, 194, 198–99
Atlantic Ocean, migration across, 165, 176–81, 207, 208–9
Atonement, 30, 34–39, 58, 62, 74, 79–80, 82, 88, 94, 113, 146
Attitude, 22
Australia, 7, 172, 220
aborigines of, 182
Australoids, 220, 222
Authority, 101
divine investiture of, 60–66, 70
Axes, 176
Aztecs, 174, 198
library of, 198

— B —

Babylonian exile, 128–29, 131
Backman, Robert L., on priorities, 17–18
"To the Young Men of the Church," 18
Bahamas, 187
Balboa, Vasco Nunez de, 196
Baldwin, J. D., 208
Baptism, 57, 82, 87, 106, 113–14, 120
of fire and of the Holy Ghost, 108, 113–14, 148
Bar Kokhba, 178–79
Bar Kokhba Rebellion, 213
Basque language, 193
Bat Creek Stone, 212
Beans, 167–68
Beirne, D. R., 176
Belief, 13, 21
Benjamin (Nephite prophet-king), 1, 55, 56, 104–5, 261
address of, 122
angel's visit to, 50, 55, 56, 120, 122, 150
on atonement, 34–35
on Christ, 28–29, 50, 74, 77
on love, 153, 161
on service, 262
on taking name of Christ, 58
people of, 144-45
priests appointed by, 101–2
Berbers (tribe), 194
Berelekh (site), 227
Bering Strait, migration across, 207, 218–36
Bible, Book of Mormon a witness for, 4
comparison with Book of Mormon, 73–90
inerrancy and infallibility of, 85
King James Version, 240, 241, 243, 244, 248
LDS 1981 edition of, 240
plan of salvation not contained in, 78–79
spelling in, 241
witness of Christ, 8, 48
Bishops, 156
Bisschop, Eric de, 208
Black, Susan, 256
on Book of Mormon references to Christ, 33
Blood sacrifice, 111
Blood types, 196, 224, 232
Blue Fish Caves (site), 229
Book of Mormon, "Another Testament of Jesus Christ," 6–7
beginnings of Christianity in, 91–99
challenges of, 1–20
Christ-centered, 74–76
Church of Jesus Christ established in times of, 100–19
claims made by, 3–4
claims not made by, 5–6
comparison with Bible, 73–90
conversion to truths of, 15
corrections made in, 239–55
cycles in, 107, 110, 257
doctrines of salvation taught in, 73–89

early editions of, 240–50
1981 edition of, 240–41, 244, 249, 251
eight witnesses of, 10
fasting in, 127–33, 136
golden plates, 10, 14
inerrancy and infallibility of, 85–86
Joseph Smith a witness of, 9
kings in, 101–2
love in, 151–63
migrations recorded in, 207
physical proofs of, 16, 18
plan of salvation contained in, 78–79
principles of righteousness in, 2, 15, 20
reading of, 14, 33
resurrection taught in, 81
scribes during translation of, 237, 239
sealed portion, 125
small plates, 92
teachings on Christ, 21–43
teachings on faith, hope, and charity, 137–50
temples built in time of, 102, 107, 114, 122, 259, 263
testament of Christ, 47
testimony of, 10–15
textual revision of, 248–50
three witnesses of, 9–10
title page, 4, 47–48, 91
translation, 237–38, 242
typesetting, 238-39
wars in, 5
witness for Bible, 4
witness for Christ, 4, 32–33
written for us, 116–17
Book of Moses, 78
"Book of Vital Messages, A" (address), 18–20
Bottle gourds, 197, 209
Bountiful, land of, 108, 111
temple at, 124
Brass plates, 77, 97, 101, 102
Brendan (saint), 195
Brigham Young University, 17, 165
Britain, 176, 182
Bronze Age, 176
Brooks, Charles Wolcott, 190
Brother of Jared, 53, 64, 112, 141, 258
Brown, Gayle O., 151
Buret (site), 227
Burgess, Don, 174
Burial practices, 210
Burnt offerings, 134
Burton, Theodore M., on language of Book of Mormon, 54–55

— C —

Cactus, 178
Campbell, Joseph, *The Way of Animal Powers,* 194–95
Calico Hills excavation site, 219
California, 219, 222
Callis, Charles A., on testimony, 23–24
Canada, 226, 231
Canary Islands, 176–77
Cannon, George Q., on the sacrament, 125
Caribbean, 179
Carlson, Roy L., 219
Carter, George F., 164, 166, 196, 197
Carthage, library at, 192, 198
Cartouches, 180
Celebes, 194
Celestial kingdom, 57, 78
Celtics, 191
Central America, 180
Cerra Sota Man, 222
Charity, 146–48, 151, 162–63, 261–63, 266
Cheesman, Paul R., ix, 165, 206
Cherokees, 212
Cherry Tree Stadial, 226
Chichen Itza, 189, 209
Chickens, 170, 172–75, 196, 197
Children, 156
blessed by Christ, 160
Chile, 173, 208
Chimu culture, 191, 193
China, 171–73, 181, 191, 193, 195–97, 208, 211, 220–22, 227
Choctaw Indians, 200
Christianity, in Book of Mormon, 91–98
Christianson, James R., 218
Church of Christ, Issaquah, Washington, 75
Church of Jesus Christ, establishment in Book of Mormon times, 100–126
Church of Jesus Christ of Latter-day Saints, The, 88, 117–19, 164, 180
prosperity of members, 256
Clairborne, Robert, 222, 223
Class distinctions, 109, 115
Cochineal, 178
Cockfighting, 175
Coconut palms, 197

Coe, Truman, 68
Cohane, John Philip, *The Key,* 193
Coins, 189, 195–96, 198, 212–13
Columbus, Christopher, 165, 171, 180, 187, 190, 195–96, 198, 210
Commandments, 154
Compass bowls, 190
Compassion, of Christ, 41, 159–60
Confirmation, 120
Consecration, 261–63, 266
Contextual assimilation, 247
Conversion, 57
Cook, Warren, 189
Corianton, 83
Coriantum, 121
Corn, 166–68
  See also Maize
Cosmology, 194
Cotton, 168, 169, 197, 210
Covenants, 4, 58, 65, 103, 104, 119
Cowdery, Oliver, 239, 247, 249
  handwriting of, 244, 247
  on translation of Book of Mormon, 238
  spelling of, 241–43, 250
  witness of Book of Mormon, 9–10
Creation, 56–57, 58, 77
Crespi collection, 189
Cuba, 187
Cuicuilco, 222
Cumorah, 116
Cupisnique-Chavin culture, 191
Cwynar, Les C., 229
Cylinder seals, 164, 180
Cylinder stamps, 198
Cyprea Moneta, 180

— D —

Dahl, Larry E., 137
Davenport Tablets, 189
David (king), 129, 130, 132
Day-Jewish Journal, The, 213
Day of Atonement, 128, 134
de Santillana, Georgio, 194
Death, 81
  second, 240
Delmar, California, 219
Dental comparisons, 222–23, 224, 232
Desire, for righteousness, 144–45, 149
  for testimony of Book of Mormon, 13, 14
Destruction, at time of crucifixion, 110, 117, 118
  of the wicked, 257, 259–60
Dibble, Philo, 125
Dictionaries, 241–42, 243
Didache, 131
Diffusionists, 170, 181, 188, 198, 199–200, 207, 212–13
Diodorus Siculus, 195
Diseases, 197
Dittography, 241, 246
Diuktai (site), 227
Divine investiture of authority, 60–66, 70
Doctrine, 73–90, 112
Doctrine and Covenants, 78
Dogs, 196
Dominican Republic, 198
Doran, Edwin J., 208
Driver, Harold, 221
Dyes, 177

— E —

Earthquakes, 22
East Africa, 191
Easter Island, 169
Ecuador, 188, 208, 209
Eden, Garden of, 78
Edwards, Clinton R., 208–9
Egypt, 176, 181, 190, 191
Ekholm, Gordon F., 209
Elders, 106
Elias, 111
Elijah, 24, 132
Elijah (oratorio), 24
Elohim, 45–47, 57, 60–66
  Father of spirits, 55
  See also God
English language, spelling variations in, 241–44, 250
Enoch, 24, 61
  city of, 119
  on creation, 56
Enos, on wickedness of Nephites, 103
  prayer of, 147
Envy, 262
Epigraphic Society, 188, 189
Epigraphy, 192–93, 199
Eriksson, Leif, 210
Eskimos, 198, 221, 233
Eternal life, 16, 57
Ether, on hope, 143, 144
Ethnology, 166
Europe, 188
Euskera (Basque language), 193
Eve, 38, 78, 187
Exaltation, 16, 78

Eyrbyggja, 195
Ezekiel, 88

— F —

Faith, 4, 10–14, 18, 21, 22, 42–43, 57, 62–64, 66, 137–50, 158
Faith Precedes the Miracle (book), 20
Fall of Adam, 34, 38–39, 42, 46, 57, 77–78, 79–80, 82, 88
False prophets, 115
Families, 78, 261, 262
Famine, 22, 108
Farley, Gloria, 193
Fast offerings, 127
Fast Sunday, 127
Fasting, 59, 140
  in Book of Mormon and Bible, 127–36
Fathers, 59
Fear, dispelled by love, 152
Fell, Barry, 180, 190, 192, 195, 205
Ferguson, Thomas, 213
First Presidency, 241
First principles, 102
First Vision, 7, 45
Fladmark, Knut R., 225, 228, 230
Flood, 232
Flora, 226
Folsom men, 221
Ford, James A., 209
France, 170
Frost, Robert, 188–89, 200
Fulness of iniquity, 258

— G —

Gadianton, 244
Gadianton robbers, 108–9, 264
Gaelic language, 188
Garden of Eden, 78
Gathering of Israel, 46–47, 84–85, 88, 121
Genealogical work, 261
Genetics, 168
Gentiles, 4, 113
Germany, 170
Giddianhi, 143
Gideon (Nephite patriot), 40
Gift of the Holy Ghost, 57, 113, 119
Gifts of the Spirit, 130
Gilbert, John H., 243, 244, 250
  on punctuation in Book of Mormon, 238–39
Gimbutas, Marija, 195
Glacial periods, 225–31
Gladwin, Harold, 220, 221
God, 64
  condescension of, 50, 55
  faith, hope, and charity bestowed by, 147
  love of, 151–63
  nature of, 44–45
  testimony of, 11
  See also Elohim; Jehovah; Jesus Christ
Godhead, 7–8, 44–45, 65–66
Golden plates, 10, 14
Gordon, Cyrus H., 212
Gospel, 43
  knowledge of, 4
  world problems solved through, 22
Gourds, 197, 209
Grammar, in Book of Mormon, 238–40
Grandin, E. B., 238
Greek language, 240, 243
Greeks, 196
Griffin, James B., 220–21, 223–24
Gulf Stream, 177

— H —

Haiti, 187
Ham (son of Noah), 187
Hamlet's Mill (book), 194
Han dynasty, 172
Hansen, George H., 164
Haplography, 241, 246
Happiness, 115
Harris, Martin, 9–10, 238
Hauksbok, 195
Hawaii, 169
Hawthorne, Nathaniel, 242
Haywood, John, *Natural and Aboriginal History of Tennessee,* 213
Healing, 160
Heart, broken, 111
  change of, 22, 58, 144–45, 148
  purity of, 152
Heaven, 146
  patriarchal order in, 57
Hebrew language, 240, 247, 248
Hebrews, 210–11
Heine-Geldern, Robert, 209
Heirship, doctrine of, 78
Helaman (son of Alma), 42
  two thousand stripling warriors of, 141–42
Hestter, Joseph A., Jr., 220
Heyerdahl, Thor, 208

Hibiscus, 170, 171–72
Hindus, 174
History of the American Indians, The (book), 211
Hokkaido (site), 227
Holy Ghost, 58, 74, 105, 115, 117, 138, 149, 154
  baptism of fire and, 108, 113–14, 148
  distinct personage, 44
  gift of, 57, 113, 119
  hope through, 143, 145
  revelator, 47, 86, 87
  witness of Book of Mormon, 10–11
Homoeoarchton, 241, 246
Homoeoteleuton, 241, 245–46
Homophones, 247
Honore, Pierre, 210
Hookworms, 197
Hooton, Earnest, 220
Hope, 13, 14, 142–50
Hornell, J., 208
Horton, George A., Jr., 237
Howard, Edgar B., 223
Hrdlicka, Alex, 220–21, 224
Humility, 153, 161, 258
Hummingbirds, 171
Huntington, Oliver B., 125
Hymns, 50
Hypocrisy, 157
Hypocrites, 131

— I —

"I Stand All Amazed" (hymn), 50
Iberia, library of, 198
Ice ages, 225–31
Idleness, 262, 263
Idolatry, 105, 149–50, 262, 264–65
Imitation of Christ, The (book), 16–17
Incas, 195
Independent inventionists, 170, 207
India, 171, 181, 198, 209, 210
Indian Ocean, 180
Indians, American, 164–236
Indians, Southwestern, 166–68
Indonesia, 221
Inventionists, independent, 170, 207
Ireland, 195
Irving, W. N., 228
Irving, Washington, 242
Irwin, Constance, 209, 210
Isaiah, 86, 88, 97, 128
  messianic prophecies of, 38, 59
Isolationism, 188–89, 198, 199–200
Israel, 112
  gathering of, 84–85
  lost ten tribes of, 25–27, 30–32, 160, 211
  scattering and gathering of, 46–47, 88, 121
Israelites, fasting among, 127–35
  rebellion of, 91–92

— J —

Jackson, Kent P., 91
Jacob (Old Testament prophet), 24
Jacob (son of Lehi), 101, 143
  name of Christ revealed to, 54, 95
  on love of God, 152
  on scattering and gathering of Israel, 84
  record of, 2–3, 92
  teachings of, on Christ, 49–50, 88, 96
  warnings of, 102
James, book of, 84
  on asking in faith, 10
Japan, 174, 188, 190, 196, 197, 208, 210, 221, 227
Japheth, 187
Jaredites, 232–33
  ages of, 121
  migration of, 208
  prophets of, 56
  record of, 62
Jarom, 102, 103
  on faith, 138
Java, 209
Jeffreys, M. D. W., 179, 180
Jehovah, 24, 27, 45–47, 50–53, 55–56, 61
  premortal, 45, 50, 51
  See also God; Jesus Christ
Jeremiah, 88, 102
Jerusalem, 52, 128–29
  destruction prophesied, 93
Jesus Christ, 44, 45, 87, 249
  abundance promised to followers of, 256
  acceptance of, 84
  ascension, 25
  atonement, 30, 34–39, 58, 62, 74, 79–80, 82, 88, 94, 113, 146
  authority of, 60–66, 75
  Bible a witness of, 8
  Book of Mormon a witness for, 4, 32–33, 47–48
  Book of Mormon teachings on, 21–43

children blessed by, 160
Church established in Book of Mormon times, 100–126
commandment on love, 156
compassion of, 41, 159–60
creator, 55–57
defense of, 23
divine sonship of, 73–75
the Eternal God, 48–53, 92, 97
faith in, 149
Father, 55–66
foreordained, 57
gospel of, 57, 91, 98
hope in, 149
hypocrites condemned by, 131, 157
knowledge of, 16
Messiah, 28, 29, 52, 55, 56, 76–77, 87, 93–95
miracles, 76
ministry among Jews, 24
ministry to spirit world, 60
name of, known anciently, 53–55
names for, 32–33, 34, 43
Nephite knowledge of, 94–98
Nephite ministry, 25–27, 29, 30–32, 56–57, 60, 65, 96, 110–15, 117, 118, 124, 130, 131, 159–60
on asking God, 10
on the Godhead, 7
on faith, hope, and charity, 149
on faith of Nephites, 138
on seeking first the kingdom of God, 16
parable of the wise and foolish virgins, 118
persecution endured by, 154
premortal, 56, 57, 61, 64, 65
prophecies concerning, 109
prophets witness of, 2–3
pure love of, 113, 146–47, 149, 162
resurrection, 30, 38, 63
Savior of all the world, 24–29
second coming, 4, 117–18
signs of birth and death of, 26
Son of God, 60–63
taking name of, 57–60, 104
temptations, 76
testimony of, 42–43
true followers of, 154
visions of, 139
visit to lost ten tribes, 25–27, 30–32
See also God; Jehovah
Jews, 4, 46, 212
Jezebel, 130
John the Baptist, 95, 131
John the Revelator, 118
Johns Hopkins University, 164, 180
Johnson, Andrew, 242–43
Jonathan (son of Saul), 132
Joseph (Old Testament prophet), 24
tribe of, 85
Joseph (son of Lehi), 101
Josephus, Flavius, 191
Joseph, Alvin M., Jr., 210
Joy, 42, 261
Juan Fernandez Islands, 208
Judaism, 79
Judgment, 4, 20
Julius Caesar, 191
Julius II (pope), 187
Justice, 34, 110
Justification, 82–84

— K —

Kelley, David, 180
Kentucky, 213
Key, Mary Ritchie, "Polynesian and American Linguistic Connections," 174
Key, The (book), 193
Kimball, Spencer W., "A Book of Vital Messages," 18–20
Faith Precedes the Miracle, 20
on Book of Mormon, 18–20
on challenges of the Church, 1
on idolatry, 149–50, 262, 264–65
on obedience, 260
on riches, 261, 262
King Follett Discourse, 45
Knives, 198
Knowledge, 4, 112, 119, 141
Korihor, 40, 51
Kroeber, A. L., 229–30
Kukulcan, 189

— L —

Laban, brass plates of, 77, 97, 101, 102
Labyrinths, 193
Lachoneus, 110, 143
Lagoa Santa Man, 222
Lake Agassiz, 231
Laman, 101
Lamanites, 4, 108, 113, 148, 232–33, 264
conversion of, 139, 155
decline of, 109–10

enemy of Nephites, 102, 259
ministry of Christ to, 110–15, 118
missionary work among, 103, 107–8
Lamoni, 159
on change of heart, 145
father of, 159
Language differentiation, 224
Language variations, 233
Languages, 192, 199
Laurentide ice pack, 229
Law of consecration, 261–63, 266
Law of Moses, 128
observed by Lamanites, 139
observed by Nephites, 92, 102, 104, 105, 107, 111, 259
Leaders, 156
Leakey, Louis, 219
Leakey, Richard, 219
Lectures on Faith, 68
Lee, Harold B., on breakdown of faith in Christ, 23–24
Lehi (prophet), 258, 259, 261
call as prophet, 93–94
dream of, 54, 94–96, 147, 161
family of, 92
first vision of, 93
Melchizedek Priesthood held by, 101
migration of, 208
on atonement, 88
on fall of Adam, 78
on God, 46
on land of promise, 207
record of, 92
teachings on Christ, 94–97
testimony to people of Jerusalem, 52
vision of, 49
Lehi (son of Helaman), 108
Lehi-Nephi, land of, 105
Lemuel, 101
Libraries, 199
Libya, 180
Limhi, 52, 106, 123
on Abinadi, 52–53
Lommel, Andreas, 193
Lost ten tribes of Israel, 25–27, 30–32, 160, 211
Love, for enemies, 156
for God, 266
for others, 146, 151–63, 261
of Christ, 113, 146
of God, 151–63
redeeming, 161
Ludlow, Daniel, 1
Luke, on sonship of Christ, 73–74
Lust, 265
Luther, Martin, 82, 83
Lying, 262

— M —

McCollum-Pratt Institute, 165
McConkie, Bruce R., on Book of Mormon, 21
on Christ, 48, 62
on condescension of God, 69
on doctrines in Book of Mormon, 88
on Godhead, 47
on revelation, 69–70
McConkie, Joseph F., 73
MacGowan, Kenneth, 220
McKay, David O., on Christ, 37–38
Madeira Islands, 176
Madoc (Welsh prince), 195
Mahan, Joseph, 194, 212
Magellan, Ferdinand, 179
Magic, 115
Maize, 167, 170–72, 179–80, 197, 210
Malachi, 65
Malaysia, 173
Mal'ta (site), 227
Man Across the Sea (book), 208
Manihiki Islands, 208
Maps, 198–99
Martin, Paul S., 220–21
Martyrs, 116
Mary (mother of Jesus), 29, 49, 55, 64, 74, 76, 77, 96
Massachusetts, 210
Materialism, 40
Mathematics, 198–99
Matthew, on Christ, 73
Matthews, Robert J., 21
Maya Indians, 179, 192, 209
library of, 198
Mayflower, 191
Mediterranean, 173, 176, 178, 223
Meekness, 154
Melchizedek Priesthood, 98
Church established with, 100
held by Book of Mormon prophets, 101, 106, 114
Mendelssohn, Felix, *Elijah,* 24
Mercy, 34, 110, 154–55
Mertz, Henriette, 212
Merv, library at, 192

Mesoamerica, archaeology in, 164
Mesopotamia, 181
Messiah, 28, 29, 52, 55, 56, 76–77, 87, 93–95
  See also Jesus Christ
Mexico, 173, 174, 178, 181, 196, 197, 209
  archaeology in, 164, 178, 180, 189
Michigan, 179
Midland Man, 222
Middle English inflections, 243–44
Millennium, 4, 66, 119
Millet, Robert L., 44
Minnesota Lady, 222
Miracles, 76, 87, 139
Missionary work, 103, 107–8, 261
Mochanov, Y. A., 227
Moche culture, 191, 193
Mongoloids, 220–25, 233
Morlan, Richard E., 238
Mormon (Nephite prophet), 250
  literary efforts of, 2–3
  love for Nephites, 160
  on Bible and Book of Mormon, 8–9
  on class system, 109
  on charity, 146–47, 162
  on decline of Nephites, 116
  on faith, 140
  on faith, hope, and charity, 88, 147–48
  on hope, 144
  on love, 152, 153–54
  on mistakes in Book of Mormon, 85
  on pride of Nephites, 265
  on visit of Christ to Nephites, 114
  on wickedness of Nephites, 110, 117
Mormon, waters of, 155
Mormon squash, 167
Morocco, 195
Moroni (son of Mormon), 152, 154
  literary efforts of, 2–3
  on atonement, 80
  on charity, 146, 162–63
  on faith, 11
  on faith, hope, and charity, 137, 150
  on hope, 143, 144
  on love for God, 155
  on the poor, 156
  on pride, 265
  on purpose of Book of Mormon, 47–48
  on seeking Christ, 67
  on testimony, 11
  on weaknesses, 86
  vision of our day, 3, 157
Moroni (Nephite military commander), letter to Pahoran, 157
Moses, 24, 56, 61, 65, 86, 91, 102, 130
  law of, 92, 102, 104, 105, 107, 111, 128, 139, 259
Mosiah (father of King Benjamin), 103, 104, 121
Mosiah (son of King Benjamin), 106–7, 261
  sons of, 59, 107, 130, 147
Mourning, 129, 134, 135, 136
Mulekites, 104, 233
Mummies, 210
Murder, 263
Muskogee Indians, 200
Mythology, 194–95, 199
Mysteries of God, 65, 114, 122, 148

— N —

Naboth, 130
Natural and Aboriginal History of Tennessee (book), 213
Nauvoo, 65
Nazca culture, 191, 193
Nebuchadnezzar, 128–29
Needham, Joseph, 208
Negroids, 221, 222, 223
Nehor, 40, 51, 157
Nephi (son of Lehi), 259, 261, 263
  brass plates obtained by, 101
  Church of Jesus Christ established by, 101–2, 112, 117
  interpretation of Lehi's dream by, 161
  king, 101–2
  large plates of, 98
  literary efforts of, 2–3
  love of people for, 158–59
  Melchizedek Priesthood held by, 101
  on baptism, 82
  on charity, 146
  on Christ, 28, 48, 55, 74, 94–96
  on commandments, 153
  on God, 88
  on land of promise, 207
  on love, 152
  on safety, 22
  on scattering and gathering of Israel, 46–47, 88
  on weaknesses, 86
  record of, 92

report of Lehi's vision by, 93–94
small plates of, 98
vision of, 49, 54, 96
Nephi (son of Helaman), 107–8
faithfulness of, 140
Nephi (grandson of Helaman), 64, 123
Nephi, land of, 104, 105, 108
Nephite Twelve, 96, 111–14
Nephites, 232–33
ages of, 121
compassion of Christ for, 159–60
cycles of, 107, 110, 257
fasting among, 127–33, 136
knowledge of Christ, 102
law of Moses lived by, 92, 102, 104, 105, 107, 111, 259
ministry of Christ to, 25–27, 29, 30–32, 56–57, 60, 65, 96, 110–15, 117, 118, 124, 130, 131, 159–60
monetary system of, 5
pride of, 256
prophets of, 56
spiritual decline of, 108–10
temples of, 102, 107, 114, 122, 259, 263
testimony of, 4
Neum, 97
New and everlasting covenant, 58
New Mexico, 190
New Testament, 24, 73–87
New World, cultural parallels with Old World, 206–17
New World Archeological Foundation, 164
Noah (Old Testament prophet), 24, 232
sons of, 187
Noah (Nephite king), 52, 59, 62, 105, 155
temple remodeled by, 122
North Africa, 194
Nyman, Monte S., 33

— O —

Obedience, 140, 145, 149, 256–62, 266
Oklahoma, 193
Old Copper culture, 179
Old Crow Basin (site), 228–29
Old Testament, 24, 73–87
fasting in, 127–35
Old World, cultural parallels with New World, 206–17
Omni, 103
Onion Portage (site), 229
Oral history, 195, 200
Oral tradition, 189
Ordinances, 82, 102, 112–14
Orthography, 241–44, 150
"Outer darkness," 81
Oxford English Dictionary, 243

— P —

Pachisi (game), 198
Pacific Ocean, migration across, 165, 181, 191, 207, 208, 232
Pahoran, 157
Paleo-Indians, 218, 222–23, 232–33
Palestine, 178, 199
Palli Aike Man, 222
Palmyra, New York, 238
Panpipes, 198
Parable of the wise and foolish virgins, 118, 125–26
Paradise, 81
Parents, 156
Patolli (game), 198
Patriarchal order, 57
Paul, 80, 84, 88
on faith, 12
on faith, hope, and charity, 137
on resurrection, 81
on witness of the Spirit, 10
Payon, Jose Garcia, 178
Peace, 115, 145
Peace offerings, 134
Peanuts, 170–71, 197
Penn, William, on American Indians, 211
Pennsylvania, 192, 211
Pentateuch, 128
Perfection, 100
Persecution, 16, 115, 154
Persia, 172
Peru, 171, 176, 178, 181, 191, 193, 196, 208, 210, 211
Peter, 110, 148
Pharisees, 131
Phelps, W. W., 240, 250
Philippines, 179, 197
Phoenician script, 212
Pilgrims, 191
Pima Indians, 167
Pineapples, 177, 197
Piri Reis map, 199
Plan of salvation, 57, 78–79, 87
Plant, William, 172
Plantains, 197

Plants, 167–72, 196–97, 226
Plutarch, 195
Polynesia, 169, 174, 197, 210
"Polynesian and American Linguistic Connections" (article), 174
Pompeii, 177, 197
Portugal, 180, 192
Potatoes, 170
Pottery, 188
Poverty, 22, 156
Pratt, Orson, 240
Prayer, 14, 41, 42, 139–40, 142, 145, 153–54
  fasting and, 59, 128, 133, 134, 136, 140
Predestination, 52
Premortal life, 11, 34, 42, 50, 51, 56, 57, 61, 64
Pride, 107, 256, 262, 264–65
Priestcraft, 40, 107
Priesthood, 91, 117
  Aaronic, 92
  Melchizedek, 98, 100, 101, 106, 114
  offices in Book of Mormon, 123
Priests, 101–3
Priorities, 16
Problem solving, 4
Promised land, 85, 258
Prophecy, spirit of, 86
Prophets, 34, 102–3, 104, 117, 140, 256–57, 260
  false, 115
  taught of Christ, 53
  testimony of, 11
  visions of, 3
  warnings of, 3
  weaknesses of, 85–86
Prosperity, 103, 107, 109, 115, 256–68
Ptolemy IV, 190
Pueblo Indians, 168
Pumpkins, 167, 169
Purity, 152

— Q —

Quebec, 222
Quetzalcoatl, 189

— R —

Ra II, 190, 208
Racism, 181, 188
Rebellion, 92, 258
Reed, Eric, 208
Religious rituals, 194
Repentance, 22, 57, 59, 107–10, 117, 119, 145
Resurrection, 30, 38, 60, 63, 78, 80–82, 87
Revelation, 21, 46, 53, 86–87, 97, 117
  scriptures understood through, 86
Riches, 157, 256–68
Richie, J. D., 229
Ricks, Stephen D., 127
Ridicule, 16
Righteousness, 17
  desire for, 144–45, 149
  hungering and thirsting after, 147
  principles in Book of Mormon, 2, 15, 20
Rodwell, Sally, 172
Roman Catholic Church, 82
Romans, 178, 179, 191, 198
Rome, 212, 213

— S —

Sackcloth, 133, 134, 135
Sacrament, 111, 125
Sacred Grove, 45
Sacrifice, 264
  animal, 175
  blood, 111
Samuel (Old Testament prophet), 132
Samuel (Lamanite prophet), 109
  on change of heart, 144
  on faith, 140
San Diego Museum of Man, 166
San Diego State College, 165, 166
Sanctuaries, 107, 123
Sariah (wife of Lehi), 158
Saskatchewan, 222
Satan, 51, 115–16, 119
Sauer, Carl, 166
Saul (Old Testament king), 129, 130, 132
School of the Prophets, 45
Scotland, 195
Scripture study, 139, 140
Scriptures, not had by Mulekites, 104
Scriptures Publication Committee, 241
Schutler, Richard, 220
Second Coming, 4, 117–18
Secret societies, 108–10, 264
Seers, 123
Seezoram, 129
Semites, 210
Semitic language, 248

Sermon on the Mount, 112
Sertima, Ivan Van, *They Came Before Columbus,* 194
Service, 262–63, 266
Shakespeare, William, 37
Sharing, 157–58
Shem, 187
Sherem, 40, 51, 143
Shiblon, 153
Shilom, land of, 105
Ships, 190–92, 207–8, 211
Siberia, 221, 223, 225–26, 229, 231
Signs, 13–14
  at birth of Christ, 26, 109
Sinclair, Henry, 195
Sinodonty, 223
Sins, remission of, 35, 104, 114, 145, 148, 154
Small plates of Nephi, 92
Smith, Emma, on translation of Book of Mormon, 237
Smith, Hyrum, 238
Smith, Joseph, 14, 23, 63, 125, 256, 264
  Book of Mormon brought forth by, 97
  Book of Mormon corrections made by, 240, 243, 247–51
  Book of Mormon translated by, 239, 249, 250
  first vision, 7, 45
  King Follett Discourse, 45
  letter to John Wentworth, 111
  on Book of Mormon, 2, 44, 66, 85, 89, 251
  on God, 65
  on Godhead, 44–45
  on nature of God, 45
  on ordinances, 82
  on prophets of Israel, 98
  on suffering of Christ, 69
  on translation of Book of Mormon, 237
  seer, 123
  witness of Book of Mormon, 9
  witnesses of, 10
Smith, Joseph F., "Vision of the Redemption of the Dead," 81
Smith, Joseph Fielding, on the Father and the Son, 46
  on priests and teachers, 120
  on revelation, 69–70
Smithsonian Institution, 195, 212
Solomon Islands, 198
Sorcery, 115
Sorenson, John, 213
Southeast Asia, 172, 175
Spain, 171, 176, 190, 192, 195, 210
Spelling, 241–45, 250
Sperry, Sidney B., on error in Book of Mormon, 249–50
Spirit birth, 55
Spirit world, 60, 81–82, 87
Spirits, 55
Spiritual rebirth, 57–59
Squashes, 167, 169
Stanford, Dennis, 219
Stealing, 262, 263
Stendahl, Krister, on Sermon on the Mount, 75
Stewardship, 262–63
Stripling warriors, 141–42
Sumerians, 211
Sunnyvale, California, 219
Sweet potatoes, 169–70, 196, 197, 210
Symbolism, 199
Symbols, 193
Synagogues, 107, 123

— T —

Tabor Child, 219
Tahiti, 208
Takhelne Indians, 188
Talgai (Australoid), 220
Talmage, James E., 240, 242
Tarahumara, 174, 196
Taylor, John, 240
  on Christ, 62
Teachers, 101–2
Technology, 176, 194
Tehuacan, 222
Temple work, 261
Temples, Nephite, 102, 107, 114, 122, 259, 263
Ten Commandments, 130
Tennessee, 179, 212–13
Teotihuacan, 178
Testament, 6–7
Testimony, 17–18, 21, 111
Texas Street excavation site, 219
Texpexpan Man, 222
Thailand, 180
They Came Before Columbus (book), 194
Thomas à Kempis, *The Imitation of Christ*, 16–17
  on living the truth, 16–17
Thomas, Cyrus, 212

Thomasson, Gordon, 136
Three Nephites, 115
Tiahuanaco culture, 194
Tibet, 221
Tithing, 266
"To the Young Men of the Church" (address), 18
Tobacco, 172
Tolstoy, Paul, 194
Toltec-Maya mural fragments, 189
Totten Norman, 187, 212
Tower of Babel, 232
Transoceanic travel, 165, 176–81, 191, 207–9, 232
Traditions, 195
Translated beings, 3
Tree of life, 147, 161
Trust, 141
Tuamotu, 208
Turkey (country), 179
Turkeys, 174
Turner, Christy, 222–24
Turner, Rodney, 100
Typography, 244

— U —

Unity, 112–13, 117–18, 119
  economic, 115
University of California at Berkeley, 166
Urim and Thummim, 14, 237–38
Utah Lake skull, 164

— V —

Valdivia, Ecuador, 188
Veil, 53
Veneti (Celtic tribe), 191
Verrill, Hyatt, and Ruth, on origin of American Indians, 211
Vikings, migration to America, 207
  sagas of, 195
Visions, 49, 93, 112
  of our day, 3
von Dechend, Hertha, 194
von Wuthenau, Alexander, 189, 196

— W —

Wales, 195
War in Heaven, 119
Warnings, 3
Wars, 5, 22, 107, 108, 115–16
Way of Animal Powers, The, 194
Wealth, 157
  See also Riches
Webster, Noah, *American Dictionary of the English Language,* 241–42
Wentworth, John, letter from Joseph Smith, 111
West Africa, 180, 197, 228
West Virginia, 181
Whitmer, David, witness of Book of Mormon, 9–10
Wicked, destruction of, 257, 259–60
Wickedness, 22, 263
Wiracocha, 189
Wisconsin glacial period, 225, 228, 231
Wise men, 26, 27
Wissler, Clark, 222, 223
Witchcraft, 115
Witnesses, 111, 112
  God's system of, 7–11
  law of, 8
  three great scriptural, 8
Word of Wisdom, 261, 266
Woodbury, George, 220
World problems, 22
Worldliness, 118
Wormington, H. Marie, 219

— Y —

Yenisei Basin, 227
Young, Brigham, on Bible and Book of Mormon, 9
Yucatan, 209
Yuchi Indians, 179, 194

— Z —

Zarahemla, 59, 104–8
Zedekiah, 129, 233
Zeezrom, 50–51, 56, 148, 157
Zeniff, 105
  priesthood held by, 122
  temple restored by, 122
Zenock, 74, 97
Zenos, 74, 97
  allegory of, 121
Zheng He, 191
Zhou Ben Xiong, 172
Zion, 117, 118
Zoramites, 51–52, 74, 139

Scripture Index

OLD TESTAMENT

Genesis
1:28 257
12:7 258
26:3–5 256
37:35 89

Exodus
34:1–2 (JST) 91
34:28 130, 134

Leviticus
16:29, 31 128, 134
23:27 128
23:27–32 134

Numbers
16:22 55
29:7–10 128, 134

Deuteronomy
9:9 130, 134
9:18 132, 135
14:2 100
19:15 7

Joshua
7:6 132, 135

Judges
13:24–16:30 268
20:26 130, 133, 134

1 Samuel
1:7 135
1:17 132
7:3–6 132
7:6 132, 133, 135
14:24 132, 135
20:34 132, 135
28:20 130, 134
31:13 129, 134

2 Samuel
1:12 129, 133, 134
3:35 129, 134
12:16 130
12:16, 21–23 134
12:20 133
12:21–23 133

1 Kings
21:4 132, 135
21:9, 12 130, 134
21:27 132, 133, 135
21:28–29 132

2 Kings
22:14–20 99
22:15–17 99
25:1 129
25:8–9 129
25:24–25 129

1 Chronicles
10:12 129, 129–30, 134

2 Chronicles
20:3 130, 134

Ezra
3 122
8:21, 23 130, 134
9:1 132
10:6 132, 135

Nehemiah
1:4 130, 133, 134
9:1 132, 133, 135

Esther
4:1, 3 132, 133, 135
4:16 130, 134

Psalm
35:13 130, 134
69:10 130
69:11 133, 134
109:24 130, 134

Isaiah
9:2 38
9:6 72
52:8 112

53 59, 62–63, 76
53:10 59
54:4 248
58:3, 5, 10 134
58:3–7 128
58:5 133
59:20 118–19

Jeremiah
5:1–10 99
14:12 130, 134
29:13–14 24
36:6, 9 130, 134
39:1 129
39:2 129
41:1 129
52:6–7 129
52:12–13 129

Ezekiel
39 124

Daniel
3:25 89
4:2–3 13
6:18 130, 134
7:13–14 118–19
9:3 130, 133, 134

Joel
1:14 132, 135
2:12–17 132, 133, 135

Jonah
3:5 133
3:5–9 132, 135

Habakkuk
1:1–10 99

Zephaniah
1:1–18 99

Zechariah
3:1–5 89
7:3, 5 135
7:5 128
8:19 128, 135

Malachi
3:10 266
4:2 249

NEW TESTAMENT

Matthew
1:18–20 73
2 27
5:23 257
5:45 258
6:10 117
6:16–18 131
6:38 (JST) 16
7:7 10
11:28 111
12:39 13
16:4 13
24:30 123
24:44–49 (JST) 124
25:1–13 118
25:21 20

Mark
8:36–37 16
11:25 257
16:17 13
16:17–18 11
16:20 13

Luke
1:32, 35 74
2:36–38 131
12:31 262
18:12 131
23:34 154

John
4:25 (JST) 55
4:25–26 46
5:30 63
5:43 60
6:38 63–64
7:16 60
7:39 (JST) 125
10:18 74–75
13:35 113
14:6 57
17:3 65–66
17:22 7
20:30 13

Acts
1:4–8 125
2:1–4 125
2:22 13
4:12 39, 55
11:26 75
15:10 111

Romans
1:17 82
8:17 147

1 Corinthians
2:11 10
13:13 137, 148
15:44 81

2 Corinthians
13:1 7

Galatians
3:24 104, 111

Colossians
2:9 65

2 Timothy
1:10 48

Hebrews
1:1–3 56
5:9 57
7:11–12 107
7:14 120
11:1 12
12:3 69
12:9 55

James
1:6 10

1 Peter
2:2 148
2:9 100
3:19–22 89
4:6 89

2 Peter
2:22 110

1 John
4:18 152
5:6 10

Revelation
12:1–3, 7 (JST) 119
16:16–21 124
18:4 118
19:7 118
20:6–10 119
22:8–13 71

BOOK OF MORMON

1 Nephi
1–22 33
1:8–10 93
1:13 93
1:14 93
1:16–17 49
1:19 93
1:20 52, 93
2 267
2:4 268
2:20 258, 258–59
2:22 101
3 (1830 ed.) 49, 53, 54
3:7 153
4:14 259
4:15–16 102
4:26 101
4:38 102
5:1–8 158
6:1, 3–5 6
7:12 139
8:4 251
8:12 147
9:2, 4 6
10:4 46, 94
10:5 94
10:6 95
10:7 95
10:9 95
10:17 95, 101
10:18–19 88
11 3
11–14 49
11:1–15:1 101
11:13 49
11:13–18 76
11:13–21 (1830 ed.) 49
11:13–21 96

11:16–21	74	4:26	249
11:17	160	5:1–25	232
11:18, 21, 32	68–69, 251	5:3–14	100
11:22	161	5:4–8	121
11:24, 28, 31	96	5:10	102
11:29	96	5:10–16	259
11:32–33	49, 96	5:11–16	263
12:4–5	96	5:16	102, 122
12:6	96, 117	5:17	263
12:7–10	96	5:18	102
12:11–12	96	5:19	101
12:18	54	5:21–23	107
13	244	5:26	101
13:40	69, 251	5:28–34	98
13:40–41	53	5:33	6
14:10	100	6:2	120
14:29	96	6:4–9	3
17:40	160	6:11	85
18:1–25	232	9	102
18:25	258	9:2	84, 85
19:1	98	9:5	49–50
19:2	248	9:6	78
19:6	86	9:6–9	38
19:7–10	27, 50	9:13	78
19:9	154	10:2–3	54
19:10	97, 98	10:2–3, 7	3
19:11–12	97	10:3	33, 95
19:12	27	10:5–7	84
19:13–15	97	10:7–8	85
19:23	97	11:2, 3	2
20:1	251	11:3	9
22:8	116	11:5	78
22:12	85	11:6–7	53
22:28	22	19:2	38
		25:3–8, 22	3
2 Nephi		25:12	56
1	267	25:16–17	46–47
1:5	207	25:19	33, 55, 95
1:9	256, 257	25:20	39, 55
1:9–13	257	25:23–30	102
1:10	50, 139	25:24	102, 104
2:6–9	34	24:24–26	76
2:17	77	26:12	48
2:22	78	26:16–24	3
2:24–27	37	26:26	123
2:25	78	26:30	146, 162
2:27	250	27:12–14	9
3:6–14	123	28:1–3	3
3:12	44	28:26–30	87
3:19–21	139	29:7–8, 11–14	25–26
4:3–7	268	29:12–14	8
4:6	268	30:2	47
4:14	6	30:6	251
4:17	152	31:5–9	82
4:21	152, 158	31:7–21	47

31:12 114
31:20 149
31:21 39
31:21 55
31–32 102, 120
32:7 3
32:9 47
33:1, 4 86
33:3 147
33:7–9 146
33:10–15 3
33:12 47

Jacob
1:9–11 102
1:10 158
1:11 102
1:13–14 103
1:15 102
1:18 101
2 259
2:11 3
2:18 262
2:18–19 16
2:19 149, 262, 266
3:2 152
3:4 102
4:4 149
4:4, 13 3
4:5 47
4:6 139
5 121
6:1, 12–13 3
7 40, 51
7:1–9 51
7:1–21 99
7:5 138, 143

Enos
1:9, 11 147
1:13 103
1:22 102
1:23 103, 260

Jarom
1:2 79
1:3 103, 260
1:3–5 102
1:3–8 259
1:4 138
1:5 102
1:7 101, 138, 259–60
1:8 257, 260
1:9 257, 267
1:10 102, 103, 122
1:11 102
1:12 103, 260

Omni
1:2 259
1:3 103
1:5 103, 260
1:6 267
1:7 103, 259, 260
1:11 103–4
1:12 104, 122
1:14–16 121
1:17 104
1:19 104
1:26 121, 131, 133, 136
1:27–30 122, 122–123
1:29 105

Words of Mormon
1:3–9 3
1:15–18 121
1:16 102

Mosiah
1:7 267
1:10 104
1:11 104, 122
2:3 104
2:4 153, 154, 156, 259
2:9 122
2:11 262
2:17 262
2:22 259, 260
2:34–35 121
2:41 260
3:2–19 122
3:5, 7, 9 50
3:5, 8 98
3:5–8 74
3:5–10 28–29, 76–77
3:8 55, 56, 76
3:11, 16–17, 19 34–35
3:14–15 104
3:17 39, 55, 150
3:19 58, 153, 261
3:22 122
4:1–3, 11 120–21
4:2–3 122
4:2–3, 11 104–5
4:2–3, 11–12, 20, 26 122
4:3 138, 145, 148

4:5–6, 11	122
4:6–8	39
4:7–8	39
4:11–12	35, 161
4:15	156
4:29	1
5:1–15	58
5:2	58, 104–5, 144–45
5:2, 7	120–21
5:2–10	122
5:3	145
5:4	122
5:4–7	138
5:7	122, 145
5:8	39, 121
5:11–12	122
5:15	122
6:1–3	102
6:2	104–5
7–22	122
7:9	105
7:24–25	105
7:26–28	52–53
7:27–28	29
8:13–17	123
9–22	122
9:1	121
9:6–8	105
11:1–15	105
11:5	105
11:5, 10–11	105
11:6–15	123
11:8	257
11:10	122
12–16	105
12:27–32	123
13:14	155
13:27–28	123
14–21	260
15:1–5	63
15:11–12	59–60
16:15	72
17:1–2	105
17:2	105
17:2–3	261
17:7–8	52–53
18:3	261
18:8–9	155
18:13	106
18:13–16	120
18:17	76, 106
18:18–19	106
18:27	120
21:28	251, 252
21:33–34	123
23:10	106
23:15	155, 156
23:16	106, 120
24:5–7	264
24:6	264
24:12–16	41
24:23–25	263
25:2	104, 233
25:13	102, 121
25:19–22	106
25:21	106
25:22	122
25:24	263
27:8	59
27:8–26	59
27:14	148
27:22–23	130, 133, 136
27:25	145
27:29	249
27:34–37	107
28:1–9	107
28:3	145, 147
28:4	59
28:16	123
29:27	103
29:41–47	102
29:42	106
29:45–46	121
29:47	106
Alma	
1	40, 51
1:12, 16	107
1:16	157
1:29	257
1:30	261
4:4	106
4:7	106
4:14	35
4:18–19	22–23
4:18–20	107
4:20	123
5:3	106
5:5	122
5:9	161
5:14	59
5:16	163
5:26	148–49, 161
5:46	130, 133, 136
5:48	47
6:1	106
6:6	131, 133, 136

7:10	74	30:2	128, 133, 136
7:10–12	77	30:3	128
7:12–13	64	30:6–60	99
7:17	148	30:13–15, 24–26, 48	51
7:22–27, 32, 48	47	30:17	263, 264
7:24	162	31:1, 8–14	51–52
8:26	130, 136	31:5	23
9:13	267	31:8–17	99
9:19–21	122	31:15–16	52
9:20	138	32	138, 163
10:3	120	32–33	139
10:7	130, 136	32:17–18, 21, 26	140
11	69	32:21	12, 142
11:21–44	50–51	32:27	13, 144, 148
11:24	157	32:30	245, 251
11:38–39	56	32:34	141
11:39	98	32:36	141
11:45	81	33:13–18	74
12:9–11	148	33:14–17	69
12:10–11	92	33:22	139
12:22, 24	35–36	34:9	78–79
12:25	78	34:9–10, 12, 14–16	36
12:33–34	47	34:10, 14	69
13:8	106	34:17, 28–29	139
13:20	249	34:41	149
13:28	153, 154	36:6	145
13:29	161	36:20–22	42
14:16	138	36:22, 24	145
14:26–28	139	36:28	145
16:13	123	37:13	267
17–26	107	38:9	39
17:3	136	38:12	153, 154
17:3, 9	130, 133	38:17	267
17:9	136	40:7, 12–13	81–82
19:10	138	40:23	81
19:33	145	41:3–4	83
19:35	107	41:13	83
20:26	159	41:14–15	83
21:9–10	52	42:2	250
21:16	123	42:5	78, 79
23:2	123	42:7–12, 14–15, 26	36–37
23:6	107	42:8	79
23:16–18	107	42:15	79
24:14	79, 160	45:1	128, 133, 136
25:15–16	139	48:15–16	138, 141
26:13	161	48:20	142
26:29	123	48:21	244
26:31	155	51:10	248
26:32	155	57:21	139, 142
26:34	155	57:26–27	138, 141–42
27:27	138	58:11	142, 149
28:6	133, 136	58:12–13	142
29:1–3, 6–8	26	60:32	157
30	40, 51	63:4–9	107

Helaman
3:14 107
3:25 107, 267
3:35 131, 133, 136, 140
4:23 107
5:9 39
5:41 140
5:43–44 113–14
5:43–45 120
5:43, 45 148
5:43–49 108
5:50 108
6:4–6 108
6:10 233
6:21, 37 108
6:26, 29 264
7:4–5 258
8:13–23 69
8:15 139
9:10 129, 130, 133, 136
10:4–5 140
11:1–2 124
12 117
13:1 109
13–15 268
14:4 26
14:16–19 37
15:5 109
15:7 140
15:7–8 144

3 Nephi
1–30 75
1:13–14 64, 71
1:14 64
1:15–19 26
1:24–25 104
1:30 109
2:12 109
3:10 143
3:16, 18–19 109
4:4 143
4:27–5:3 109
5:12 105
6:6 109
6:10–12 109
6:14 109, 138
7:7 110
7:8 110
7:15 110
7:18 123–24
8 258
8:5 124
8:5–9:12 110
9–10 26–27
9:11, 13 110
9:15 56–57
9:16–17 60
9:17 110
9:19 111
9:20 108, 113, 120, 148
10:4 245
10:12 110
10:18 110, 124
10:18–19 30
11:1 111
11:6–17 30–31
11:7 111
11:14 65
11:15 111
11:18–22 124
11:26, 32, 36 8
11:27, 36 47
11:28 112
11:31–32 65
12:1 113, 124
12:6 113
12:19 65, 111
12:44 156
13:5 157
13:16–18 136
13:17 133
13:21 265
13:24 265
13:33 265
15 25
15:4–5 29
15:5 65
15:13 65
16:1–3 31
16:5 65
16:9 65
16:16 65
16:18 112
17:1–3 41
17:4 32, 160
17:5–6 159
17:5–9 41–42
17:25 31
18:4–5, 9 113
18:32 123
19:13–14, 20 114
19:25 114
19:28 114
19:35 112, 138

20:8 113
20:8–9 113
20:27 65
21:5–6 116
21:22 84
22:4 248
24:1 65
25:2 249
26:1–4 112
26:6–12 114
26:11–12 3
26:13 114
26:17–18 114
27:1 131–32, 133, 136
27:16 113
27:19 138–39
27:20 114
27:27 114, 261
27:32 115
28:10 47
28:26 3
30 100
30:1 3

4 Nephi
1 264
1:1 124
1:1–17 112
1:1–45 233
1:2 114
1:3–18 115
1:7 260
1:12 131–32, 133, 136
1:15 161
1:20 114, 121
1:23–24 115
1:26–29 115
1:30–34 115
1:35–38 115
1:45 115
1:46 264

Mormon
1–8 264
1:8 115
1:13–14, 16 115
1:15 2
1:19 115–16
2:1 268
2:10 116
2:15 116
3:2 116
3:9–6:22 257
3:12 160
3:14, 20–22 3
3:19 124
4:12 116
4:14, 21 125
5:9, 13 3
7:8–9 9
8:10 115
8:11 3
8:17 86
8:24 139
8:25–35 3
8:35 116
8:35, 37 157
8:35–37, 40 265
8:37 156
9:12 72
9:13–14 80
9:26, 30–31 3
9:28–31 100
9:30–31 86

Ether
2:8 258
2:9–10 258
2:10 257, 267
3:9 139
3:14 53, 57, 60, 69
3:19 141
3:21–22 112
4:1 251
4:1–2 112
4:4–5 124–25
4:6 125
4:7 139
4:7–8 53
4:12 64
5:2–4 9
5:4 11
6:1–12 232
6:13–21 232
8:24–26 3
9:24 121
10:22 268
10:28 268
12:4 143, 144
12:6 12, 14, 138
12:8, 19–20, 31 139
12:9 143
12:13 139
12:14 108, 120
12:16, 18 139
12:22 139

12:22–23, 38–39	2	7:28	139
12:23	116	7:30	139
12:23–36	86	7:36–37	87
12:28	149, 162	7:40–42	143–44, 144
12:30	139	7:44	163
12:32	149	7:45	147–48
12:33	160	7:45–46	146–47
12:33–34	146	7:45–47	162
12:34	162–63	7:46–47	261
12:35	162	7:47	146, 149, 162
12:41	67	7:48	146, 153–54, 154
13:13	3		
		8:16	152
Moroni		8:17	162
1:2–3	116	8:26	154
1:4	3	8:27	265
2:6	124	9:8	125
4:3	47	9:9–10	125
5:2	47	10:3–5	11, 14
6:1–20	233	10:11	148
6:5	131–32, 133 136	10:19	150
		10:20–21	137
7:1	123	10:21	143, 146, 163
7:3	147, 149	10:23	139
7:6	266	10:24–34	3
7:10	266	10:32	155
7:21–25, 28–32	140	10:33	114

DOCTRINE AND COVENANTS

1:35–36	118	63:54	118
5:9–10	14	65	119
5:10	89	65:6	117
5:11–15	9	66:2	58
6:28	7	76:58	70
17:6	254	76:67, 92–94	100
18:8	258	82:3	116
20:17–19	46	82:14	118
29:1	61	84:19–27	120
29:42	61–62	84:23–27	91, 98
33:17	118	84:26–27	104
38:16	258	84:38	147
38:17	257	84:54–57	15
38:18	258	84:57	119
38:27	117, 117–18	86:8–10	116
38:39	256, 266	87:6	123
45:47–53	124	88:29	114
45:56–57	118	88:110–115	119
45:59	119	89:2	266
45:64–71	119	89:20	261
49:5	62	93:4, 12–14	63
49:28	62	97:21	118
59:18, 20	257	100:16	118

101:6	117–18	128:24	118–19
101:32–34	119	130:22	45
105:1–6	117–18	132:19–20	70
105:19	14	132:24	65–66
109:74	118	133:2	118, 118–19
112:23–26	118	133:5	118
113:8	116	133:10	118
121:26	114	133:57	58
121:26–29	67	138:12–19	60
121:26–33	119		

PEARL OF GREAT PRICE

Moses
- 1:4, 6 — 61
- 1:31–33 — 56
- 1:32–33 — 61
- 4:2 — 57
- 5:7–8 — 53
- 5:8 — 55
- 5:9 — 71
- 6:51–52 — 61
- 6:52 — 55
- 6:59 — 57–58
- 6:62 — 78
- 7:16–18 — 119
- 7:30 — 56
- 7:39–40 — 61
- 7:65 — 119

Abraham
- 2:9–11 — 116

Joseph Smith—History
- 1:19 — 45
- 1:30–54, 59, 67 — 9

Articles of Faith
- 1:4 — 149
- 1:8 — 85